**Gerard DeGroot** was born in California and is Professor of Modern History at the University of St Andrews. He has published fourteen books and dozens of articles on various aspects of twentieth-century history. His book on nuclear weaponry (*The Bomb: A Life*) was published to considerable acclaim and won the Westminster Medal for Military Literature. *The Sixties Unplugged*, an iconoclastic history of the decade, won the Ray and Pat Browne Prize in 2008 for the best book on American cultural history. DeGroot is also a freelance journalist, contributing frequent op-ed columns and reviews to national newspapers in Britain and the USA.

'A scintillating analysis of how American politics in the 1960s and the changing nature of the state of California came together to transform a third-rate Hollywood actor into a first-rate politician. DeGroot's sharp and witty analysis of the state of American politics in the 1960s entertains as it enlightens. A brilliant achievement.'

Marilyn B. Young, Professor of History, NYU
and author of *The Vietnam Wars*

'Whether Democrats or Republicans, American politicians habitually compare themselves to Ronald Reagan. Gerard DeGroot's bold and fast-paced book explores how that past-it Hollywood actor converted himself into a silver-tongued politician and president. In telling this entertaining and important story, DeGroot explains why Ronald Reagan's transformational career matters today, perhaps more than ever.'

Nick Witham, University College London,
author of *The Cultural Left and the Reagan Era: US Protest and Central American Revolution*

# Selling RONALD REAGAN

## The Emergence of a President

**GERARD DeGROOT**

I.B. TAURIS
LONDON · NEW YORK

Published in 2015 by
I.B.Tauris & Co. Ltd
London • New York
www.ibtauris.com

Copyright © 2015 Gerard DeGroot

The right of Gerard DeGroot to be identified as the author of this work has been asserted by the author in accordance with the Copyright, Designs and Patents Act 1988.

All rights reserved. Except for brief quotations in a review, this book, or any part thereof, may not be reproduced, stored in or introduced into a retrieval system, or transmitted, in any form or by any means, electronic, mechanical, photocopying, recording or otherwise, without the prior written permission of the publisher.

References to websites were correct at the time of writing.

ISBN: 978 1 78076 828 1
eISBN: 978 0 85772 930 9

A full CIP record for this book is available from the British Library
A full CIP record is available from the Library of Congress

Library of Congress Catalog Card Number: available

Typeset by JCS Publishing Services Ltd, www.jcs-publishing.co.uk
Printed and bound in Sweden by ScandBook AB

To Charlie Roe:
a lovely man, and a believer in government
★
and to Marilyn Roe:
of course

# Contents

Introduction 1

1 The Speech 7
2 Hardening of the Categories 24
3 'You Guys Are Absolutely Crazy' 55
4 Old Tactics, New Faces 85
5 Those Boys from BASICO 107
6 The Great Pretender 137
7 Drowning in Milk 164
8 'What Are You Going to Do About Berkeley?' 179
9 'Who Shot Lincoln?' 208
10 'Hey, This Guy Could Be President Someday' 248

Notes 269
Bibliography 293
Index 301

# Introduction

There once was a time when the idea of Ronald Reagan in politics provoked ridicule and scorn. (For some it still does.) The problem was not just that he was an actor, but rather that he was a bad one who, instead of giving up and implementing Plan B, hung around Hollywood for decades in the pathetic hope that his big break would come. The roles he played never suggested a capacity for leadership. He lacked the toughness of John Wayne, the cerebral charm of Gregory Peck, or the quiet solidity of William Holden. He was, quite simply, too mushy – the guy who always fell in love but never got the girl. 'Ronnie for governor?' the studio mogul Jack Warner quipped when rumours circulated of a Reagan candidacy. 'No. Jimmy Stewart for governor. Ronnie for best friend.'[1]

As we now know, Reagan had a nasty habit of making his critics eat their words. Again, and again, and again. Yet the incredulity that his first foray into politics inspired is entirely understandable. Growing up in San Diego, I recall radio ads in which he tried to suggest that six terms as president of the Screen Actors Guild (SAG) was legitimate qualification for the new role he coveted – governor of the most populous state in the Union. I was only 11 at the time, yet I could sense that there was something wrong with that logic. The problem, however, was not just Reagan's lack of experience; it was also that his politics seemed Mesozoic. He was a pal of the arch-conservative Barry Goldwater and, on certain issues, more extreme than his friend. Since Lyndon Johnson had trounced Goldwater in the 1964 presidential election, that seemed proof that America wanted nothing to do with the loony politics of the far right. How, then, could an extremist like Reagan dare to think he could gain election at a time when America seemed fundamentally liberal?

Reagan was right and his doubters wrong. In 1966, a far-right candidate with no political experience triumphed by nearly a million votes over the two-term incumbent, Edmund G. (Pat) Brown. That clearly qualifies as a mammoth achievement, yet how did this happen and what does it mean? Was this just another example of capricious California, or was Reagan a harbinger of a trend that would soon sweep across the United States?

'What happens in California today often happens in America tomorrow,' wrote the journalist Joseph Lewis not long after the Reagan landslide. 'California is a social laboratory for the other forty-nine states.'[2] Lewis was correct, even though some still deny the implications of that statement. The most successful political revolution of the 1960s was not conducted by students, nor was it left-wing. It was instead a populist revolution from the right, with Reagan in the van. Some analysts, frightened by the implications of that phenomenon, insisted that California was just being silly. They assumed that if the people supported this Hollywood lightweight something must be wrong with the people. 'Perhaps only the capricious California electorate could stage such a political jest,' Emmet John Hughes remarked in *Newsweek*. Reagan's victory, he decided, 'dramatizes the virtual bankruptcy, politically and intellectually, of a national party ... The political point should not be more sharp. Some men learn from history. Some men run from it. And the GOP has chosen feckless flight.'[3] To an extent, Hughes was right. The GOP, with Reagan in front, *was* running from history. What many failed to realize, however, was that voters were running in the same direction. To paraphrase Bob Dylan, Reagan did not need a weatherman to know which way the wind was blowing.

This is the story of the 1966 election, when the first rumblings of the Reagan revolution were heard. It was the moment when America turned rightward and liberalism became a dirty word. Historians have not paid sufficient attention to this election, to what it reveals about Reagan and to what it says about political trends in America. Reagan's biographers have given only nodding attention to 1966, being eager, apparently, to get to the eventful presidential years. The best book so far written on the election itself is Matthew Dallek's *The Right Moment*. It is an impressive piece of research, but leaves us wanting more, since it is concerned mainly with why Brown lost, rather than why (or how) Reagan won.

The historian Garry Wills has suggested, in *Reagan's America*, that the 1966 campaign had a sinister, Orwellian quality, introducing tactics of behaviour engineering, voter profiling and negative campaigning. If true, that would make for an interesting story, but unfortunately Wills is wrong. The Reagan victory was indeed an impressive example of professional campaign management. The candidate employed the firm Spencer-Roberts, a new breed of political technicians with skills in public relations, advertising, communications, market research, etc. Their role makes the 1966 effort one of the first 'modern' campaigns; they provided a playbook for election management still relevant today. Yet none of these 'new' developments was actually new, nor particularly sinister.

The campaign was equally notable as homage to the past. Reagan was, for instance, a superb stump speaker. His television ads were surprisingly old-fashioned – the very opposite of the slick, Madison Avenue products one might have expected from a candidate out of Hollywood. Even more striking was the campaign's superb grassroots organization – a very low-tech phenomenon. Thousands of volunteers knocked on doors to mobilize support, walking precincts in the glaring heat of a California summer. The campaign broke records for the number of individual donations and, interestingly, for the lowest average size of donation. In other words, hordes of ordinary people gave what they could afford (sometimes as little as a quarter) in order to fund the Reagan revolution. This aspect of the campaign, perhaps because it seems mundane, has received little attention.

It is difficult to exaggerate what was achieved in 1966. At a time of apparent liberal ascendancy, an arch-conservative captured the Golden State. Reagan achieved this feat in part because he was one of the best campaigners in American history. The 'Great Communicator' was just that. Yet skilled communication is not just articulation; it also requires sensitivity to the mood of the electorate. Reagan understood the voters, particularly the white working class, better than any politician of his generation. He knew precisely what the people wanted to hear. When this book was conceived, the goal was to show that Reagan's election had less to do with the man himself than with the faceless men around him – the fixers and manipulators of a modern campaign. Yet that aim proved unsustainable. In the end, we come back to the argument made in almost every Reagan book: he was extraordinary. Nevertheless, the story of how his special qualities played out in this particular contest will still prove surprising. And recognition of those qualities should not blind one to the wider political trends which his candidacy highlighted. A simple fact needs emphasis: Reagan was a brilliant campaigner, but he could not have taken California in a direction that it did not already want to go.

Finally, we need to remind ourselves that the 1960s was the decade of consumerism and Reagan a product to be sold. In order to appeal to the voters, he needed to be packaged. Leaving aside his personal skills, Reagan won because his campaign team figured out how to make an extremist seem moderate. They understood how to sell Reagan, and he, wisely, allowed himself to be sold. Thus, the 1966 election victory should not be reduced to singular phenomena – the perfect candidate or the most high-tech, manipulative campaign. It was, instead, a synthesis: a skilled campaigner voicing a relevant message, backed by a gifted sales team.

Here follows the story of how Reagan was sold to California and to America.

# 1

# The Speech

Small incidents often carry big meaning. In the autumn of 1954, Ronald Reagan was working for General Electric (GE) as a goodwill ambassador visiting factories around the country. Since he was frightened of flying, he travelled exclusively by train, making the itinerary all the more exhausting. Earl Dunckel, his General Electric minder, accompanied him. 'We hit Erie, Pennsylvania, one morning coming in on the redeye special New York Central train,' Dunckel recalled. 'They met us at the station at six-thirty in the morning, grabbed us and put us in a car ... We never saw the hotel ... until after midnight. All that time we were walking plant floors, talking to employees.' Throughout the day, Reagan was the Good Humour Man – nothing disturbed his light-hearted demeanour. When he and Dunckel finally got to the hotel, they felt like zombies. Passing the front desk on their way to the elevator, they heard the clerk clear his throat and timidly announce that a young lady had been waiting for Reagan in the lobby for nearly three hours. 'Ron,' Dunckel interjected, 'you can't afford it. You're dead now. We have a tough day tomorrow. Let's just ask this gentleman to do regrets.' Reagan shook his head. 'Dunk, I'd better find out what it's all about.'[1]

The young lady fancied herself the next Rita Hayworth. Reagan sat patiently while she unreeled her dreams. 'This was the typical stage-struck, small-town girl,' Dunckel recalled. 'She was all set, had it in her mind, tickets and everything, she was going out to Hollywood.' Reagan spent an hour and a half convincing her to stay home and first make a name for herself in community theatre or local radio. 'He kept drumming it into her, "Always remember, if you can command an audience in Erie, Pennsylvania, you can command an audience anywhere. You don't have to go to Hollywood to prove it."' His job done, Reagan walked her to the door, bade her farewell and good luck. As they dragged themselves to their rooms, Dunckel said: 'Ron, you couldn't afford that time.' Reagan replied: 'Dunk, I couldn't not afford that time. I'd do almost anything to keep another one of these little girls from going out there and adding to the list of whores out in Hollywood.' Dunckel later reflected: 'We were both exhausted, but that wasn't enough to quench his humanity. It quenched mine, but it didn't quench his.'[2]

We start with a simple, but important, fact: Reagan was a nice guy.

Before World War II, Reagan had toiled through forgettable films, always believing his big break would come. 'I was the Errol Flynn of the B's,' he recounted, 'as brave as Errol, but in low budget fashion.'[3] A breakthrough of sorts came when he landed a big part in *Kings Row* (1942), but the war then intervened. When he resumed acting after 1945, Hollywood had moved on, leaving Reagan behind. He took whatever came his way, including a demoralizing stint at a Las Vegas nightclub. Never a great actor, by 1954 he was an unemployed one. Down on his luck, he eagerly grabbed the lifeline handed him by General Electric. They wanted him to present *General Electric Theater* and be a cheerleader at plants around the country. 'They weren't beating a path to my door offering me parts and this television show came riding along, the cavalry to the rescue.'[4] GE offered a steady income, an important requirement after he married Nancy Davis and their first child, Patti, was born in October 1952. They paid him $125,000 a year, a bargain for the firm. '[We got] a Cadillac at Ford prices,' an executive admitted.[5]

Reagan, perhaps because he was so desperate, didn't see it that way. Included in the deal was a complete remodelling of his Pacific Palisades home, turning it into a showcase of GE technology. 'We benefited to no end from their generous intention,' he admitted.[6] In addition to presenting the show, he occasionally got to star in the dramas. In one episode, he played a United States Information Service official who helps a downtrodden Asian village rebuild its library after nasty communists torched it. The role was easy because Reagan got to play himself. All he had to do was act naturally.

GE was scrupulous when it came to choosing its spokesman. 'We had been very, very definite as to the kind of person we wanted,' Dunckel explained. 'Good moral character, intelligent. Not the kind with the reputation for the social ramble. A good, upright kind of person.'[7] Reagan fit the bill perfectly. He was delighted to work for GE, 'a vast corporation, but as human as the corner grocer'.[8] The experience was like a homecoming. 'When I went on those tours', he reflected, 'I was seeing the same people that I grew up with in Dixon, Illinois. I realized I was living in a tinsel factory. And this exposure brought me back.'[9] The workers were:

> a cross-section of America and, damn it, too many of our political leaders, our labor leaders, and certainly a lot of geniuses in my own business and on Madison Avenue have underestimated them. They want the truth, they are friendly and helpful, intelligent and alert. They are concerned, not with security as some would have us believe, but with their very firm personal liberties. And they are moral.[10]

On those tours, Reagan morphed from actor into politician. He discovered the constituency on which he would later build his populist crusade. Their virtue lay in their mundanity. Decent, honest, hard-working, they had, Reagan decided, been ground down by an oppressive government.

Perhaps because Reagan was not a good actor, he never behaved like one. Dunckel confessed that 'It was a great and pleasant surprise when this tall, slim, handsome ... fellow shook hands with me and smiled and was not posturing and was as natural as anyone else you would meet ... there was nothing ... of the "I am a star"; he was a regular guy.'[11] Over the eight years he worked for GE, Reagan visited 139 plants in 39 states. The visits brought ersatz stardom – at the factories, at least, he was still famous. Women would rush up, demanding autographs and jockeying to get close to him. On at least one occasion, an assembly-line worker pulled out her breast and asked him to sign it. He handled the situation with typical aplomb.[12] Men, on the other hand, feigned disinterest. 'I bet he's a fag,' they'd mutter. After chatting with the 'girls', he'd walk over to the guys and ramp up the charm. 'When he left them ten minutes later, they were all slappin' him on the back saying, "That's the way, Ron."'[13] Reagan looked every bit like a politician on the campaign trail. When he talked to these workers, he had the knack of making every one of them feel like the most important person on earth.

He projected a genuine sensitivity, despite being rather shy and very private. The fact that he actually did care about people made it easy for him to seem sincere. For critics and opponents, his innate goodness was perhaps his most annoying feature – it made him difficult to despise. 'They used to say about him that he could charm anybody,' Caspar Weinberger quipped, 'but for people who really hated him it took ten minutes.'[14] His simple good nature made his humanity credible; there seemed nothing fake about him. From the start, he was an effective politician precisely because he never seemed like one. He had a remarkable ability to make everyone think he was a friend.

In truth, then, Reagan did not 'become' a politician; no dramatic transformation took place. He was, in fact, a natural. His uncanny ability to connect with ordinary people was perfectly suited to the populist he would become. Weinberger, who worked on both his gubernatorial and presidential staffs, remarked that Reagan 'could talk to an audience of three or four, or he could talk to an audience of 10,000 people. Yet you always felt that he was talking right at you, that *you* were the one he wanted to talk to.'[15] According to his brother Neil, this made campaigning easy: 'If you've got a good communicator ... [a crowd of] 20,000 will get the same kind of feeling ... as the ten people around him on the street corner while he's shaking hands.'[16]

Dunckel discovered another important attribute while watching Reagan present live on television. He'd get a script, quickly memorize it and then expand or contract it according to the time slot given. 'This was the most amazing thing. This man has a sense of timing almost as if there's a clock in his head ... All they'd do is tell him how many seconds, and he'd say what he had to say, and he'd be almost always right on the dot. There was never any problem of breaking in or adapting or anything else with him at all.'[17] The timing was perfect, but so too was the emotion. Reagan could make a stock list sound moving. A joke went round about a viewer who listened to Reagan talk about a nuclear submarine built by GE: 'I didn't really need a submarine, but I've got one now.'[18]

On those tours, 'The Speech' evolved. It was Americana distilled, a well-crafted mix of anecdotes, homespun homilies, inspirational advice and bits of *Reader's Digest*. According to Dunckel, biographers have misunderstood 'The Speech', often assuming it was GE's big plan for Reagan, a carefully devised strategy to 'sway the nation to conservatism'.[19] In reality, it was a fortuitous piece of improvisation. Plant managers, keen to further connections with the local community, would often ask Reagan to speak at Rotary, Kiwanis or PTA meetings. Reagan, being Reagan, couldn't say no. He proved so adept that, before long, the talks became part of his itinerary. He'd usually speak on whatever moved him, but was occasionally asked to expound on a specific topic. These requests never fazed him. In one town, with little preparation,

He got up there and gave a speech on education that just dropped them in the aisles! He got a good ten-minute standing applause afterward. This is when I finally began to realize the breadth and depth of his knowledgeability. I subsequently came to know that virtually everything that went into that mind stayed there. He could quote it out like a computer any time you wanted. He ... read widely, and he remembered what he read ... It was an amazing tour de force.[20]

Reagan would later be famous for what he forgot. In these early years, however, he had the closest thing to a photographic memory. 'He was a very, very quick study,' Weinberger recalled. 'He always said [that] was part of his heritage as an actor.'[21]

GE originally wanted Reagan to recount Hollywood anecdotes to workers, mixed with inspirational stuff designed to encourage company pride. He, however, went his own way. Stories about political interference in the film industry morphed into morality tales about the threat of big government. Listeners would often respond with their own complaints about interference, incompetence and profligacy by politicians. Reagan eventually became 'convinced that some of our fundamental freedoms were in jeopardy because of the emergence of a *permanent government* never envisioned by the framers of our Constitution: a federal bureaucracy so powerful it was able to set policy and thwart the desires not only of ordinary citizens, but their elected representatives in Congress'. Fate was pulling him in a direction he was already inclined to travel. 'Those GE tours became almost a postgraduate course in political science for me.'[22] He discovered the perfect populist constituency of heroic workers betrayed by a heartless, despotic government. His mission was to convince those workers that their best friend was not the government, but GE, that the fate of the company was their fate and, likewise, that the destiny of the company depended on the defence of the free world. Everything was connected. No one was unimportant in the war against tyranny.

Reagan is often credited with bringing populist conservatism to America during his presidency. While that is true, the phenomenon did not suddenly materialize in 1980. Reagan was always a populist. His party affiliation changed, his sympathies never did. Populism is usually defined as an appeal to the common man, often expressed as an attack on an elite. When Reagan campaigned as a Democrat for Harry Truman in 1948, he defended the common man against corporate greed and Republican policies that favoured plutocrats. In the late 1950s, he switched parties, but not constituencies – he still defended the little man, but his disdain had shifted from big business to big government.

While Reagan always insisted that his political beliefs were rooted in the American Revolution, he had a muddled understanding of what the founding fathers actually believed. His heroes, figures like Thomas Jefferson and Alexander Hamilton, had a very low opinion of the masses. As the historian Richard Hofstadter argues, secret discussions at the Constitutional Convention were characterized 'first and foremost [by] a distrust of the common man and democratic rule'.[23] That distrust eventually became an abiding characteristic of conservatism in America. As the prominent conservative cleric Bernard Iddings Bell argued in 1952, the 'chief threat to America come[s] from within America ... from the complacent, vulgar, mindless, homogenized, comfort seeking, nouveau riche culture of the common man'.[24] For most conservatives, that had always been gospel.

Traditional conservatism was characterized by a paternalistic attitude toward the common folk, who were assumed to be incapable of looking after themselves. A movement that promoted the common man, as Reagan's would, therefore necessitated a profound shift in attitude, a discovery of virtues overlooked by Bell. This was facilitated by improvements in the condition of the working class – better education and health – but was also helped along by the faith increasingly placed in the free market. Conservatives had once believed that the class system was God's construction – a deterministic ordering of society. Free-market theory, on the other hand, presupposed a more fluid society in which the individual shaped his own destiny. By implication, this meant that class differences were attributed not to fate but to real inequalities in ability – the rich were rich because they had talents the poor lacked. The duty of government, these conservatives believed, was to remove the obstacles to individualism and mobility, one of them being government itself.

Removing obstacles would enhance individual liberty. Thus, the founding fathers were themselves redefined, with their contempt for the masses subsumed in favour of their belief in freedom. While government had previously been seen as a way to protect the masses from themselves, it was now seen as a way to set the masses free from those forces that constrained them. This also meant convincing the mob that they were poor because they were not free. The best government was by definition small – the smaller it was, the less it could interfere in the lives of the masses. In contrast, liberal social welfare, in trying to improve the lot of man, inevitably impeded the freedom of the individual. As Reagan was fond of arguing, 'For every ounce of federal help we get we surrender an ounce of personal freedom.'[25]

Conservatives discovered wisdom in the mob. The redemption of ordinary people meant the sanctification of the values they held dear, in particular family, God, tradition and patriotism. These were co-opted as conservative values. Those who adhered to traditional ideals were considered morally superior and therefore better equipped to succeed in the free market. Those ideals, once a matter of personal choice, became a social code. Freedom, in other words, did not extend to behaviour that contradicted majority custom. A culture war developed: those who ignored mainstream values were deemed to be immoral, or at least too tolerant of immorality. Among the miscreants were liberals, intellectuals, the media and intrusive government. As will be seen, this led smoothly into an anti-intellectual crusade, with the universities presented as elitist, alien and too permissive of social and political deviancy. The purity of the masses lay in their simplicity and practicality – education had not corrupted them. Recall what Reagan said of the simple folk he met on GE factory floors.

The ethic looked back to a prelapsarian idyll, usually associated with colonial or frontier America, when morals were pure and freedom unhindered. By implication, modernity was feared because it was laced with multiple threats to morality and freedom. Americans, it seemed, had been corrupted by progress. Social welfare had destroyed the purity of self-reliance. Affluence had made Americans soft. The media and entertainment industries were like sirens luring Americans onto the rocks of decadence. Yet there is a fundamental contradiction in this fusing of the free market with traditional values since unfettered capitalism produces the enticements that supposedly undermine those values. Thus, the more dynamic and unencumbered the capitalist system, the greater the threat to morality. As the conservative thinker George Will pointed out in 1980: 'capitalism undermines traditional social structures and values; it is a relentless engine of change, a revolutionary inflamer of appetites, enlarger of expectations, diminisher of patience … Republicans see no connection between the cultural phenomena they deplore and the capitalist culture they promise to intensify.' The slide into immorality was, Will argued, the result of the 'unsleeping pursuit of ever more immediate, intense and grand material gratifications' – the very thing the capitalist encourages.[26]

Reagan never understood these connections. As Robert Dallek wrote, 'It is a peculiar facet of [his] personality that a man who is so much the product of a consumer culture should be so strong a proponent of rugged individualism and other traditional values.'[27] Reagan perceived no contradiction. He loved to debate issues of freedom and seems to have been an avid reader of political philosophy. But, while he read widely, he did not think deeply. He never perceived the need to protect the noble masses from the monsters that capitalism begat. His greatest strength, politically, was his steadfast belief that life is simple. His political toolkit contained a few basic principles and a handful of moral absolutes. Complex philosophical problems were distilled into glib aphorisms or heart-warming morality tales. Thus, 'Just Say No' seemed the perfect creed whether the problem was big government, tax policy, welfare or, eventually, drugs. As Rick Perlstein has written rather perfectly, 'Ronald Reagan was an athlete of the imagination, a master at turning complexity and confusion and doubt into simplicity and stout-hearted certainty.'[28] He was never afraid of sounding simplistic. 'They say the world has become too complex for simple answers. They are wrong. There are no easy answers, but there are simple answers. We must have the courage to do what is morally right.'[29]

'I have heard more than one psychiatrist say that we imbibe our ideals from our mother's milk,' Reagan wrote in his autobiography. 'My breast feeding was the home of the brave baby and the free bosom.'[30] While that toe-curling sentence makes less sense each time it is read, Reagan seems to have been saying that, despite his switch in party allegiance, his ideals were hard-wired to his soul. Originally a New Deal Democrat and an admirer of Franklin Roosevelt, Reagan was once a self-confessed 'near-hopeless, hemophilic liberal'. The period after 1948 – the last time he voted Democrat – was 'the story of my disillusionment with big government'.[31] In truth, his conversion was not as dramatic as he pretended. At the core of his beliefs was a steadfast faith in individualism and self-reliance – he worshipped the revitalizing struggle symbolized by the frontier. That never changed. Since the greatest threat to social harmony in the 1930s was bankers and rapacious corporations, it was only natural that he supported Roosevelt. Back then, he was Jimmy Stewart in *Mr Smith Goes to Washington* or *It's a Wonderful Life*. Yet his support for Roosevelt never implied a theoretical conversion to Keynesian economics or social democracy. Reagan was pragmatic: New Deal reforms and aid seemed appropriate in the 1930s, but redundant after the war. By the 1950s, the welfare state was a tiresome guest who wouldn't leave. On his tours, he reminded audiences that: 'Today there is hardly a phase of our daily living that doesn't feel the stultifying hand of government regulation and interference. We are faced with a collection of internal powers and bureaucratic institutions against which the individual citizen is absolutely powerless. This power, under whatever name or ideology, is the very essence of totalitarianism.'[32] Reagan, as will be seen, was an absolute master when it came to apocalyptic hyperbole.

Reagan's experience as president of the Screen Actors Guild compounded his disillusionment with the left, since he became convinced that communists were bent on taking over the guild, and Hollywood, aided by Democrats too scrupulous in their protection of free speech. Since Hollywood had a unique ability to sway American opinion, a communist takeover of Tinseltown frightened him. His brother Neil recalled that 'the beating ... he took mentally during the Screen Actors Guild strike' of 1946–7 was instrumental to his political enlightenment. He 'saw ... pickets swinging three-foot lengths of log chain at people's heads who were just trying to go in and go to work.' Neil feels that 'It finally brought him around to the place where he thought maybe the country needed some change.'[33] In October 1947, he warned the House Committee on Un-American Activities (HUAC) about a 'small clique' within SAG that was 'following the tactics that we associate with the Communist Party'.[34] Cooperating with HUAC seemed like sublime duty given the threat the country faced. His first wife Jane Wyman complained at their divorce hearings that Reagan was 'obsessed with the Screen Actors Guild and political activities' and that he forced her to attend meetings, though her ideas 'were never considered important'.[35]

Big businessmen – like those he met at GE – were Reagan's new heroes, the front line in the war against communism. Long hours on the road sharpened his political consciousness. The message delivered during those tours was conservative even though Reagan did not yet identify himself that way. He thought he was simply speaking common sense about individual liberty. In time, 'the portion of my speech about government began to grow longer and I began to shorten the Hollywood part. Finally, the Hollywood part just got lost and I was out there beating the bushes for private enterprise.' He later concluded that 'it wasn't a bad apprenticeship for someone who'd someday enter public life – although ... that was the farthest thing from my mind.'[36] Dunckel, a self-confessed 'arch-conservative', helped to exorcize the liberal ghosts. 'Whenever he tried to defend New Dealism, or what was passing for it at the time, we would have some rather spirited arguments. I think this helped him to realize, as he put it later, that he didn't desert the Democratic party; the Democratic party deserted him. They had turned the corner and gone a different direction.'[37] Reagan came to realize that the gap between him and the Democrats 'had widened just too far to be bridged'.[38] He would eventually discover that a great many Americans shared his disillusionment. Shifting allegiance to the Republicans did not involve a change of heart, but rather a simple realization that beliefs were more important than labels. Nancy once said of her husband's conversion: 'Some men change their party for the sake of their principles; others their principles for the sake of their party.'[39]

What had been a job became a mission. 'There is no point in saving souls in heaven,' Reagan once remarked. 'If my speaking is to serve any purpose, then I must appear before listeners who don't share my viewpoint.'[40] He seemed to crave discordance, loved to toss perfect one-liners back at hecklers. 'The Speech' was always a flexible thing tailored to the audience. Dunckel marvelled at Reagan's uncanny ability to gauge the mood and adjust his message accordingly. 'He would start down let's call it Street A, and if he wasn't getting the vibes back, he would segue without any hesitation into Route B. Generally, he'd get it then, but if he didn't, he'd move to Route C ... It's an absolutely uncanny, extrasensory ability the man has.'[41] What made 'The Speech' remarkable was Reagan's ability to deliver a basically conservative message to an audience of working-class trade unionists and yet convince them that he was a friend who understood their predicament. He did not preach, nor did he try to convert. He instead forged a personal bond with his listeners and that bond made his message seem like common sense rather than politicking. 'One of the things that I drew', Dunckel recalled, '[was that] he's proud of the country ... [and] he thinks the American people are much better than they conceive themselves to be. He wants them to recognize how good they are.'[42] He gave his audience a Neverland version of their world in which they could feel comfortable and secure.

'He is intelligent but not brilliant,' the journalist Bill Boyarsky wrote of Reagan. He thought that Reagan had a quick wit, but not much intellectual curiosity. Reagan would find a simple and satisfactory answer to a problem and then stick with it for the rest of his life. 'He will use it over and over again, clinging to familiar words as if they are part of a movie script. The same phrases, and even the same paragraphs, appear in speech after speech.'[43] Through endless repetition, 'The Speech' hardened into dogma, wearing a groove into his mind. 'There was a formula,' admitted Paul Gavaghan, who handled Reagan after Dunckel. 'His speech was always the same, he had it polished to perfection. It was old American values ... but it was like the Boy Scout code, you know, not very informative. But always lively, with entertaining stories.'[44] Reagan reckoned that he visited every GE plant during his eight years as front man. The company had around 700,000 employees in 1954. Add in all the people Reagan spoke to in the community, and that equalled a lot of exposure. It was easy to mistake him for a budding politician testing the waters for an election run. 'You should go into politics' was a frequent reaction after 'The Speech'. 'Nah,' came the reply.

Ralph Cordiner, the General Electric CEO, originally told Reagan: 'I am not ever going to have GE censor anything you say. You're not our spokesman ... You're speaking for yourself. You say what you believe.'[45] Cordiner did not, however, quite anticipate what Reagan would do with that assurance. Though GE executives admired his conservative values, they eventually grew uneasy about the direction 'The Speech' was going and the attention it got. A favourite target was the Tennessee Valley Authority (TVA): it was, Reagan insisted, a bad example of big government that needed to be dismantled and privatized. 'The annual interest on the TVA deal', he claimed, 'is five times as great as the flood damage it prevents.'[46] Unfortunately, the TVA was one of GE's biggest customers. When Cordiner complained, Reagan agreed to target his wrath elsewhere. 'Dropping TVA from the speech was no problem,' he admitted. 'You can reach out blindfolded and grab a hundred examples of overgrown government.' That was perhaps true, but at least 90 of those 100 examples were GE customers.

Before long, liberals started accusing Reagan of being the front man for a virulently right-wing crusade. '[He] was being portrayed in the liberal press as a combination of Attila the Hun and Genghis Khan,' Dunckel claimed. 'Editorially the press commented, "Here's somebody who hates the little man, who would turn us back to the Dark Ages" – all that nonsense.'[47] This was not the type of publicity GE wanted. Keen to muzzle Reagan, the management demanded prior approval of his speeches. When Reagan refused, GE abruptly cancelled his contract. The firm offered the convenient excuse that the programme had run its course and was facing insurmountable competition on Sunday night from *Bonanza*, which, unlike *General Electric Theater*, was filmed in colour.

The real explanation, however, was that Reagan had become too controversial. As he admitted, 'I was suddenly being called a "right-wing extremist".'[48] GE might have also been worried because MCA, Reagan's agents, was facing indictment by the Justice Department for federal antitrust violations, with SAG named as a co-conspirator. There was every possibility that Reagan would be sucked into an ugly trial. He left with no hard feelings, but he did turn the episode into a useful allegory about the dangers of big government. In bygone days, 'GE stood up against government threats ... [and] government was less prone to use force and coercion.'[49] He blamed his misfortune on 'liberal Democrats [who] wanted to rein in the energy of free enterprise and capitalism, create a welfare state, and impose a subtle kind of socialism'.[50] The communists, the American Federation of Labor and Congress of Industrial Organizations (AFL-CIO), liberals in Hollywood and Attorney General Robert Kennedy had conspired to get him dismissed. 'Of course Bobby Kennedy's behind it,' Nancy reassured her husband. 'It's obvious.'[51]

*General Electric Theater* died, but 'The Speech' lived on. Reagan was now financially secure. He did some acting and also hosted *Death Valley Days* in 1965, but spent most of his time delivering speeches on what he called the 'mashed-potato circuit'. He felt a genuine purpose that had been missing in Hollywood: 'I had always believed that you pay your way for how good life has been to you. So, being a performer, and therefore having some ability to attract an audience, I ... campaigned for causes and people that I believed in.'[52] No longer needing to please his employers, he said what he liked, with the result that his message became even more apocalyptic. Behind every problem was the creeping threat of communism. He warned one audience:

> The Communist party has ordered once again the infiltration of the picture business as well as the theatre and television. They

are crawling out from under the rocks, and memories being short as they are, there are plenty of well-meaning but misguided people willing to give them a hand ... Most people agree that the ideological struggle with Russia is the number one problem in the world ... and yet, many men in high places in government and many who mold opinion in the press and on the air waves, subscribe to the theory that we are at peace ... the inescapable truth is that we are at war, and we are losing that war simply because we don't or won't realize we are in it.[53]

Every expansion of the state was a sacrifice of freedom and a step towards socialism. Programmes like Medicare were 'one of the traditional methods of imposing statism or Socialism on a people'.[54] Progressive taxation had 'no moral justification'; it was 'an idea hatched in the Communist revolution'. Federal aid to education was a 'tool of tyranny' and people on welfare 'a faceless mass waiting for a handout'.[55] Though the exact content of each speech varied, he usually ended in the same way, warning that, if government was allowed to grow unimpeded, 'one of these days you and I are going to spend our sunset years telling our children and our children's children what it once was like in America when men were free.'[56] For years, that was Reagan's favourite closing line.

The GE years were enormously important to Reagan's political development. He took the job because he was a mediocre actor no longer able to land parts. The factory tours revealed that the qualities that made him a bad actor also made him a great politician. He was far too transparent and one-dimensional ever to be a huge success in Hollywood. He could not escape himself – an ordinary guy liked for his simplicity and trusted for his honesty – 'the guy who always loses the girl in every picture he's in'.[57] He was convincing precisely because he was incapable of pretence. The plant visits also caused his political beliefs to coalesce. From this point on, he would follow his heart, which would take him in a resolutely conservative direction. Working for GE also brought him into contact with a constituency of opinion that would eventually form the bedrock of his populist campaigns. He found that he had a talent for communicating with 'the unwashed public'.[58] 'The trips were murderously difficult,' he reflected. '*But I enjoyed every whizzing minute of it.* It was one of the most rewarding experiences of my life.' Reagan sensed that the experience had transformed him from an actor into an activist: 'No barnstorming politician ever met the people on quite such a common footing. Sometimes I had an awesome, shivering feeling that America was making a personal appearance for me, and it made me the biggest fan in the world.'[59]

# 2

# Hardening of the Categories

The 1964 Republican National Convention was held at the Cow Palace in San Francisco. Jackie Robinson, the first black man to play Major League baseball and an honorary delegate from Connecticut, watched in dismay as his party tore itself to shreds. Robinson was unusual in being a black man who supported the Republican Party, but then, he prided himself on being an integrationist. He believed sincerely that 'It would be a terrible thing if every Negro voted Democrat. Then we'd be on the way to having a white party and a black party in America.'[1] That was the main reason why he went to San Francisco. He feared that the nomination of Barry Goldwater 'would ensure that the GOP became completely the white man's party'.[2]

His worst fears were realized. By the time the first gavel pounded, Goldwater had all but sewn up his party's endorsement. His rabid followers saw their victory as an opportunity to purge the party of its moderate wing and symbolically lynch the losing candidate, Nelson Rockefeller. Purity was more important to them than electability. Moderates who tried to inject some rationality into the proceedings were shouted down, and often threatened with violence. Robinson could not bear to watch the bloodletting. The Goldwater supporters were 'full of such hatred toward us Rockefeller people that surrounded by them I thought I felt a little of what it must have been like to be a Jew in Hitler's Germany'.[3]

To many, the Republican Party seemed in terminal disarray in the early 1960s. Moderates like President Dwight Eisenhower had accommodated New Deal reforms in order to establish a political consensus near the centre of American politics. Those on the right, however, deplored this betrayal of conservatism; they complained that the party had become a poor imitation of the Democrats. Phyllis Schlafly, the right's favourite harpy, argued in 1964 that the party needed to offer 'a choice, not an echo'.[4] Reagan fully agreed. Instead of appeasing liberalism, he wanted to destroy it. 'The Speech' was the battle hymn of the new conservatives, sung in major key.

In 1958, internecine warfare within the GOP brought an end to the party's secure hold on the governor's office in California. During that election, radical conservatives in the south revolted against moderates who had long controlled the party from their base in the Bay Area. Disunity was blatantly manifested when the popular incumbent governor, Goodwin Knight, a moderate, was rudely pushed aside by the conservative William Knowland. Exploiting Republican disunity, Pat Brown, the Democrat nominee, engineered an unexpected victory. The election should have been a lesson in the need for consensus, but far-right ideologues interpreted it differently. Like true zealots, they took defeat as proof that Republicans needed to distance themselves even further from their opponents – instead of fighting for the centre, the party should seek ideological purity on the far right.

Meanwhile, the retired candy baron Robert Welch took the right's vague resentments and turned them into a movement, fuelled by rampant paranoia. An inveterate peddler of conspiracy theories, he accused Eisenhower of being a Soviet agent, demanded the imprisonment of Chief Justice Earl Warren and alleged that water fluoridation was a communist plot. From his stronghold in Southern California, Welch launched the John

Birch Society in 1958. Three years later, California Attorney General Stanley Mosk accurately described the Birchers as a group:

> formed primarily of wealthy businessmen, retired military officers and little old ladies in tennis shoes. They are bound together by an obsessive fear of 'communism', a word which they define to include any ideas differing from their own ... In response to this fear they are willing to give up a large measure of the freedoms guaranteed them by the United States Constitution ... They seek, by fair means or foul, to force the rest of us to follow their example. They are pathetic.[5]

Pathetic or not, the society always punched above its weight. 'They weren't just your ordinary, average, small group of noisy dissidents,' Weinberger argued. 'Everybody was ... terribly alarmed by them, the way people were terribly alarmed by Senator McCarthy.' Mainstream Republicans feared that any attempt to move the party rightwards would take it into Bircher territory. It seemed entirely possible that the party might be hijacked by 'a small group of very fanatical people'.[6]

At his inauguration, Brown promised 'responsible liberalism'. He wanted to use government to improve the lives of ordinary people – not just the poor or dispossessed, but all those who would benefit from better schools, transport, parks, etc. During his first term, he made good on his promise by delivering a Fair Employment Practices Commission, more funding to education, new road and highway schemes, tighter pollution standards and the beginnings of a state healthcare system. Conservatives, alarmed by the tide of progressive reform, warned of a socialist Leviathan rising in Sacramento. One particular project would have ironic effect. Brown pushed through construction of the California Aqueduct, which brought water to the most parched areas in the south, thus making possible the immigration of those who would become bitter opponents of his policies.

Voters at first seemed to welcome 'responsible liberalism'. Thanks to a steadily expanding population, Brown's ambitions did not place a huge burden on the taxpayer. It was nevertheless fortunate that the GOP was still at war with itself when Brown sought re-election in 1962. The selection of a candidate to oppose him again tore the party apart. A group of arch-conservatives led by Representative H. Allen Smith tried to persuade Reagan to run, but he declined. That was probably fortunate, since it meant he did not have to endure a bloody battle against Richard Nixon in the primary, nor face Brown at the peak of his strength. Nixon's emergence as the frontrunner annoyed conservatives in the south, who turned to Joe Shell, an oil executive and former football star. The slow-witted Shell was a good man, but one whose ambition outstripped his ability. He was not a Bircher, but, when Nixon openly attacked the society, Birchers enthusiastically backed Shell, much to Nixon's delight. Uninterested in compromise, Nixon let the hatred fester.

Reagan, who felt that Nixon was ideologically vague, had reluctantly supported his 1960 presidential bid. During that campaign, he urged Nixon to expose John Kennedy's 'socialism'. 'Under the tousled boyish haircut it is still old Karl Marx', he warned. 'There is nothing new in the idea of a government being Big Brother to us all. Hitler called his "State Socialism" and way before him it was "benevolent monarchy".'[7] Nixon probably recognized that that made absolutely no sense and wisely ignored Reagan's febrile warnings. When Nixon lost by a narrow margin, Reagan blamed the defeat on his party's failure to offer a clear alternative – Nixon was too moderate, his anti-communism too muted. For that reason, he backed Shell for governor in 1962. His loathing intensified when Nixon attacked Birchers instead of Democrats.

Many years later, the wounds of 1962 still pained State Assemblyman William Bagley:

it was a strident primary. The right-wing accused Nixon of being a left winger ... people of that right-wing mold and mode would come up to me ... and would give me the heavy finger on the shoulder and say, 'You're some kind of a Com symp [communist sympathizer] because you are a friend of Nixon. He's a liberal!' ... I couldn't stand these right-wing, bug-eyed, blithering, bigoted Birchers! ... these fringe groups are destructive ... They think with their glands; they suffer from 'hardening of the categories'.[8]

Nixon won the nomination, but his attack on Shell so alienated right-wingers like Reagan that they refused to work for him in the general election. Weinberger struggled to find sense in this attitude. 'It's sort of ironic because I always regarded myself as philosophically very conservative but not aligned with the rather fierce presentation of that viewpoint that seemed to accompany them,' he reflected. 'I wanted the party to win. I wanted the party to be strong and I wanted that much more than so-called ideological purity.'[9]

Reagan was sailing very close to the wind. Rumours that he was a Bircher were credible precisely because he acted like one. He had much in common with the society, though not its fondness for conspiracy. He was more unashamedly extremist than at any time in his life. Politically naïve, he was unable to see that he would be judged on the friends he kept. In the early 1960s, he appeared at rallies of extremist groups like the Christian Anti-Communist Crusade, Project Prayer, Project Alert and the Town Meeting for Freedom, often sharing a podium with Birchers. Members of Project Alert were notorious for advocating that Warren be hanged for treason. In 1961, Reagan delivered the keynote address at a rally for John Rousselot, a congressmen and member of the society, describing him as a 'warm personal friend'.[10] When questioned about that endorsement, Reagan explained that he did so 'automatically, because he [is] a Republican'.[11] He also accepted awards from governors Orval Faubus and Ross Barnett, two notorious segregationists and Bircher favourites. While he probably never actually joined the group, neither did he denounce it. Opponents of the society equated his tolerance as sympathy with its aims, a fair assumption. Meanwhile, Birchers loved Reagan because he offered the best opportunity for wider recognition. 'The Speech' articulated their anti-communism beautifully, while the man himself possessed the charisma that they sorely lacked.

The situation facing California Democrats in 1962 looked ominous since Nixon had taken the state two years earlier when running against Kennedy. Much to Brown's good fortune, however, the Republican split had since widened. In an effort to court conservatives, Nixon cast Brown as a 'willing puppet of the left-wing'. Some of his lunatic supporters even released a clumsily doctored photo of Brown bowing to Nikita Khrushchev – an image of the Soviet leader had been pasted over that of a visitor from Thailand. Adding his voice to the tirade, Reagan accused Brown of ignoring the most pressing issue of the campaign – that of 'totalitarianism versus freedom'.[12] In truth, however, few voters saw communism as a problem in California and fewer still believed that Brown was pink. Thanks to Republican disarray, he swept to a comfortable victory by over 300,000 votes, in the process becoming the state's first two-term Democratic governor. Nixon rightly blamed his defeat on his failure to woo the right.

'We were at the low ebb [in 1962],' party activist Gaylord Parkinson recalled, 'probably the lowest the Republican party has ever been in the state, both vote wise, financial wise, and every other way.'[13] Appearances, however, were deceptive – in truth, prospects were more promising than anyone understood. While Brown interpreted his victory as a mandate for further liberal reform, the state was in fact moving steadily rightward. That made the governor seem increasingly leftist with each passing day. The journalist Hale Champion noticed that there was 'a strong impression in the second four years of the

Brown administration that he was more liberal than his past image'.[14] On so many issues, he was seriously out of step with the electorate. Thus, time was on the side of the right, though hardly anyone realized it.

Demographics favoured the Republicans. By 1962, California was the most populous state in the Union. In the election that year, Brown lost comprehensively to Nixon in Orange and San Diego counties, and managed to carry the other southern counties by very narrow margins. This was ominous, since the south was growing at a much faster rate than the rest of the state, and new arrivals were predominantly conservative. During the 1960s, California's population increased by around 2,800 people per day, more than a third of whom were migrants from conservative states. By the start of the new decade, only one-fifth of the population lived in the Bay Area, while one-half lived in the south coastal region. Suburban houses could hardly be built fast enough to accommodate the flood of migrants. The population of Orange County more than tripled during the 1950s and then grew at an annual rate of 10 per cent from 1960 to 1965.[15]

For many migrants, California embodied the American Dream – the logical corollary of the advice 'Go West, young man.' They came from the Midwest and South, drawn to jobs in Southern California's aerospace, manufacturing and construction industries. The migration, which began during the Dust Bowl days, gained pace during World War II, when new defence firms sprouted up in the Golden State. Those factories thrived in the early years of the Cold War, as the US consolidated its Great Power status. Each new threat from abroad brought new defence contracts and new migrants. The 'bomber gap' was closely followed by Sputnik, then the 'missile gap', then Vietnam. Each threat was meat and potatoes for workers in Southern California.

The newcomers brought their politics with them. The Midwest had a long tradition of populism inspired by rugged frontier individualism. As for the migrants from the Deep South, they were technically Democrats, but distinctly different from those elsewhere. 'Dixiecrats' had deeply conservative values and a long memory – their beliefs resembled Republicanism, but they still rued the betrayal of 1860. 'An awful lot of registered Democrats out there are conservatives,' the journalist Lyn Nofziger remarked.[16] The campaign strategist Stuart Spencer echoed this judgement:

> When you analyze the data of where those people came from, a lot of them came from the south. Their daddy was a Democrat, their grand-daddy was a Democrat. But their thinking processes ... were much closer to the Republican party philosophy in the state of California than they were to ... the California Democratic Council. So, they were out here for a couple of years and they'd [say] ... 'I'm a Democrat, but that's not me!'[17]

These migrants confounded the pollsters. New arrivals from the South did not immediately switch parties on entering California. They remained Democrats, often formally registering as such. Yet they despised Brown's liberalism. In Orange County, Democrats briefly outnumbered Republicans from 1960 to 1962 because of migration from the South. Yet this did not change the fundamentally conservative nature of the county. These trends were, however, apparent only to those willing to deconstruct the data. Brown's team, dominated by men from the Bay Area, failed to notice what was happening. Confusion and ignorance suited the far right, since it allowed them to slip under the radar. They played the long game, their confidence bolstered by two certainties: as time passed, their support base would expand and satisfaction with Brown would shrink.

To up stakes in search of a better life is an avowal of the American Dream, affirmation of a faith in self-reliance. Success in their new home convinced these migrants that anyone could prosper, without need of state help. Echoing their values, Reagan declared: 'the man on the street ... [is] supporting too many families not his own.'[18] These were the people Reagan had met on his GE tours. A *Washington Post* reporter accurately described them as 'people who like to complain about the 20th century'.[19] They espoused homespun values, were suspicious of minorities and were intolerant of government interference. To them, social welfare undermined the structure of society by cushioning the adversity that made people strong. Law and order was always high on their agenda, since crime seemed out of control. Because basic morality seemed threatened, politics took on the characteristics of a quasi-religious spiritual revival. Their complaints comprehensively changed the politics of the Golden State. A huge opportunity awaited the politician able to voice their outrage.

As the Tea Party has recently demonstrated, those obsessed with self-reliance are seldom able to notice the benefits that government provides. California's attractiveness owed much to the beneficent big government that the new migrants angrily derided. A well-developed network of highways meant that industries could locate where land was cheap. The California Aqueduct allowed the south of the state to support a much larger population than should have been possible. The public education system was the best in the nation. This meant that industries could draw upon an educated workforce, while universities provided the research necessary to high-tech development. Migrants, however, failed to notice what liberalism had achieved. They instead saw Southern California as the best example of free enterprise and frontier individualism. Government expenditure on infrastructure was dismissed as creeping socialism. 'Dump the tea and save California,' a supporter urged Reagan.[20]

The new arrivals were anti-communist, but not rabidly so. They loved America, hated socialism, but the Soviet threat seemed distant. For this reason, the virulent anti-communism of the Birchers had limited appeal. The new migrants might have considered Eisenhower a bit too moderate, but could not accept that he was a Soviet stooge. Thus, the Society was ill-equipped to capitalize on the demographic change occurring in California. The attention Birchers received camouflaged the much more successful grassroots efforts of less controversial right-wing groups. For instance, the mega-wealthy Orange County businessman Walter Knott (of Knott's Berry Farm fame) founded the California Free Enterprise Association, which reached out to factory workers. Pamphlets argued that big government was eating into disposable income through high taxation, while jeopardizing economic growth by inhibiting entrepreneurs. Reagan regularly lent his services to these organizations; Knott and others were impressed by his unique ability to communicate with workers. These groups were actively trying to turn working-class voters, whose natural sympathies should have been with the Democratic Party, into Republicans. This meant undermining class identity by encouraging disharmony between those in stable employment and those in need of state support. New Deal assumptions about the duty of the state to look after the downtrodden were steadily eroded. Since those in need of assistance were often black, arguments over the shape of government took on a racial dimension.

From the outside, California looked like a state that had taken leave of its senses. In Berkeley, activists campaigned against the atom bomb and loyalty oaths. In San Francisco, the Beats celebrated bohemian excess. In the south, however, a very different revolution was materializing on the right. That, in particular, frightened Weinberger, a northern Republican. 'Extremist groups ... would tie up the party with all kinds of silly resolutions,' he recalled. As a result, 'we had trouble getting the proper impression around ... of what we were trying to do. I was worried about extremist viewpoints giving the party basically a bad name.'[21] Those on the fringes needed one another: leftists warned of a resurgence of McCarthyism in Southern California, while those on the right used the lifestyle revolt in the Bay Area as proof of moral degradation.

In truth, California was more stable than appearances suggested. As the journalist Joseph Lewis argued, 'the quintessential California, for all its distractions, is a quiet and self-preoccupied place, a kind of national suburban retreat.'[22] It was a haven for white people and white values. In 1962, 83 per cent of the population was non-Hispanic Caucasian. Blacks were concentrated in poor pockets of San Francisco, Los Angeles and San Diego, with integration still a long way off. The Hispanic population were transient, or at least seemed so. They were the migrant workers who laboured on the farms of the Central Valley, or in the gardens and homes of white suburbanites. They were phantoms – where they came from, and where they went after work, hardly concerned whites. Despite the small size of the minority population, race was an increasingly important issue because a disproportionate number of new residents were ethnic minorities. Whites feared a black 'invasion'.

California was not a racist state, but could easily be turned into one. Brown inadvertently managed that early in his second term. Intent on extending 'responsible liberalism', he pushed through a Fair Housing Bill. Originally drafted by William Rumford, the bill sought to outlaw discrimination on the basis of race, sex, marital status or physical handicap when private owners sold or rented property. Richard Kline, one of Brown's closest advisers, thought fair housing was a minefield. 'It would be unsound to initiate any major specific housing legislation at this time,' he warned Brown in December 1960. 'We are simply not prepared for it ... Housing is such an explosive social subject ... The question is not what has to be done in this field, but what can be done from a politically realistic standpoint.'[23] Brown at first heeded that advice, but then decided after his re-election that the time had come to act upon his principles.

Despite fierce opposition, the bill passed the committee, Senate, and Assembly stages on the final day of the 1963 legislative session. Then the real battle began. Brown mistakenly assumed that legislative opposition was not representative of popular opinion. His aide, Arthur Alarcón, recalled a common assumption that fair housing was a 'mom and apple pie' issue 'that no one could possibly be against', except for a few 'totally foolish' people 'not worthy' of serious consideration.[24] That assumption proved catastrophically mistaken. The Brown team was probably led astray by the fact that extremists – Birchers and members of the American Nazi Party – were conspicuous at rallies calling for repeal. Their claims that the bill was a communist or UN plot reassured Brown that the even-tempered majority would be supportive.

Birchers and fascists camouflaged mainstream resentment. Opponents of the Rumford proposal were not all bigots, though many were. Antagonism was rooted in white fears that property prices would fall and crime rise in neighbourhoods where blacks purchased homes. More fundamentally, the measure made it possible to hide racial prejudice behind noble assertions of freedom. 'Conservatives', according to Parkinson, 'felt that the Rumford Act, because of the compulsive side of it, was a foot in the door for more government involvement in … forcing them to do things.'[25] Republicans cleverly avoided the race dimension by arguing that every individual had an inalienable right to dispose of his property as he wished.

Brown steered his administration into a perfect storm of populist anger. The Rumford Act, Champion felt, 'was probably, *sub rosa*, the single most important issue in California'.[26] The right immediately mobilized a grassroots campaign that foreshadowed Reagan's own effort in 1966. Over a million people signed a petition calling for a proposition to overturn the act and prohibit the state from denying any person the right to sell or rent his property as he chose. Realtors dubbed Proposition 14 the 'real fair housing initiative'.[27] At the election in November 1964, 65 per cent supported it. 'You could draw but one conclusion from the vote on 14,' Brown wrote candidly to his wife, 'and that is that the white is just afraid of the Negro.'[28] While that was probably true, the anti-Rumford reaction was strong because it was more substantial than simple fear.

The 'people's victory' was short-lived. The federal government responded by cutting off all housing funds to the state. A 5–2 decision by the Supreme Court of California then overturned Proposition 14 on the grounds that it violated the equal protection clause of the 14th Amendment to the federal constitution. All this merely fuelled populist hatred of big government. 'I am greatly disturbed by the Supreme Court's decision,' Reagan commented. 'They have established the right of government to interfere in the individual's personal property rights. The right of the individual to the ownership and control of his own property is the basis for individual freedom.'[29] He insisted that those who had voted for Proposition 14 had done so 'not through bigotry or prejudice ... They are right-thinking and fair-minded people.'[30] He wanted to 'repeal or amend' the Rumford Act and replace it with 'constructive legislation which protects the free choice and constitutional rights of all citizens'.[31] With the weight of popular anger behind him, he did not have to explain what he meant.

The chief benefactor of this debacle was the far right of the Republican Party, whose platform was rooted in a defence of individual freedom against the threat of big government. While Democrats still supported the act in principle, they came to lament the quagmire they had created. 'It never really was effective, never really was the law,' Don Bradley, a Brown adviser, complained. 'It was so contested that it was never put into effect ... Then Prop. 14 nullified it. Then the Supreme Court knocked that down. And by that time there was a federal housing law ... So, in effect we had fought a battle over nothing, and it was a hurtful battle. It really divided people in this state.'[32] Brown fell victim to his own good intentions.

'I had been governor six years, and I wasn't sure whether I would run again,' he reflected. 'As a matter of fact, I enjoyed the freedom of doing what I wanted to do and taking positions that I felt were idealistic ... I did things because they were the right thing to do.'[33] The behaviour of his fellow Californians perplexed and embarrassed him. 'It told the black people of the state of California, "The whites don't want you to live next to them."'[34] Black discontent over Proposition 14, he felt certain, was manifested in the Watts riots of the following year. Whether that is true or not, it is certain that Proposition 14 exposed the chasm separating the governor from the people. 'We felt that if we could educate the people they'd vote our way,' Kline explained. 'Well ... we did educate them and they voted against us two to one.'[35] Lucien Haas, a press assistant to Brown, felt Proposition 14 was a turning point. 'Liberalism ... was dead. Liberalism died in '64, if you want to pick a date.'[36]

The Rumford disaster demonstrated what could happen if the right in California united behind an issue. As yet, they had not been able to unite behind an individual. The split in the party was underlined during the 1964 presidential campaign. In the Republican primary, moderates backed Nelson Rockefeller, who perfectly suited the temperate nature of Northern California. Republicans in the south, however, preferred Goldwater, a genuinely radical alternative. Reagan saw Goldwater as Birchism by other means – extremism without damaging affiliations. He was, he claimed, 'one of the very early ones' to urge Goldwater to run. 'I met Barry Goldwater and began saying that I thought he should be a candidate.'[37] Goldwater's apparent ability to swim in the political mainstream made Reagan feel more confident about distancing himself from the Birchers.

Senator Barry Goldwater was the grandson of a Jewish émigré who traded a Polish ghetto for the Arizona desert. His father was a dry goods merchant who built a lucrative retail empire in Arizona. For the Goldwaters, becoming American meant ditching the Jewish faith in favour of Presbyterianism. They turned themselves into typical Westerners, paragons of American individualism, pugnacious men who liked guns for the frontier self-reliance they symbolized. That individualism in turn encouraged a virulent hatred of the federal government. Goldwater agreed with Southerners on states' rights, which meant that he saw civil rights legislation emanating from Washington as a fundamental violation of federalist principles. Like so many mega-wealthy heirs, he somehow convinced himself that he embodied the virtues of a self-made man. A *Washington Post* cartoon poked fun by showing Goldwater telling a homeless black woman, 'If you had any initiative, you'd go out and inherit a department store.'[38] Goldwater insisted he was not racist, offering as proof the fact that he played football with 'Negroes' when he was a kid. He was not, however, prepared to use federal power to improve the lives of blacks. In a recent article in *Salon*, the linguist and social commentator Noam Chomsky argued that American racism has been characterized by '"intentional ignorance" of what it is inconvenient to know'.[39] Goldwater exhibited something similar, namely an inability to visualize the consequences of his rigid orthodoxy. He was, in other words, a racist who lacked the imagination to realize he was one.

In a more logical world, Goldwater would never have won the Republican nomination in 1964. He did not seem like a very nice man; his demeanour was as bleak as the desert in which he lived. While he occasionally smiled, for most people his name brought to mind a man in perpetual scowl. He was also not very politically astute: his pronouncements emanated from his glands rather than his brain. For instance, he failed to realize that it would be unwise to rail against Medicare when talking to pensioners in Orlando. He wanted America to carry a big stick, but opposed the military draft. Crime, violence and race riots were blamed not on social conditions, but on federal immorality – they all stemmed from the fact that Johnson was a liar. Likewise, sexual assault was the fault of the over-lenient Warren Court. Anyone willing to use taxpayers' money to build a new highway was suspected of being a socialist radical. The Viet Cong problem, he felt certain, could be solved with gallons of defoliant and a few low-yield atomic bombs. Every time Goldwater opened his mouth he lost a few supporters. Comments such as 'I think a general war is probable' made the nation tremble in fear.[40] His main problem was that he had built his political reputation on being a mean son of a bitch and never understood how that image was unattractive outside cowboy country. Most people saw Goldwater as the scariest man in America.

Goldwater benefited enormously from Nixon's defeat in the 1960 presidential election. Nixon had defied labelling; he was a pragmatist who, according to Spencer, 'kept a lid on a lot of people'.[41] When the lid was removed, pragmatism gave way to zealotry. Like moths to a flame, new activists were drawn to the prospect of a fundamentalist crusade. Bagley watched in horror as Goldwater jihadists hijacked the party. 'Some of these people were absolutely nuts and I mean that literally ... literally weren't in their right mind. I mean, they were almost fascists. They were bigots.'[42]

In the race for the Republican nomination, everything hinged on how California would vote. Realizing this, the far right cleverly infiltrated the California Republican Assembly, eventually getting their man, Nolan Frizzelle, elected president at the CRA convention in Fresno on 13 March 1964, completely wrong-footing the complacent Rockefeller group. Rockefeller loyalist William Nelligan complained to reporters that 'Fanatics of the Birch variety have fastened their fangs on the Republican Party's flanks and are hanging on like grim death.'[43] The histrionics were entirely appropriate. 'I don't consider the John Birch Society extremist,' Frizzelle shouted. 'Except maybe extremely American.'[44] On hearing that, moderates shuddered, shook their heads and despaired for the future of their party.

'It was a very bitter fight,' Weinberger recalled. 'It was very apparent that we would weaken the party seriously if we didn't recover from it quickly.' Prior to the convention, he had worked hard to persuade delegates of the need for unity regardless of the winner. Unfortunately, 'not very many people would take that pledge or support it because the Goldwater people, by that time, had control of all the volunteer organizations and were strongly opposed to anybody else.'[45]

The primary pitted two distinct conceptions of what it meant to be a Republican and two very different styles of campaigning. Rockefeller relied on old-fashioned loyalties – the assumption that Republican supporters were easily identifiable and did not need much shepherding. Goldwater, in contrast, conducted a grassroots campaign that played to the fierce individualism of the new migrants, many of whom had never voted Republican before. His team tried to establish face-to-face contact with every potential supporter. Thousands of volunteers poured through suburban neighbourhoods, especially in Southern California. 'Goldwater had a corner on the volunteer talent,' recalled Spencer, who managed Rockefeller's campaign. 'You have to hand it to the Birchers: they are great little workers. Our volunteers just couldn't match their energy.'[46] The personal contact gave the new residents a sense of their own importance and suggested to them that a revolt against the Republican mainstream was the logical extension of the ethos that had brought them to California in the first place. Voting Goldwater was, essentially, a cultural revolt.

That revolt harmonized perfectly with Reagan's own beliefs. 'I'd met Barry at the home of Nancy's parents in Phoenix several years before and admired him greatly. His book, *The Conscience of a Conservative*, contained a lot of the same points I'd been making in my speeches and I strongly believed the country needed him.' Goldwater was essential because 'Lyndon Johnson had begun to make most of the tax-and-spend Democrats of the past seem miserly by comparison.'[47] Reagan was therefore delighted when asked to serve as co-chairman of Goldwater's campaign in California. This was, in essence, his first formal entry into politics – a step beyond delivering 'The Speech' on the mashed-potato circuit. His contribution was instrumental in the grassroots effort to drum up support. 'I had no idea – never kept track – of how many appearances or speeches I made, but believe me, I covered the state of California from top to bottom.'[48]

While the campaign was superbly organized, the candidate left much to be desired. Vernon Cristina, excited by the rise of the new right, watched in horror as Goldwater wilted in front of television cameras, especially when journalists got aggressive. 'He never did handle the press well. That Arizona mafia that ... dictated all the way that the campaign was going to be run was just, as far as I was concerned, just idiots, just plain damned political idiots.' In retrospect, Cristina felt that rabid enthusiasm for Goldwater's policies blinded his supporters to his serious character flaws. The lesson, he concluded, was that a successful campaign needed a strong grassroots effort *and* an inspiring candidate. 'That was one of the reasons I went so quickly and so strongly with Reagan.'[49]

Meanwhile, other lessons emerged from the Rockefeller campaign, organized by Spencer-Roberts, the state's premier campaign-management firm. At the beginning of the California campaign, Rockefeller trailed Goldwater badly, so badly that Spencer and Roberts initially turned down the opportunity to represent him, since they refused to work for losers. When Rockefeller dangled an obscenely large cheque, they reconsidered. Rockefeller's seemingly hopeless situation nevertheless necessitated an aggressive approach. 'Our strategy ... was simple,' Spencer explained.

> We had to bring Barry back down to us. There was no way we were going to catch him in a straight-out, heads-on, positive campaign. We had to attack him, bring him down to our level,

and then rebuild ourselves into something that was feasible as a presidential candidate. So we attacked. We attacked, we attacked, we attacked. I mean we attacked everything. Some of it was valid. Some of it was borderline.[50]

Goldwater was portrayed as a madman, a bomb primed to explode. 'It was the nuclear aspect of it,' Spencer recalled. 'This man is going to be President of the United States. He's going to have access to these materials and yet he is a little bit deranged. He's not quite there. He'll do something scary. It was scare tactics.'[51] Getting that message out was expensive, but Rockefeller had money to burn. The negativity appalled Reagan, who called it the 'most vicious and venomous campaign against a candidate in our party we have ever seen'.[52]

The endless attacks on Goldwater's character were designed to distract attention from skeletons in Rockefeller's own closet. In 1962, he and Margaretta (aka 'Happy') Murphy had both obtained quickie divorces in order to marry the following year. The fact that Happy had worked on Rockefeller's staff fuelled speculation that they had been carrying on an affair while still married to their first spouses. Nor did it help that she yielded custody of her four children to her former husband when she married Rockefeller. The affair, Goldwater argued, was proof that Rockefeller had no respect for family values. As for Happy, what sort of woman would abandon her kids just to satisfy her own lust? Senator Prescott Bush, father of a president and grandfather of another, thought it symptomatic of national decline that the 'governor of a great state', who aspires to the presidential nomination, 'can desert a good wife, mother of his grown children, divorce her, then persuade a young mother of four children to abandon her husband'.[53] All this should have been old news, but the scandal was revived because Happy was pregnant during the campaign. 'We were trying to confuse the issue,' Spencer confessed.

Nelson had marriage problems. He was divorced. He'd just married Happy ... we certainly weren't on the right side of the family morality question at that time ... We had to confuse that.

We could do it by attacking Barry Goldwater and his weaknesses. Frankly we did a very good job of it. All of a sudden they forgot all about Happy and the potential baby. I'd say 48 hours out, or something like that, our polling data showed us dead even.[54]

Just when the momentum had shifted to Rockefeller, Happy gave birth to a son on 30 May, three days before the primary. The birth shifted attention from Barry to Happy. Voters in California did not appreciate being reminded that Rockefeller was a divorcee and philanderer. 'I am convinced today that we would have won California and ended Goldwater's chances for the nomination for the presidency had Mrs. Happy Rockefeller not had the baby on that Saturday before the election,' Roberts reflected. He sensed that female voters, in particular, concluded that 'he was a wife-stealer, and ... she was a home-wrecker.'[55]

Goldwater edged Rockefeller by just 3 per cent. The victory owed everything to grassroots efforts in Southern California. In the week prior to polling, activists made contact with every registered Republican in metropolitan areas of the south to gauge their support. Then, on election day, volunteers made sure that potential supporters got to the polling stations. This effort would not seem unusual today, but it was at the time. As it turned out, Goldwater won only 4 of the state's 58 counties: Los Angeles, Riverside, Orange and San Diego. Yet large majorities in those counties (especially Los Angeles and Orange) allowed him to carry the state. Goldwater left California with the Republican nomination virtually assured.

Despite the defeat, Spencer and Roberts felt proud of what they had achieved. Unashamed of the negativity, Roberts concluded that it was 'the best campaign that we ever ran, before or since. I think we did more things right in that campaign, coming from a very long way back.' The primary did, however, reveal that winning an election in California was expensive:

> I think we wound up spending a million and a half, or $2 million I don't remember exactly on that primary, which in those days was an enormous amount of money. Of course, Goldwater matched us dollar for dollar. In fact, he might have outspent us in the ultimate count of the money spent. And he [Goldwater] did it with much smaller contributions, of course, which made a lot of ... difference here in California.[56]

Though it was clear that television had transformed campaigning, the firm had not placed all their eggs in that basket. 'I believe in broad-based campaigns where all aspects are involved,' Spencer later explained. 'I see too many candidates today that are strictly media campaigns.'[57] Limitless money meant that they could try new techniques. Huge rallies, some in excess of 10,000 people, resulted in thousands of formal pledges of support. 'We ... built up our own organization that way,' Roberts recalled. 'We sent out a lot of direct mail, we did some television spots, radio, billboards.' Before long, word got out that something interesting was happening in California. The national press took notice. 'Many of them from the East had never seen the phenomenon of professional campaign management. And so a number of them took the time out from their Rockefeller/Goldwater reporting and did a story on professional campaign management.'[58] While Spencer and Roberts were proud of their efforts, they also absorbed lessons from Goldwater's campaign. Their next big client, Reagan, would benefit from a synthesis of both campaigns.

Conservatives in California thought Goldwater the perfect embodiment of their dreams. He seemed a genuine radical, not a misguided Republican intent on courting the centre. In *The Conscience of a Conservative*, he articulated the libertarian sympathies of the new right:

I have little interest in streamlining government or in making it more efficient, for I mean to reduce its size. I do not undertake to promote welfare, for I propose to extend freedom. My aim is not to pass laws, but to repeal them. It is not to inaugurate new programs, but to cancel old ones that do violence to the Constitution, or that have failed their purpose, or that impose on the people an unwarranted financial burden. I will not attempt to discover whether legislation is 'needed' before I have first determined whether it is constitutionally permissible. And if I should later be attacked for neglecting my constituents' 'interests', I shall reply that I was informed that their main interest is liberty and that in that cause I am doing the very best I can.[59]

The new right swooned when Goldwater shouted that big government was evil, that citizens had to be set free. Cristina found the message entrancing:

I was a fiscally conservative person ... nobody talked about abortions, a dirty word, so that didn't come into our deliberations and discussions, but Medi-Cal, God, that was a very liberal thing. All of the social welfare programs were just extremely liberal. Well, those are the things that I didn't approve of, because I thought it took a man's independence away from him.[60]

The beauty of these beliefs lay in their extremism – the refusal to fudge. At the 1964 Republican Convention, Goldwater shouted: 'I would remind you that extremism in the defense of liberty is no vice! And let me remind you also that moderation in the pursuit of justice is no virtue!'[61] Zealotry obliterated logic: supporters could not understand that most of the country found Goldwater frightening, dangerous, misguided or simply bizarre.

With moderation taboo, the party embarked on a purification campaign. Goldwater fanatics watched vigilantly for any hint of deviation. The new party motto was 'rule or ruin, purity over pragmatism', Robert Walker concluded.[62] 'It was rather curious,' Weinberger reflected. 'They felt they had to demonstrate repeatedly their absolutely permanent attachment to the most extreme-right-wing philosophy.' Politics on the far right became a test of machismo, with courage measured in the willingness to edge further rightward. 'I didn't feel I had to put a large badge on that said "I am a conservative" and parade it around every day,' Weinberger recalled. While hardly a cuddly moderate, he realized that the party needed the centre in order to win. That seemed heresy to Goldwater enthusiasts, however. 'They didn't want to have that kind of neutrality or non-ideological fervor.' They took the view that:

> if you weren't with me, you were against me. And if you were against me, you had to be crushed ... It was a fierce sort of philosophy. It was totally antithetical to anything that might have been described as a way to win. It wasn't a winning strategy – it wasn't designed to be ... They'd much rather lose with their ideological purity ... They were quite frank about that.[63]

'Goldwater does not seem to be a man of hatred but hatred surrounds him this autumn,' wrote Roger Kahn in the *Saturday Evening Post*. 'Wherever and however fast he travels, the hatred of both his supporters and his opponents travels with him.'[64] Walker thought that Philip Davis, co-chairman (along with Reagan) in California, 'was the leader of the "crazies", those who wanted to go down in flames at all costs'. At a particularly acrimonious meeting in August, Reagan tried to soothe tempers. His famous charm hit a brick wall because Davis wanted the opposition crushed, not mollified. The zealots 'more or less ignored [Reagan] because he was just a movie star'.[65] Purification efforts purged the ranks of devoted volunteers – the campaign bled to death. For instance, Weinberger was quite prepared to speak on behalf of

Goldwater, but his overtures were rebuffed by the candidate's inner team. 'Of course, you see, that's why they lost. They spent all their time discussing stupid questions like that instead of getting out ... the vote.'⁶⁶

California conservatives loved Goldwater, but he wasn't particularly fond of them. The arch-extremist ironically found them too extreme. The ugly side of Republican politics in the state was revealed when far-right hooligans attempted to shout down Rockefeller during the Cow Palace convention in mid-July. Goldwater, rattled by that experience, decided that Californians were an embarrassment. Since he couldn't bring them under control, he decided to ignore them. This explains the reluctance to make use of Weinberger and Reagan during the national campaign. Goldwater's advisers feared that giving Reagan a larger profile would focus attention on shenanigans in California. In addition, Reagan's outspoken opposition to the TVA and his advocacy of a voluntary social security programme were too radical even for Goldwater.

Snubbing Reagan, however, was problematic since he had been enormously successful at fundraising. The state committee, annoyed at the rebuff, refused to hand this money over to the national campaign, proposing instead to buy Reagan a slot on national television. Goldwater's people stubbornly resisted, forcing the Californians, led by Henry Salvatori, to take unilateral action. In mid-October, they announced that they had bought a slot and Reagan would use it. A script was sent to Goldwater aides William Baroody and Denison Kitchel, who judged it too controversial. The senator, acting on their advice, vetoed the idea. Reagan, however, pleaded with Goldwater to read the speech and judge for himself. When he did so, and failed to find anything objectionable, Reagan was allowed to go ahead.

The speech was broadcast on 27 October. After all the worries about what Reagan would say, he managed to sound a lot more moderate than Goldwater. This was achieved through tone, not content. The address, called 'A Time for Choosing', was essentially 'The Speech' in its most refined form. Reagan began by assuring listeners that he had written it himself, thus asserting his independence from the party and indeed from politics itself. He then launched into a tirade against Johnson's 'tax and spend' policies, which had resulted in a situation where 'our national debt is one and a half times bigger than all the combined debts of all the nations of the world.' Then came his trademark anti-communism:

> We're at war with the most dangerous enemy that has ever faced mankind in his long climb from the swamp to the stars, and ... if we lose that war, and in so doing lose this way of freedom of ours, history will record with the greatest astonishment that those who had the most to lose did the least to prevent its happening.

The speech was mainly a populist attack upon big government and the dangers of letting irresponsible politicians have access to the public purse:

> We set out to help 19 war ravaged countries at the end of World War II. We are now helping 107. We have spent 146 billion dollars. Some of that money bought a $2 million yacht for Haile Selassie. We bought dress suits for Greek undertakers. We bought 1,000 TV sets, with 23-inch screens, for a country where there is no electricity, and some of our foreign aid funds provided extra wives for Kenyan government officials.

Was any of this true? That hardly mattered since it sounded so good. Reagan understood the power of anecdote. Dozens of small facts – some true, some fabricated, all exaggerated – were used to make real the monster growing in Washington:

> Since the beginning of the century our gross national product has increased by 33 times. In the same period the cost of federal

government has increased 234 times, and while the work force is only 1½ times greater, federal employees number nine times as many. There are now 2½ million federal employees. No one knows what they all do.

Big government threatened freedom. This argument, hardly a new one, was presented in a manner that appeared non-partisan – in stark contrast to most other Republicans, and especially to Goldwater. Reagan quoted a Cuban refugee recently arrived in the United States: 'If we lose freedom here, there's no place to escape to. This is the last stand on earth.' The struggle for survival rendered party loyalties irrelevant:

> This is the issue of this election: Whether we believe in our capacity for self-government or whether we abandon the American revolution and confess that a little intellectual elite in a far-distant capitol can plan our lives for us better than we can plan them ourselves.
> You and I are told increasingly we have to choose between a left or right. Well I'd like to suggest there is no such thing as a left or right. There's only an up or down – up, man's old ... dream, the ultimate in individual freedom consistent with law and order, or down to the ant heap of totalitarianism. And regardless of their sincerity, their humanitarian motives, those who would trade our freedom for security have embarked on this downward course.

He moved seamlessly to what he perceived as the concrete manifestations of totalitarian drift. The New Deal and Johnson's Great Society were the thin end of the socialist wedge, and socialism the thin end of communism:

> Back in 1936, Mr. Democrat himself, Al Smith, the great American, came before the American people and charged that the leadership of his Party was taking the Party of Jefferson,

Jackson, and Cleveland down the road under the banners of Marx, Lenin, and Stalin. And he walked away from his Party, and he never returned till the day he died – because to this day, the leadership of that Party has been taking that Party, that honorable Party, down the road in the image of the labor Socialist Party of England.

In other words, communism was not simply an external threat. It was a disease spreading outwards from Washington, fostered by well-meaning liberals. 'It doesn't require expropriation or confiscation of private property or business to impose socialism on a people.'

The speech's strength lay in the connection Reagan made with his audience. He used the phrase 'you and I' 10 times, 'we' 67 times, and 'we're' 25 times, thus pulling his listeners into his crusade. The message was at least as apocalyptic as any that Goldwater had delivered, yet Reagan made it seem like an invitation to heroic adventure. He concluded:

> You and I ... do not believe that life is so dear and peace so sweet as to be purchased at the price of chains and slavery. If nothing in life is worth dying for, when did this begin – just in the face of this enemy? Or should Moses have told the children of Israel to live in slavery under the pharaohs? Should Christ have refused the cross? Should the patriots at Concord Bridge have thrown down their guns and refused to fire the shot heard 'round the world? The martyrs of history were not fools, and our honored dead who gave their lives to stop the advance of the Nazis didn't die in vain. Where, then, is the road to peace?

The 'simple answer' lay in each person realizing a duty to defend American values. 'You and I have a rendezvous with destiny. We'll preserve for our children this, the last best hope of man on earth, or we'll sentence them to take the last step into a thousand years of darkness.'[67]

'When it was over', Reagan wrote, 'the others in the room said I had done well. But I was still nervous about it and ... I was hoping I hadn't let Barry down.'[68] He needn't have worried; the speech was an instant success, so much so that a jealous Goldwater could not muster the humility to thank Reagan for it. At this late stage in the election campaign, nearly everyone, except the most ardent Goldwater supporters, accepted that Johnson would win resoundingly. Yet Reagan's speech still managed to inspire a surge of donations for Goldwater, with $8 million received in the final week. The journalist David Broder concluded that Reagan had emerged as 'a political star overnight'; the performance was 'the most successful national political debut since William Jennings Bryan electrified the 1896 Democratic convention with the "Cross of Gold" speech'.[69] Reagan had delivered Goldwater's message in a spirit of camaraderie, inspiring rather than frightening voters. Looking to the future, what was important was that he had promoted Goldwater without being contaminated by him. The experience was for Reagan 'one of the most important milestones in my life – another one of those unexpected turns in the road that led me onto a path I never expected to take'.[70]

The speech revealed just how important was personality. Far-right ideologues, obsessed with principle, had failed to notice that Goldwater was scary. His uncompromising attitude alienated voters. 'Barry never minced words,' Spencer reflected. 'He said it like he felt and he said it in a harsh way ... Barry was a hard-nosed, up-front Arizonan cowboy, and that's what scared people. So you took his style and put it with the issue of the hot button, you made some headway.' In other words, Goldwater wore well the madman image that his opponents hung on him. 'If it were Ronald Reagan running, we could've never pinned it on him because of his style,' Spencer felt. 'People would not have believed us.'[71] Reagan had trouble frightening a baby.

Johnson made light work of the worst candidate the Republicans ever ran for president. Despite growing fears about the

Great Society, urban unrest and the Vietnam War, he coasted to one of the biggest landslides in history. In the wake of that defeat, the Republicans looked doomed. Conservatives, *Time* argued, had 'suffered a crippling setback ... The humiliation ... was so complete that they will not have another shot at party domination for some time to come.'[72] This seemed especially true in California. The party, most commentators argued, would have to move toward the centre. Nixon, however, realized that the issue was not quite so simple. The main problem facing the party was that it had to find unity, which could not be achieved simply by moving in one direction or another. 'If Barry showed that the Republicans can't win with just the right wing,' he remarked, 'I showed in 1962 that we can't win without them.'[73] Parkinson, soon to take over as state party chairman, echoed that analysis.

> I was able to finally say, after Mr. Goldwater was defeated, that now ... we should understand that both factions of the party need each other, in order for us to win an election. We lost with Mr. Nixon because Joe Shell and the conservatives sat on their hands. We lost with Mr. Goldwater because the liberals sat on their hands.[74]

The key was to find a candidate who could tap the energy of the radical right without alienating moderates. Reagan was unfazed by the colossal defeat. 'Well, it's over and we lost,' he concluded in the *National Review*. 'We lost a battle in the continuing war for freedom, but our position is not untenable.' They were not simply fringe extremists. 'First of all, there are 26 million of us and we can't be explained away as diehard party faithfuls. We cross party lines in our dedication to a philosophy.' He rejected the idea that the huge majority for Johnson accurately represented American opinion. Refusing to blame the defeat on Goldwater, he instead credited it to the mistaken impression of Goldwater that Democrats had peddled. Salvation lay in coaxing back 'the millions of so-called Republican defectors':

> those people who didn't really want LBJ, but who were scared of what they thought we represented ... [they] did not vote against the conservative philosophy; they voted against a false image our Liberal opponents successfully mounted. Indeed it was a double false image. Not only did they portray us as advancing a kind of radical departure from the status quo, but they took for themselves a costume of comfortable conservatism.

It would be easy to dismiss this as typical post-defeat bluster, but Reagan was right. There were indeed millions of Americans uneasy with what liberalism – as represented by Johnson or Brown – meant in 1960s America. In 1964, their discontent with Johnson was less powerful than their fear of Goldwater. But the balance of emotions could easily shift, especially if conservatism found a more congenial candidate. In a blatant swipe at Johnson, Reagan argued that 'our job beginning now is not so much to sell conservatism as to prove that our conservatism is in truth what a lot of people thought they were voting for when they fell for the cornpone come-on.' Goldwater's 'extremism', he insisted, was an 'optical illusion' since conservatism was decidedly mainstream. 'We represent the forgotten American – that simple soul who goes to work, bucks for a raise, takes out insurance, pays for his kids' schooling, contributes to his church and charity and knows there ... "ain't no such thing as free lunch".'[75]

Reagan had voiced what quite a few conservatives felt. Shortly after Goldwater's defeat, Cristina was commiserating with friends in Los Angeles. 'We were talking: "what shall we do now?" ... We've got a pretty good movement going. So we lost an election, we lost a candidate, but we didn't think our cause was that bad.' Along came Reagan, whose speech remained fresh in the minds of those mourning defeat. 'The idea hit each of us about the same time. Why doesn't he run ... for governor? He's got all the ingredients to make a goddamned electable person. I don't give a damn how smart you are, if you're not electable, forget it. You've got to have that charisma to get elected.'[76] They immediately put the idea to Reagan. Though this was not the first time the suggestion had been made, Reagan feigned surprise. He argued that he couldn't possibly run since he was frightened of flying. Cristina and his friends piled on the pressure. Reagan's reluctance began to dissolve.

'One thing led to another.'[77]

# 3

# 'You Guys Are Absolutely Crazy'

In the late summer of 1964, Roger Kahn, while reporting on the Goldwater campaign for the *Saturday Evening Post*, met a Bircher in a bar. They shared a few drinks and talked a lot of politics. The Bircher had that myopic confidence, typical of zealots, that caused him to assume that his bigotry was commonplace. 'I'll bet you've gotten where you are on your own,' he said to Kahn. When Kahn replied in the affirmative, he assumed that he'd found a fellow traveller. That prompted a tirade against Medicare, civil rights, Commies and the federal government. 'We've got to kill welfare and make the colored go to work just like the rest of us, or the whole country will go under.' Kahn – first and foremost a reporter – just listened, sensing that the Bircher had not yet hit his stride. But then came a surprise. 'We're not happy with Goldwater,' he announced. 'He's just the best that we could do – this time.'[1]

'Well, the hell with this election,' the man slurred. 'We know we're going to lose. But at least we've gotten control of a party. Whatever happens, we aren't letting go.'[2]

Reagan held similar views, minus the bourbon-soaked belligerence. Despite Goldwater's disastrous defeat, he retained confidence in an inevitable conservative ascendancy. In a blatant stab at Republican Senator Thomas Kuchel, a moderate who had refused to endorse Goldwater, Reagan remarked on 10 November 1964 that: 'We don't intend to turn the Republican Party over to the traitors in the battle just ended.' The problem, he insisted, was not ideology, but presentation. He rejected any move to the centre. 'We will have no more of those candidates who are pledged to the same goals of our opposition ... turning the Party over to the so-called moderates wouldn't make sense at all.'[3]

Reagan's obduracy defied electoral logic, but that did not diminish his status within the party. Many Republicans saw him as the lifeboat that would rescue them from the sinking of Goldwater. 'They kept ... insisting that I offered the only chance ... to bring the party back into something viable.'[4] It all came down to packaging. Cristina noticed how, once the idea of a candidacy was mooted, support for Reagan expanded exponentially. 'Some more people got talking about it, and some more people got talking about it, and we started having meetings, and that's how ... Ronald Reagan got launched in California for governor.'[5]

Not everyone, however, was prepared to anoint Reagan. Joe Shell still saw himself as the conservative heir-apparent and was still holding tight to his pathetic dreams of stardom. Cristina, however, had already dumped Shell, complaining that he 'had no personality at all'. The dire state of the party left no room for sentiment. At a meeting with Shell, Cristina did not mince words: 'I just told him ... "Joe, I love you like a brother, but like a brother I have to talk ... some sense into your head. You don't have the ingredients to win. Nobody's going to argue with me or anybody else about your ability and your knowledge, but that don't win elections."'[6] 'The farthest thing from my mind was running for political office,' Reagan later claimed. 'I liked my life. I thought it was an exciting life. I loved what I was doing.' Soon, however, he found it difficult to ignore the clamour. 'It wasn't a case of ... party leadership,' he insisted.

'Groups and people who knew me started coming, and were just very insistent that I should be the gubernatorial candidate. I dismissed them lightly and quickly to begin with, but they just kept coming back.'[7]

Leading the push were three prominent businessmen – Holmes Tuttle, Henry Salvatori and Cy Rubel. Each exemplified the American Dream that Reagan worshipped. Salvatori was born in Italy and, after immigrating to the United States, studied physics at Columbia University. After graduation, he started his own company, Western Geophysical, and became enormously wealthy by plundering oil fields in California. Rubel, also an oilman, was at that time head of Union Oil. Tuttle, born on an Indian reservation in the Oklahoma Territory, hopped a freight car to the promised land – California. He took a job washing cars and eventually built his own auto empire, initially through wartime contracts supplying dump trucks to the government. After the war, he moved seamlessly into the private market, just in time for the postwar boom in ownership. Because they had succeeded on their own, all three men believed that anyone could do so, without need of government help.

Spencer described Tuttle as 'a man of tremendous energy, tremendous drive and strong feelings ... about how the world should be run, how the country should be run'.[8] That description applied equally to Salvatori and Rubel. All three shared Goldwater's distaste for big government; all were prepared to use their resources to fund a revolution in California. While they were disappointed by Goldwater's failure, they were more pragmatic than others on the far right. Power, not purity, drove them. '[They] were Republicans', Nofziger recalled, 'without any hyphenations ... They saw Ron as a man who not only shared their general philosophic views, but was a very effective spokesman and a very effective campaigner.'[9] 'When I saw Ronnie on television,' Salvatori remarked after the Goldwater speech, 'I knew he was our boy!'[10]

This optimism inspired them to form the Friends of Ronald Reagan in 1965. The Friends were all wealthy and powerful people. Some brought quintessential California glamour, including William Randolph Hearst, Walt Disney, James Cagney, William Holden, John Wayne and Robert Taylor. 'They ... were tired of seeing the kind of candidates they had for governor up to then,' Parkinson reflected. While Reagan was steeped in Goldwater's ideological certainties, that was not what the Friends found attractive. 'I don't think [it was] for ideological reasons,' Parkinson remarked, 'they simply wanted to get [Pat] Brown out of there.'[11] Reagan, they felt, could be turned into a winning candidate. Their vision did not extend beyond November 1966: none of them thought very hard about whether Reagan actually possessed the good leadership qualities that were essential. 'I don't think ... [they] ever gave much thought to whether Reagan had the ability to govern effectively,' Nofziger admitted. 'They assumed that it would just happen ... they were more interested in a winner than in a governor. Besides, they didn't know anything more about governing than he did.'[12]

As William French Smith reflected, the Friends provided Reagan with 'the one thing that he could not do without, namely ... a political organization'.[13] They were wealthy, but more important was their ability to raise money. 'Holmes Tuttle is probably the best fundraiser in the history of the Republican party in California,' Nofziger argued.[14] Spencer felt that Tuttle's ability made him 'the biggest single force in the early part of Ronald Reagan's career'. Before long, he emerged as leader of the Friends. 'Reagan was the first legitimate person that Holmes was absolutely, totally, in synch with, and who he totally loved,' Spencer recalled. 'He raised millions and millions and millions of dollars for Ronald Reagan's political efforts.'[15]

In the early months of 1965, Tuttle, Salvatori and Rubel intensified their efforts to persuade Reagan to run. 'Holmes was the most persistent,' Reagan recalled. 'He just was firmly convinced that I could [win].'¹⁶ Incessant pressure gradually eroded Reagan's reluctance. 'It got to the place where I said no, and no, and no. And Nancy and I couldn't sleep any more. You know, we wondered, "Are you making the right decision? Are you letting people down? What if they're right?"' He agreed to explore the possibility:

> I said, 'If you make it possible for me to spend ... six months accepting these speaking engagements all over the state, I'll make the decision whether you're right or wrong. I think you're wrong.' And I really meant that. I said, 'I think that you're wrong about me being the candidate. But I'll come back. By December 31, I'll tell you whether I should or should not be.' And they agreed.¹⁷

Six months on the road inevitably ate into Reagan's earning power. The Friends therefore made up the shortfall – he became their employee. The work was not that different from the GE years. He would travel from town to town delivering 'The Speech'. He was running, but not running.

The freelance effort of the Friends was possible because of the peculiar nature of California politics. This was frontier electioneering, with few steadfast rules. Since the Republican central organization was structurally weak and poorly funded, it had little influence over candidate selection. 'There was no unified state central committee,' Parkinson explained.

> It was ... the most screwed-up system I ever saw in my whole life ... we could never do in Connecticut or New York or North Carolina what we can do in California, precisely because we are so unstructured, you see. This gives a tremendous opportunity to ... anybody who wants to get in and make something in the party in California ... California is wide open.¹⁸

A candidate, such as Reagan, who could mobilize a formidable organization had an enormous advantage. 'There's nothing comparable to the Eastern parties here,' Weinberger explained. 'There the party structure is pretty well able to say who will run and who won't.' In contrast, in California, 'the real decision is always made by the individuals, not by the party. Because there isn't any one party. The party is not a monolithic thing in California. There's a whole raft of volunteer organizations and a whole raft of official state organizations, but there isn't any unifying factor.'[19] During the primary, central organization was essentially invisible. 'They pick up after the nominating primary is over,' Weinberger explained. 'They react and they try to elect people who are nominated, but they don't do very much before.'[20] This meant that a powerful candidate could easily take the party in a direction it did not actually plan to go, as Reagan would demonstrate. 'He did not accept our philosophy,' Parkinson admitted. 'He came full-blown with a philosophy to prominence ... He was more conservative and more concerned about Americanism than a lot of us were at the time.'[21]

Tuttle and his friends 'controlled the campaign as the money always controls the campaign,' Parkinson explained. 'Money buys the professional skill, and then they find the candidate, and they manufacture the candidate, and they put him over.'[22] While the Friends felt confident that Reagan had the personality to succeed, they still understood the need to turn him into a politician. That meant hiring Spencer and Roberts, a move ironically supported by Goldwater. On hearing that Reagan was thinking of running, he advised: 'I'd hire those sons of bitches, Spencer-Roberts.'[23] For Reagan, that was endorsement enough.

Stuart Spencer and William Roberts met in the 1950s when both were Young Republican activists. At the time, Spencer worked as director of parks and recreation for the city of Alhambra and Roberts was a TV salesman. While canvassing for Eisenhower, they discovered that they shared a talent for political organization and good instincts about modern communication. 'Politics was a hobby, an avocation, but I loved it,' Spencer recalled. 'I just got more mired in it every day.'[24]

By 1960, they felt confident enough to ditch their day jobs and start their own consulting firm.

The concept of professional campaign management emerged in California in 1933 when the husband-and-wife team of Clem Whitaker and Leone Baxter applied basic public relations techniques to the challenge of winning elections. They were hired guns: in 1942 they helped Earl Warren get elected governor and then, three years later, worked for the American Medical Association in the successful campaign against Warren's compulsory health insurance bill. California was a trendsetter in the campaign-management field, but when Spencer and Roberts started, only a few firms were established in the state. 'We didn't want to run for public office,' Spencer explained. 'This [was] the best opportunity to be in the game, to play the game and ... make a living ... So we went that route. We started a business on 500 bucks each and never looked back.'[25] The firm was simply the creative minds of two highly talented individuals. 'We ran it on a very low budget,' Roberts recalled. 'We didn't have a secretary for a long time, we didn't have a very big show.'[26] A perfect symbiosis developed. Spencer was a tough-talking, hard-driven, earthy man who was always angry. Roberts was polite, soft-spoken, emollient and patient. Their characters determined their roles. 'Stu is more content in the back room,' a colleague remarked, 'Bill up front leading the troops.'[27]

Spencer and Roberts were, essentially, marketing managers selling a product. This meant finding out the priorities of voters in a given area and crafting their candidate's message to that constituency. This required research, but also, more importantly, intuition. 'Politics is an art and not a science,' Spencer boasted. 'Bill Roberts and I ... just had a feel for it.'[28] Before long, the firm became noted for slick, expensive, media-driven campaigns perfectly suited to ultra-modern California. 'We brought what you call full management ... to the campaign; strategic planning, campaign plans, survey research, media production, media buy, press relations.'[29] They enjoyed enormous freedom to improvise because the Republican Party machinery in the state was too weak to get in the way. 'Stu and I have both been innovators,' Roberts explained.

> We have not always gone with the status quo. Not that it's been a flamboyant thing, it has not. We were probably one of the first in the country to be using survey research, we set up our own company, we went through the whole gamut of studying electronic data processing as to how it would affect political campaigns. We discarded most of it because we found it was not workable, but we were trying everything.[30]

Pragmatism was their greatest strength. 'We were out there to win,' Spencer recalled. 'We weren't involved with philosophies as much as we were into the technique of winning.'[31] They worked only for Republicans, but were not otherwise fussy. 'We never hyphenated Republicanism,' Roberts reflected. 'We didn't classify ourselves as conservative or liberal, but Republicans.' Or, as the straight-talking Spencer explained: 'I don't care about the issues. I care about the votes.'[32]

The advent of professional campaign management coincided with and fuelled four important trends in 1960s California. The first was populism, which feeds on the grievances of the common people in their struggle against a powerful elite. The first task of a firm like Spencer and Roberts was to identify the 'common people', so that their hopes and fears could be specifically targeted. Public relations techniques, adapted to politics, suited this task. Rule number 10 in Whitaker-Baxter's 50 rules of political campaigning perfectly encapsulated the need for a common touch: 'More Americans Like Corn than Caviar.'[33] This meant keeping things simple and always paying attention to what ordinary people wanted. Critics might call this 'dumbing down'. Al Gardner, a campaign manager who worked for Robert Kennedy from 1964 to 1968, confessed that the best copywriter they had 'was a girl who was politically naïve'. Faced with an issue, 'she'd go to the politicians and say "Explain this to me so I can understand it." Then she'd reduce the issue ... to a language which would explain it to the average citizen.'[34] There was no room for pretence or condescension. 'California politics abound with opportunities for self-dramatizers and over-simplifiers, who rely on charisma instead of character,' Lewis observed. 'The intricate questions are reduced to black-and-white slogans and personalities, and everything else is remote and ill-defined.'[35]

The second trend was the increasing importance of the individual candidate, in contrast to the party. Campaign managers found parties cumbersome, hidebound and difficult to control. They preferred striking out on their own with a handpicked person who could be moulded to the mood of the electorate. A survey of campaign-management firms conducted by *Congressional Quarterly* in 1968 found that 'From the viewpoint of a professional campaign manager, the ideal candidate is an attractive young Republican or Democrat who has accumulated no political "record" or possible liabilities.'[36] It helped if that candidate already had star quality, perhaps because of a reputation in business, sports or entertainment. This meant that the difficult and time-consuming process of building name recognition could be bypassed.

The third trend, evident nationwide but especially in California, was the decline of party voting. Prior to the 1960s, it was common to vote a 'straight ticket' – checking the boxes of all the Democrats, or all the Republicans, without much consideration of the actual individuals. In the 1960s, party loyalties began to weaken. Voters were increasingly inclined to split their vote after careful consideration of the candidates. Lewis remarked:

> California's personalized style of politics is breaking down the old loyalties of party, precinct and ward as voters become more sophisticated, more mobile, more 'politicalized'. The old ties of

labor unions, ethnic blocs and geography are dissolving. The change reflects, in part, the voter's (correct) suspicion that most of the dogma and doctrine of conventional American politics is so much rhetoric; that the labels 'liberal' and 'conservative' are obscured by the momentous and unanticipated problems of the Sixties; that doctrinaire assumptions stultify the public servant's attempt to confront and solve problems.[37]

This erosion of party loyalty was most evident among blue-collar whites who identified themselves as Democrats but were uncomfortable with civil rights and welfare legislation. This made campaigning much more complicated, since it was no longer simply a case of targeting Democrats or Republicans. Instead, the predominant concerns of individual voters in each area had to be discovered, and these had to be played upon, regardless of party identity. This was a complicated task suited to marketing professionals. 'Too many campaigns try to fly by the seat of their pants,' Roberts remarked. 'Good old Charley Brown who knows that district like the back of his hand just isn't good enough for this day and age.'[38]

The fourth trend – the rising influence of television – magnified the first three. As Lewis argued, television 'makes ideology and party label seem even more like excess baggage as it brings the campaigner into the home and gives the voter a chance to study his personality and appearance. If a candidate can sway millions on television he doesn't need the party; it needs him.'[39] While it was perhaps premature to say that the candidate unable to perform impressively on television was doomed, it was undoubtedly true that an enormous advantage went to the individual who was comfortable with the medium. Yet being good in front of the camera was not enough on its own; the candidate also needed the good sense to hire professionals able to use television effectively.

The art of campaign management thrived in California because the state was perfectly equipped to nurture it.

California had never been dominated by big party machines, nor by complex webs of patronage. An old adage held that 'There is no political machine [in California], just a lot of moving parts.'[40] It was a state of newcomers, where the past was unimportant. Californians had always tended to vote for the man, not the party. What was not yet apparent, however, was that California, far from being an aberration, was instead a trendsetter. The party machines were in decline everywhere, providing opportunities for manipulators like Spencer and Roberts, and for upstarts like Reagan.

Given all these trends, it is fair to say that Reagan fit the criteria of what Spencer and Roberts might have called the 'perfect candidate'. Roberts recollected when the Friends came calling:

> Our general policy had always been to talk to everybody, whether we get involved with them or not. So we said, 'Yes, we'd be very happy to talk about it.' In fact, we had a good feeling about Reagan because we thought he'd done awfully well previously ... We thought he was going places and we were impressed with the way he had handled himself in the Goldwater campaign.[41]

For Spencer, the fact that Reagan was open to hiring the firm, after their involvement with Rockefeller, was impressive in itself. 'That showed me the practical side of Ronald Reagan. People thought he was such an ideologue.'[42] A meeting was arranged. Then another meeting. Then another meeting.

Reagan meanwhile still pretended that he was not officially running. Spencer, however, saw through the charade: 'I personally think that Ron was committed, emotionally, to running for governor in 1965, but wanted an escape hatch.'[43] Roberts agreed: 'He had decided, I'm sure ... he had gotten a huge reaction from the general public all over the country. He showed me some boxes of letters that he had gotten from literally all over the nation thousands of them asking him to do something, run for something.'[44] The firm only dealt with committed candidates – Reagan fit the bill. 'He was ... sold on the whole project of doing it way before we ever showed up or else we wouldn't have had our meetings and the thing wouldn't have gone that far,' Roberts explained. 'If he had had just a passing interest, he wouldn't have gotten as aggressive on the whole organizational thing as he did.'[45]

The partners had some misgivings. 'We had heard a lot of things ... from people that he was difficult to get along with, that he was a martinet,' Roberts recalled. They quickly discovered something entirely different. Reagan seemed eager to learn, open to advice. His character especially impressed. 'He is a person of great compassion ... [and] tremendous sense of humor,' Roberts felt. 'You've got to be able to laugh at your own mistakes once in a while. You don't have to take everything so deadly serious ... He was just an easygoing person. Obviously bright. Very retentive.'[46] His politics nevertheless caused concern. 'We wanted to know, is this a right wing nut or what because we didn't want to get involved in that kind of situation,' Roberts explained.[47] They grilled Reagan on his beliefs, interrogating him on 'economics, and how he'd run the state, and why he thought he ought to be governor ... and a whole bunch of other questions. He satisfied our questions.'[48]

Reagan's connection to the Birch Society nevertheless worried the partners. '[It] was an extremely hot issue,' Spencer explained. 'The *L.A. Times*, *Santa Barbara News Press*, both had done big exposés seven days in a row. All the dirt was out there.' Having earlier represented Rousselot, Spencer and Roberts were wary of drawing close to the society. 'John ... was one of the best candidates we ever worked with.'[49] Spencer had tried to persuade Rousselot to ditch the group, but he refused. 'He paid the price ... Here's a young man who could have been Senator from California, could have been ... Governor of California.'[50] The problem was especially complicated in California, Bircher territory. As the Nixon–Shell debacle had revealed, a successful candidate had to deny affiliation without alienating supporters of the Society.

Spencer and Roberts were confident that Reagan was not a Bircher. 'That wasn't the problem,' Spencer explained.

> The problem was, are they going to be able to hang this on him? Is he going to let them? What's his state of mind? We spent a lot of time asking him those questions and going over those things. He satisfied our qualms about it; if that issue comes up, how he would handle it, and that he had no involvement with it ... He knew pretty well where [the Society] was going to go and that was nowhere.

The partners were eventually satisfied. Reagan was a right-winger, but not a lunatic. 'He was a big connoisseur of the *National Review*,' Spencer recalled. 'That was his beginning point philosophically ... There was nothing wrong with the things that [William] Rusher and [William] Buckley and those guys were putting into the *National Review*. They were the cutting edge of conservatism.'[51] Their doubts now answered, Spencer and Roberts became excited by the possibilities. At their third meeting, in May 1965, Reagan pressed them to make a decision. 'He said, "Well, are you or aren't you?" So we said, "Yes, we think we will."'[52] Some ground rules were set: 'We made it clear that ... a candidate cannot be a star and treat his staff like dirt. We were not an entourage, we were consultants, and we made it clear that we don't work for dogmatists, or prima donnas. Ron respected us for laying our cards out, and he agreed all the way.'[53] A fee of $150,000 for the primary campaign was agreed.[54] That perturbed Neil Reagan, who assumed that his firm, McCann-Erickson, would get the account. A bone was thrown their way. Spencer and Roberts 'took care of the purely political,' Neil Reagan explained. 'We took care of the media writing and the media placement.'[55]

Reagan, though a loyal family man, was pragmatic enough to know when to give his brother the swerve.

Spencer immediately sensed that the client was Ron *and* Nancy. 'The Reagans are a team politically. He would have never made the governorship without her.' Their relationship enhanced Reagan's solidity. 'It was not Hollywood. At that time I thought, *oh, boy*. It's not only a partnership, it's a great love affair.' Nancy attended those first meetings when a possible partnership was discussed. 'She was quiet. With those big eyes of hers, she'd be watching you. Every now and then she'd ask a question, but not too often.'[56] She needed reassurance about what lay ahead:

> How is he going to be protected, who's going to take care of him, what are these two guys sitting in my living room, Spencer and Roberts? What's their agenda? When things get tough, are they going to run? Are they going to tell us the truth? Are they going to work 24 hours a day? Those are the questions that were in her mind.[57]

Spencer and Roberts applied four factors when analysing a candidate's potential: his communication skills, his access to money, his stand on the issues, and the organization backing him. On communication, 'Reagan was extremely articulate, the most articulate guy, not only then but since then.' His finances were obviously solid. 'If you put Henry Salvatori, Justin Dart, Holmes Tuttle, Jack Hume, Jack Warner in one room, I think you know you're going to get some money.' Those same men were essentially his organization, so that, too, was settled. That left issues:

> That's ... where we spent most of our time, worrying and thinking. After many discussions with him, we realized this guy was a basic conservative. He was obsessed with one thing, the

communist threat. He has conservative tendencies on other issues, but he can be practical.

When you look at the 1960s, that's a pretty good position to be in, philosophically and ideologically. Plus, we realized pretty early on that the guy had a real core value system ... The best candidates have a core value system ... A lot of them have it and a lot of them don't, but Reagan had it.[58]

In other words, the firm had no qualms about going with a conservative just six months after Johnson's demolition of Goldwater. They sensed that America was turning, but they also realized that Reagan could be groomed.

The firm was simultaneously negotiating with George Christopher, the former mayor of San Francisco. Christopher was a Rockefeller Republican with long experience and a solid reputation within the party. Nearly everyone assumed that he would easily win the nomination and pose the most formidable challenge to Brown. That assumption was, however, distinctly retrograde: it ignored the changes taking place in the southern part of the state and therefore underestimated the problems a moderate would encounter – the same problems that had plagued Rockefeller. 'Christopher was ... a good, decent man,' Nofziger felt, but not a good candidate. 'He came from the wrong part of the state.'[59] He also lacked the persona for the television age. 'He was a good mayor, but he was dull,' Spencer explained. 'California politics is a little bit of Hollywood. You can't be dull in California politics and be very successful.'[60]

When asked why Spencer and Roberts chose Reagan over Christopher, Nofziger quipped: 'Maybe they wanted a winner ... Reagan was an exceptional candidate. He was a highly unusual candidate, and I think that any unbiased reporter, as I was in those days, would clearly have said that this guy is going to win it.'[61] Spencer echoed that judgement:

we definitely felt that Reagan was a new face, that Reagan could beat Pat Brown if it was done right, that the party would coalesce around him and we didn't feel that George Christopher could bring those things about. He was not a new face ... he didn't have the financial support that Ron would have ... time had passed George by.

The choice seemed clear cut, but was not easy. 'The big wrenching thing ... was the fact that ... we were walking away ... from ... our allies,' Spencer recalled. 'We got a lot of nasty mail.'[62] Moderates felt understandably betrayed. Bagley recalled both bewilderment and anger when 'Stu Spencer and Bill Roberts, who had run the Rockefeller campaign, suddenly became the Reagan ... team.'[63]

The decision also seemed idiotic. 'George Christopher laughed when he heard about it,' Spencer recalled.[64] When Cristina first discussed a Reagan candidacy with his friends the reaction was: '"You got to be out of your mind." "You gotta be kidding," you know? Then I would talk to their wives and they'd say, "Oh, wouldn't he be great?"'[65] Contradicting Nofziger, Spencer thought that there wasn't a journalist anywhere who believed Reagan could get elected. The reporter Jack McDowell, who knew the state as well as anyone, was flabbergasted. 'I had a high regard for [Spencer and Roberts] ... When they got onto this Ronald Reagan thing, I thought they were absolutely bonkers ... I said, "You guys are absolutely crazy." ... Because George Christopher was the front-runner ... Christopher seemed to be the establishment guy.' Yet that was precisely why Spencer and Roberts rejected him; they understood that an establishment guy would not do well in iconoclastic times. Such a man would not fare well in the south, where the voters were rebellious, nor could he be easily moulded to suit the changing tastes of the electorate. They wanted a fresh face, a man willing to be marketed. Their decision was motivated not by ideological zealotry (which had been overabundant in 1964) but a cold, hard, practical sense of what could be achieved in the political temper of 1966. 'Bill and I were the only two people that had a lot on the line professionally,' Spencer recalled. 'We did a lot of soul searching. Finally we said, "You know, this guy could do it. If we do it right, this guy could do it."'[66]

Spencer and Roberts understood that the biggest challenge was to court moderates without alienating the right. This was a problem of packaging. The very idea, however, annoyed zealots in the California Republican Assembly. The CRA was delighted that Reagan was (perhaps) running, but they wanted to make him *their* candidate, who would follow *their* directions, and remain true to *their* ideals. At a meeting in July 1965, CRA president Cyril Stevenson warned members of the danger of surrendering control of the selection process to Spencer and Roberts, cynical spin-doctors. Stevenson had in mind another conviction-based campaign. 'How do we know we will even know the candidate when the P.R. men finish him?' he asked.[67] That outburst provoked a ferocious riposte from the Reverend W. S. McBirnie, who attacked what he called 'cannibalism in the Republican Party'. 'He really took these boys apart,' one witness, O. L. Bane, recounted.[68]

Undaunted by McBirnie's attack, Stevenson wrote to Reagan, demanding that campaign appointments be cleared with the CRA, the United Republicans of California and the Young Republicans. If Reagan refused, those groups would withhold support: 'Mr Reagan, since your entire excuse and strength for running comes from the grassroots conservative movement, why is it you refuse to accept them as "General Partners" in your campaign? Are you ashamed of the Volunteers? ... Do you feel the Volunteers are a liability?'[69] Reagan, realizing that the CRA needed him more than he needed the CRA, simply ignored the threats. On 28 October 1965, Stevenson, disgusted with Reagan's refusal to obey, threw his support behind Goodwin Knight. That stunt backfired when Knight subsequently announced that he wasn't running.

Now firmly in charge, Spencer and Roberts outlined their plans. The most important necessity was to get Reagan to follow directions. The relationship was explained in terms he could understand. He was an actor; they were the directors:

> I found it very, very helpful to take his past profession and project it to his present profession whenever I was explaining something to him. I explained it to him in Hollywood terms ... I would say, 'This is like a stage play ... we'll take it out of town. We're going to go out of town to Visalia and to all these little burgs up in northern California and try out your act. If you screw up, only a small number of people will see it, and if it's good, we can keep it.[70]

Roberts took charge of the campaign – an indication of the firm's expectations. As Spencer explained, 'Bill is very good at taking an established candidate, a front runner, and holding the lead. I won't say I'm not good at it ... but I don't enjoy it that much. I'm better at taking somebody that's behind and blitzing the thing and winning it.'[71] They had already decided they had a winner.

In an interview with KTTV's George Putnam on 1 June, the partners explained their plans:

> Reagan, they say, is very new in politics, but he's a hot product. He's hot now, because he's supplanted Goldwater in people's minds, but they aren't going to try to shift that image in order to win until about mid-June [1965] ... they're going to let Reagan go on making his own talks up 'til then, and then they're going to put him under wraps for a two month course on the key State issues, education, welfare, taxation, water problems, health, transportation and labor. Spencer and Roberts hope to modify the impression that Reagan is a right-winger ... The moderates will be solicited, the same group that backed Rockefeller in his primary battle with Goldwater. Roberts and Spencer say people

are going to be surprised when they see the liberals and the moderates are going to come out for Ronald Reagan.'[72]

While the main thrust in the early weeks was to showcase a potential candidate, Spencer and Roberts also laid the foundation of a grassroots campaign. They understood that Reagan had a unique ability to inspire enthusiasm among a new cohort of supporters. 'It's a word of mouth thing,' Spencer explained. 'He hit everything in the state, every region. And we would have pledge cards, sign-up cards ... for all the people who would show up ... A lot of new people would show up at those things.'[73]

Brown ridiculed suggestions that Reagan might be marketed as a moderate. 'The other day Ronald Reagan complained that the "image" of ultra-conservatism has been pinned on him as a result of his campaigning for Barry Goldwater. Well, if Ronald Reagan is not an ultra-conservative ... we should get out of politics.' The governor nevertheless warned that Reagan needed to be taken seriously, reminding supporters that Goldwater had won nearly 3 million votes in his primary battle with Rockefeller. This had been achieved because 'his precinct workers rang millions of doorbells and telephones. And they carried his message to every corner of the state.' He cautioned supporters not to be complacent because of Goldwater's subsequent thrashing by Johnson. 'The Goldwater spirit is as alive and vibrant today as it was last fall. And 1966 will be the year of decision for its future in California.' The state would be a bellwether for the presidential campaign of 1968. 'A victory here next year will provide a new resurgence of conservatism that – even if partially successful – could stop President Johnson's program in its tracks and turn back progress in California.'[74] That was precisely what Reagan had in mind.

'During the summer months and into the fall of 1965,' Roberts recalled, 'we were busily moving Reagan around, having him speak to Republican groups a lot and having him do some public stuff, doing a lot of organizational work.'[75] Roberts witnessed a trust develop:

> it started out slowly, and during time more and more responsibility was placed with us and ... they came to respect our judgment, and as a consequence we were given a lot more freedom. But we still functioned with a steering committee, and we still had the finance committee to report to. We still had a candidate to talk to, and our attitude has always been that the candidate has veto power over whatever recommendations are made.[76]

While Reagan remained his own man on issues of policy, he was perfectly willing to take technical direction:

> he just totally left that up to us. Ron was a man trained ... in the movie business, where you have a director and a producer and everybody carries their load. And because of that environmental background, he was a very easy candidate to work with ... But on issues, he had beliefs, he had thoughts. You might convince him: let's don't discuss that one, and it's non-productive and he'd see the merits of it, but in terms of how he felt about Berkeley, how he felt about welfare programs, how he felt about size of government, he had strong feelings.[77]

'We tried out speeches,' Spencer explained, 'we tried out everything. He would adopt those things that he felt [worked].' Surveys and polls gauged reaction, but Reagan 'never took survey research very seriously. He liked all the good numbers, didn't like the bad numbers, really didn't care.' In truth, he trusted his gut reaction. 'He was very good at reading a crowd.'[78]

The reaction was overwhelmingly positive. In the first few months of the campaign, mere personality was much more important than policy. Walker felt that 'A guy as articulate as

Reagan (as white-hat a guy as Reagan, if you will) could excite enough attention so that you could penetrate the electorate.'[79] Weinberger agreed:

> His enormous magnetism showed almost immediately. People flocked around him. Californians love celebrities, and he was a certified celebrity, having been in the movies, which was a double dividend for Californians. He stood out immediately ... had an enormous amount of charm and excited a great deal of almost immediate support just by being there.[80]

Smith felt that he answered a yearning for something new. 'He had a definite ... glamour. Probably mystique is a better term. He was really quite different from anything that anybody had seen ... before.'[81] His newness allowed the voter to strike a blow against the political establishment. Since he seemed like an ordinary guy, he could sell himself as a direct expression of popular will. Reagan's strength, according to State Senator Vernon Sturgeon, lay in his ability to project honesty. 'What he says, he believes. You can agree or disagree, take your pick, but he believes what he's saying, he really believes that. He really is a very sincere, honest guy.'[82]

The more attention Reagan received, the more he became a target. Early in the game, Democrats decided that the best response was derision, mocking the very idea of an actor running for governor. Some of the worst abuse, however, came from fellow Republicans. Party officials resented how he had ignored them and gone his own way. The ill-will surprised him, especially since he was accustomed to a world in which he could make everyone like him. 'One of these days I think it would be wonderful to just sit down and let you hold my hand,' he wrote to Goldwater on 11 November 1965. 'Even in these few months I have acquired a new understanding of the frustration you must have felt so many times, particularly when the blows are coming from our own side.'[83]

By mid-summer 1965, Reagan's newness began to wear thin. He was still delivering 'The Speech', endlessly repeating his warnings about government interference. Seasoned journalists, now accustomed to the lament, questioned its relevance to California. Did Reagan, in fact, know anything about the state? As he recalled, 'there used to be columns and editorials to the effect that, well, if Ronald Reagan doesn't start talking about state affairs, state problems, he's not going to have any votes – he'd better get off these national, international problems. Of course, that wasn't the point. The point was that I was simply continuing to express my overall philosophy.'[84] Journalists weren't missing the point: they simply wanted something more substantial than vague philosophy. Worried by the criticism, the prominent Republican John Harmer protested when a Reagan speech in July 1965 contained 'no reference to any new proposal or program; there was no new ideas presented on the old issues.' Harmer warned Roberts that, very soon, 'the magic of Reagan's presentation ... [will] have to be augmented by some ideas that could conceivably catch the imagination of the public.'[85]

Spencer and Roberts refused to tinker with the message at this stage. 'They didn't interfere ... with that,' Reagan recalled. 'They never tried. They knew what their job was. They ... delivered me to the places where I was to speak, and they told me what the schedule was.'[86] That wasn't quite true, since the firm was doing more to manipulate his image than he perhaps appreciated. They had, however, decided that it was best for Reagan to keep talking generalities, so as to underline that he was not a politician. They wanted to preserve for as long as possible the innocence of a neophyte. Slick, well-informed answers would not have resonated with the public at this stage. While the journalists were not unanimously impressed, the ordinary voters seemed to be.

While Reagan was great at communicating with audiences, he was uncomfortable one-on-one. He did not, in particular, enjoy small talk with politicians, journalists or money men. 'Ronald Reagan is a shy person,' Spencer explained. 'People don't understand this. He was not an introvert. Nixon was almost an introvert and paranoid. That's a bad combination. Reagan was shy.' With strangers, he used humour as a shield.

> He's not going to tell you about what he's doing. He doesn't think it's any of your damn business ... he's not comfortable and so he uses his humor. He can do dialects. I mean the Jewish dialect, a gay dialect. He can tell an Irish ethnic joke. The guy was just unbelievably good at it and he'd break the ice with it. You'd listen to him. But ... you'd walk out of there and you'd say, 'What the hell were we talking about? He didn't tell me anything.'

Spencer found Reagan an interesting contrast to Rockefeller, who was superb at bonhomie. Reagan 'was a shy person and he didn't want to walk up to you and say, "I'm Ronald Reagan and I'm running for Governor."' In contrast, Rockefeller would 'work a room if there were three people in it. It was always, "Hi ya, fella. Hi ya, fella."' The firm encouraged Reagan to develop this ability, but he was never comfortable doing so. 'At communication, one-on-one, he was not very good. At global, big communication, the stage, he was fabulous.'[87]

Even though he seemed, in many ways, a perfect candidate, there was still so much to do. 'Reagan was literally a one-man band when we met him,' Roberts recalled.

> He didn't have any help; he had one secretary that came in a couple of times a week in his home to answer some letters. He literally opened, read, and answered all his mail. He'd answer all his phone calls, he'd handle his own schedule, and he drove himself to meetings ... I was amazed. I said, 'Who's helping you on this? Who's helping you on that?' He said, 'Nobody. Me. I'm doing it.' We naturally had to change that ... very quickly to get ... that detail work off of him.[88]

Politicians were now products moulded for public consumption. Reagan's background in Hollywood rendered him ideally equipped to thrive in such a campaign. His honesty and sincerity camouflaged the fact that he acted the part that Spencer and Roberts devised. His strength lay not only in his ability to carry off his role convincingly, but also in his willingness to accept direction.

The talks at Elks Lodges, PTA meetings and Chambers of Commerce generated media attention that ordinary politicians could not command. As Spencer explained, 'he'd be on television, he'd be on the radio, he'd be in print ... He had really not announced yet, but he was building his base.'[89] Those first few months exceeded all expectations. A California Poll conducted by the Field organization in early August 1965 showed that he was the first choice among Republicans for the nomination, with Kuchel, Christopher, Knight and Senator George Murphy trailing well behind. In head-to-head match-ups, he led Christopher by 17 points, Knight by 30 and Kuchel by 6.[90] Another poll, conducted in May, suggested that his lack of party identity was an asset, since 54 per cent stated they would vote for him if he ran as a Republican, 58 per cent if he was the Democratic nominee and 51 per cent if he ran as an Independent.[91] These polls persuaded other candidates that it was futile to challenge Reagan. Shell took his cue and bowed out. Efforts to lure Knight into the race failed miserably. Some Republicans, including Parkinson, wanted Murphy to run, but he wisely declined. By the beginning of August, the only credible challenger seemed to be Kuchel, though he feigned disinterest. In any case, a California Poll suggested that Reagan offered a better hope of uniting the party, with a higher percentage of Kuchel supporters claiming they would support Reagan in the general election than vice versa.[92] The efforts to woo moderates were clearly bearing fruit.

Kuchel was certainly interested in running. He had ambitions for the presidency and felt that the governor's mansion would provide a better platform than the US Senate. Given that goal, he could not afford a defeat in 1966, especially not in the primary. For this reason, he refused to declare his candidacy, preferring instead to wait for a groundswell of popular support to materialize. That never happened. When the enthusiasm for Reagan refused to dissipate, Kuchel decided to bow out of a race he had never officially entered. On 20 September 1965, he formally announced that he would not seek the nomination and went on to slam the 'extremists' who had hijacked the party. 'The tragic fact is that within our California Republican Party is a fanatical neo-fascist political cult overcome by a strange mixture of corrosive hatred and sickening fear, recklessly determined to control our Party or destroy it.' He stressed that 'All reasonable Republicans have a duty for the sake of our State and for the sake of our Party to unite behind one reasonable candidate untainted by extremism, and then to nominate him and elect him.'[93] While he refused to mention names, it was clear that he wanted someone to stop Reagan. Kuchel's misgivings were given credence when the notoriously extremist Los Angeles County Young Republicans declared nearly unanimously on 7 September that the senator had 'by his own behavior voluntarily resigned from the Republican Party'.[94]

Kuchel and others wrongly assumed that Reagan was the front man for big money's attempt to take over the state. Granted, he did have a few wealthy benefactors like Tuttle and Salvatori, but they did not buy themselves a candidate. Their actual contributions were small. 'I don't think anybody in the Reagan campaign put in over $25,000,' Roberts insisted. Furthermore, 'no money was ever accepted ... with any kind of a string attached to it.'[95] The evidence suggests that, rather than being manipulated by his backers, Reagan was the manipulator. Early in the campaign, he and his sponsors were in perfect accord, particularly as regards anti-communism, free enterprise and the liberal threat. Those were, however, already Reagan issues; he did not stress them because of money he received.

The real proof of the relationship was the way Reagan would distance himself from those who assumed that they could control him. Salvatori, for one, eventually grew annoyed with Reagan's refusal to play the poodle.

Reagan's ability to attract thousands of small donations gave him the freedom to be his own man. The way money was collected demonstrated how politics was changing. 'Big industry ... is a whore,' Nofziger explained.

> Big industry goes to where it thinks the power is ... Big industry works very closely with big government because they feed off of each other. And big business is not necessarily Republican any more ... Surprisingly, the strength of the Republican party is little business. People in the mid-level economic strata. People who make somewhere from $20,000 up ... they are salaried people or they are small business people. They are not the big bankers, they are not the big oil people.[96]

Parkinson agreed that the thrust in fundraising had shifted. 'The tops of those big things [companies] are very apolitical,' he remarked. 'They've got about as much Republican philosophy as Democrat philosophy. It just depends on who is winning. That's not the people we're after.' The Goldwater campaign had demonstrated the advantage of targeting small donors: 'That's what we were after; that's where your money is ... I felt when a man puts in $2 in the Republican party, he's not going to vote Democrat. He's going to vote Republican ... We've done better than the Democrats ... on getting more small money ... The Democrats are getting all the big lump sums.'[97]

Big backers often assume they're buying influence. Small donors have no such expectation. For them, money is simply an expression of loyalty, a symbolic confirmation of membership in a crusade. 'It's very important to get a lot of money from small donors, for two reasons,' Smith discovered. 'You raise a lot of money that way. The second reason is you get people interested.'[98] The gesture, in other words, was as important as the money. Each donation was an expression of faith. This is evident from the thousands of letters from small donors Reagan received. Mr and Mrs Alberts sent $10: 'Perhaps you can use [it] on taxi fare to get some couple to the polls to vote for you.'[99] 'I only have $1.85 and I am sending you a dollar,' wrote Daniel Arthur. 'When I get paid I will send you more.'[100] 'Enclosed is a quarter to further your campaign,' Rita Brown wrote.[101] Jan Phillips, a secretary from Huntingdon Beach, sent a dollar, explaining that Reagan, while a lifeguard on the Rock River in Illinois, had saved her mother from drowning. 'If it hadn't been for Ronald Reagan', she wrote, 'I would not even be here.'[102]

Direct-mail campaigns drummed up support and raised even more money. A Reagan speech at a local gathering would get the ball rolling by raising interest within that locality. The firm would then target that area. 'We started doing some mailings to find out how we were doing with the public in various assembly districts,' Roberts explained.

> We'd just pick an assembly district and mail the whole district and see if we couldn't get enough returns out of it to mail to the next one. And we did. We would get more than enough, maybe by five or six or $7000 over the cost to mail the next one. So we would mail the next one. We just kept doing that, mainly around the L.A. area and that helped get a lot of interest going and a lot of people signed up.[103]

'Money was not hard to raise,' Roberts recalled. In addition to the direct-mail campaigns, they 'raised it with a lot of gatherings, parties of various kinds – cocktail parties, dinners, and so forth. Also we did a lot of direct eyeball, one-on-one, will-you-give-me-some-money type of phone calls and meetings.'[104] The campaign spent a huge amount, but ended up with surplus funds.

In one rather imaginative scheme, a four-page genealogical pamphlet was sent to individuals with selected family names.

The booklet included a history of the surname, a list of prominent Americans and Californians with that name and a picture of the family crest. 'Please accept this personal gift with my most sincere compliments,' the accompanying note from Reagan read. Also included was a missive from campaign chairman Philip Battaglia: 'The enclosed brief history of your family name is sent to you as an indication of Ronald Reagan's interest in the individual – you. We hope that it will serve to impress upon you Mr. Reagan's strong faith in the individual and the importance that he places in the family.' Then came an appeal: 'For a contribution of $5 or more we will send you a quality reproduction of your family coat of arms suitable for framing ... We feel that it is a most worthwhile investment for good government and your personal pleasure.'[105]

Money made Reagan uncomfortable. 'You don't talk money in the company of the candidate, not this candidate anyway,' Spencer explained. 'He just glazed over.'[106] Nofziger saw nothing wrong with Reagan's aversion. 'You keep the candidate doing his thing, which is campaigning ... You've got to keep him above [the money matters] ... You just don't want him mixed up in that kind of nonsense.'[107] He especially hated big fundraising events. 'The first time in '65, we took him to West Covina ... for a fundraiser,' Spencer recalled.

> They probably had fifty to seventy-five people there. He walked in with Nancy ... He goes over to the corner of a room and stands there ... I'm watching all this ... Finally I walked over to him and I said, 'Ron, you've got to get out and mix. You've got to rub shoulders.' He was used to people coming to him. I said, 'You've got to go press the hands. You've got to move it.' He didn't like doing that.[108]

Reagan's role was thus restricted to giving speeches designed to inspire people to donate. 'He would make great presentations,' Smith felt. 'But he just didn't want to then ask them for the money. That's when Holmes Tuttle and the rest of us would jump in and do the asking. And that's perfectly normal.'[109] In truth, Reagan did not need to be good at asking for money since there was already so much eagerness to give. The novelty of Reagan's campaign inspired a new cohort of supporters to donate. Those inclined to give were the same people who found Reagan's attacks on big government, high taxes and welfare so appealing. His crusade was theirs.

Spencer felt that the primary was won long before Reagan actually announced his candidacy. 'He had won … by the time filing had closed, in my judgement. Everything he did in 1965 is what won the primary for him. It's not what we did in the campaign.'[110] Reagan and his handlers had originally agreed to give the trial run six months. Within weeks, however, everything seemed in place: a charismatic candidate, backed by an efficient organization and limitless money, was wooing voters all over the state. The great contrast to 1962 and 1964 was that a conservative Republican was finding enthusiastic support all over the state. Spencer and Roberts thought that the trial run had become a pretence. 'Roberts and I looked at each other one night and said, "This guy's running. To hell with this exploratory stuff, he's made his mind up." … It was obvious to us that he'd caught the bug. He was running.'[111]

Ten weeks into the experiment, a circular to the Friends proclaimed that 'the effort has gone way beyond the fondest hopes of all those concerned.'[112] That was certainly the message Reagan was receiving:

> people would come up to me. They'd say, 'Oh, you ought to run for governor—' and I would say, 'Oh, no,' and I'd name people prominent in the party and say, 'Why not so-and-so or so-and-so, and we'll all go campaign for them?' They just dismissed that and came right back to me. So I told [Nancy], 'They're right. I think I do offer the best chance of winning. Now, do we want to do this?'[113]

> Why he ran — in his own words)

In mid-September, Reagan accepted that he had 'burned all of [my] bridges career-wise'.[114] Yet he later claimed that it was not until late November that 'I knew that I was going to say yes.'[115] His motives, he insisted, were pure:

> I'm honestly fearful that unless we restore the balance of power, we could, and will, see great changes in our fundamental system. I had to ask myself whether continuing to make speeches and sound warnings was enough, or whether I had not reached the point in which I must supplement words with more positive action. The difficult part of the choice had to do with my personal desires to spend more time, which I now can't do, on the farm, [and] jump into a way of life that has never been particularly appealing. Perhaps my own children were part of the decision because I would hate to think that they would grow up in a different America than I have known.[116]

He realized that there were huge implications for the way he lived. He had been semi-retired, spending one day in Hollywood and four at his ranch. 'I loved every minute of that.' Since the acting money would dry up, he would probably have to sell the ranch. 'That broke my heart.' In truth, however, he was so consumed with campaigning, that he did not fully consider the consequences. 'I have to confess something … when I said yes, I had not actually thought beyond November … It wasn't until after I had agreed, and I said, "Wait a minute. I'm talking about the next several years."'[117]

# 4
# Old Tactics, New Faces

'There was nothing new about the '66 campaign,' Caspar Weinberger grumbled. 'It was a good campaign, well-organized, but there was nothing new or unusual about it at all.'[1] That seems a strange statement given the campaign's shiny exterior. It might be explained by Weinberger's ornery nature, not to mention his reluctance to praise something in which he played a minor part. Yet there is a germ of truth in what he said. No aspect of the campaign was genuinely new; every element had been seen before. What made it special, however, was the whole package – the efficiency, the professionalism and the way sophisticated techniques were integrated so effectively. Reagan, the 'Great Communicator', was such a huge presence that he tended to overshadow those who helped him become governor. Yet their expertise was essential to his victory.

Strategy meetings were held at Reagan's house at least once a fortnight. Roberts, Spencer, Tuttle, Salvatori and Battaglia usually attended, and Nofziger joined in after he became press secretary. Reagan would sit quietly while others formulated strategy. He was 'a very good listener', Nofziger felt. After hearing everything, he'd ask questions or make proposals. 'He was there and he participated, and he agreed. When he didn't agree, he said so.'[2] Tuttle and Salvatori were actively involved in grand strategy, as their regular attendance at these meetings attests, but did not interfere with the mechanics. Roberts was satisfied with this relationship: 'I think they all had a nice, even healthy interest ... and I would have to say had quite a bit to contribute to the direction of the effort. I don't think they dominated it, or wanted to dominate it, but I think they wanted to have their say.' He insists, however, that 'They were never pushy ... They always generally bowed to the pure political decisions and policy in most matters, but always wanted to be aware of what was happening and, on occasion, put in their recommendations.'[3]

Spencer and Roberts created their own organization, separate from the party machine, designed with the single purpose of electing Reagan. 'They [did] ... something very smart,' Nofziger described. 'They ... said, "To heck with all the old hack Republicans out there, we'll go out and get some bright, new faces."'[4] Roberts elaborated:

> We surrounded him with a lot of new young fellows on the way up because we wanted to present Ron as a positive guy. We kept him away from the old-fogey element. We didn't want to encourage the kind of hysteria that attached itself to the Goldwater campaign. In 1964 you saw a lot of feverish people working for Goldwater. Every Goldwater volunteer was hoarse and red-eyed. We deliberately kept our campaign low-key and friendly. We wanted a nice friendly buzz around the headquarters, but none of that Holy War feeling. We weren't going to give the Democrats anything to hang their extremist charges on.[5]

The management team was divided into northern and southern committees to oversee local organizations and plan Reagan's tours. Philip Battaglia served as Southern California chairman during the primary, with Tom Reed managing the north. During the general election campaign, Battaglia became campaign committee chairman for the entire state, while Thomas Pike and Dirk Eldredge became Southern California co-chairmen and

Fred Haffner supervised operations in the north. Each county then had its own organization, with the bigger counties divided into separate regions. For example, Los Angeles County had seven regions and San Bernardino five. Within the regions, local organizations, often corresponding to separate precincts, arranged efforts that reflected the specific interests of voters. This was Reagan's army, the people who knocked on doors, distributed campaign literature and manned tables outside grocery stores.

The predominantly decentralized, grassroots effort contrasted markedly to the top-down style of Republican operations before 1964. The old approach involved expensive dinners geared toward wealthy contributors, with the money raised going toward advertising, direct-mail shots and further big events. The Reagan campaign did have its $100-a-plate dinners and speeches to huge crowds, but the main effort was directed toward smaller events designed to establish direct contact with the voters. These gatherings highlighted Reagan's populist, 'citizen-politician' message. It was all very labour intensive, with Reagan himself one of the hardest workers. Though his fear of flying had at first proved an obstacle, he quickly overcame that. Mervin Amerine, an enthusiastic supporter, lent Reagan his DC-3, along with his services as a pilot. The plane was nicknamed 'The Turkey' because its regular remit was transporting baby turkeys from Amerine's San Joaquin ranch to markets around the state.

While the strain on the candidate was enormous – he often attended five or six events a day – these small events inspired not just a willingness to vote for Reagan, but often a desire to work for his campaign. 'As your campaign gets under way', wrote James Alleman immediately after Reagan declared his candidacy, 'I would like to help out, by word of mouth or with literature. Also financially to a small extent. I cannot get away from home, on account of an arthritic wife, but I will do what I can.'[6] In contrast to the Goldwater campaign, in which activists were not mobilized until well into the primary, the Reagan team had a network of volunteers established long before he formally announced his candidacy. All this surprised journalists covering the campaign, since they had expected something decidedly different. As Morrie Ryskind remarked in the *Los Angeles Times*, 'there were more volunteer Reagan organizations for the primary than all the rest of the candidates in both parties put together.'[7]

Spencer surmised that a huge number of voters were inclined to support Reagan who had not formally registered Republican and were not, therefore, qualified to vote in the primary. The 'Register for Reagan' drive solidified the voter's commitment to the candidate, providing a sense of belonging to a cohesive group of like-minded people. A pyramid scheme was devised in which each new registrant was urged to find an additional six supporters, the goal being to sign up more than a million people. At the time of registration, individuals were asked if they also wanted to volunteer. Existing volunteers would then quickly contact the new registrant to outline what help was needed. All registrants were asked to make a one-dollar contribution, though this was not mandatory. The entire approach was a great deal more intimate than customary registration drives, which often consisted of blind mailings to individuals identified as potential supporters, with little follow-up involved.

A Speakers Bureau, headed by Assemblyman Charles Conrad, was established to provide a pool of politicians and activists ready to speak to local organizations. In an attempt to guard against gaffes, much effort went toward keeping speakers carefully briefed. A detailed manual provided strict instructions on how to prepare for these events and also served as a primer on Reagan's policies, designed to prepare the speaker for question-and-answer sessions. Speakers were also given detailed information about the characteristics of the constituency and the issues important to it. They were discouraged from speaking negatively about other Republican candidates: the aim being to present Reagan's views in a positive manner. Speakers were also urged to bring along a few sympathetic individuals to ask pre-determined questions in order to move the Q&A session in the right direction. These plants also helped to trigger an enthusiastic ovation.

Very little help was provided by the Republican Party machine, which was poorly funded and badly organized. In any case, according to its own rules, it could not be seen to be aiding any specific candidate during the primary. This meant that, by the time the primary was over and the party organization could throw its weight behind the nominee, there was little it could contribute since the candidate's direction was already set in stone. Groups like the Young Republicans and the Federated Republican Women did not, however, have to maintain impartiality. These organizations were wooed, but always with a clear sense that they were helpers, not policy-makers. They were, according to Spencer, 'a very important ingredient … You've got to have rapport with them; you have to understand what motivates them; and you have to understand who the leadership is.'[8] These groups tended to be right-wing; ultra-conservative beliefs often went hand-in-hand with a crusading mentality. The team tapped their energy and Reagan himself inspired volunteers with a new enthusiasm he was uniquely able to arouse. He did, however, caution against a repeat of 1964. 'It is wrong to fly off the cliff with all flags flying,' he told Young Republicans in early February 1966. 'It is wrong to believe that you would rather be right than win.'[9]

Democrats outnumbered Republicans in California by about four to three. This meant that Republicans, in order to win, had to be better organized. 'We were a smaller party', Weinberger explained, 'but we managed to win a great deal. I always attributed a large part of it to the effectiveness of the women's organizations … They were the ones who worked. The men talked a lot, the women got out and really worked. They were one of our … secret assets.'[10] Women were instrumental in every aspect of grassroots organization. 'Never knock the ladies,' George Murphy remarked, 'they can cover a block like a pack of beavers.'[11] For the women, many of whom were housewives, working for Reagan was like joining a club. It provided a chance to socialize while doing something important. Women's clubs would host coffee mornings and luncheons which would usually be attended by Reagan, his wife Nancy, or a close associate. These events drove home the 'citizen-politician' message because he was actually talking to ordinary people rather than communicating through television or the larger party machine.

Young Republicans had enormous energy but their puerile antics had often negated any benefit they brought. Their fondness for the John Birch Society caused considerable disquiet. Parkinson wanted to utilize their enthusiasm in the grassroots campaign, but this proved difficult because they were often immune to control. 'They were always making adverse publicity,' he recalled. 'My problem was to try and keep them in harness and to get them to do something positive.'[12] Through careful management, he 'was able to keep a lot out of the press and a lot of controversy under cover by convincing them that they need us and we needed them'. The Reverend John Sorenson was recruited to act as a minder in order to 'kind of keep the lid on'.[13]

Young Republicans were attracted to Reagan because of his past association with Goldwater. He appealed directly to this group, emphasizing that 'to have an effective campaign, we must have the help and support of California's youth'.[14] A new body, called Youth for Reagan (YFR), was formed, a calculated effort to sidestep the official Young Republican organization and bring its exuberance under control. A central YFR organization was established within each county, whereupon that body then established individual chapters in high schools, colleges, churches, workplaces and community groups. 'We worked right alongside the Federation of Republican Women,' Thomas Fuentes, a recent high-school graduate, recalled. 'We helped out at rallies, we helped out at events, we walked precincts, we registered voters, we helped get out the vote – hands on, grassroots activity.'[15] This was another side of youth activism in the 1960s, a movement that probably had more impact than the campus groups that protested the war in Vietnam.

A subgroup of YFR was the Reagan Girls, established to provide 'eye candy' at events. Founded by Cherie Adams, the club replicated a similar effort during the Goldwater campaign in California. As its literature boasted:

> The Reagan Girl program is a major step forward in political promotional programs and has already won the hearty approval of the public. Reagan Girls represent the young, wholesome, vivacious, natural, all-American girl. She is a sincere individual genuinely interested in civic affairs, better government for California, and the election of Ronald Reagan as Governor. She is an attractive, friendly and charming girl between the ages of 16 and 25.[16]

The main function of the Reagan Girls was to provide 'beauty, personality and energy'. Not every girl could join: suitable members were selected on the basis of their 'appearance, intelligence, and friendliness' after a rigorous vetting process that resembled a beauty contest. 'A 25 inch waist maximum has been established. Any girl with a waist measurement over 25 inches should be asked to participate in the Reagan Pep Squad.'[17] Nancy Reagan oversaw the selection of the uniform, reputed to be 'the most attractive campaign outfit ever designed'. The girls' behaviour was rigidly monitored and those who strayed from the strict moral standards were discharged. Evidence of gum-chewing, alcohol or smoking brought immediate dismissal. Jewellery ('except rings and watches') was not allowed, nor was 'excessive make-up'. Though mild flirtation was the unofficial purpose ('[your] presence is an added attraction for the males in your group!'), actual congress was forbidden – 'giving out of phone numbers and addresses, and making dates is not permitted during appearances'.[18] Reagan Girls were highly visible at every campaign event, riding in parades or sitting prominently on stages. They also acted as 'usherettes' at campaign events, hostesses or waitresses at dinners and receptionists at campaign headquarters.[19] 'I'm not old enough to vote, so I feel that this is my contribution,' Reagan Girl Tammy Zebold told a reporter. 'I have to do s*omething* ... I mean, he's just so fabulous. He's my main reason for being in this. I'm just so dedicated to Ronald Reagan.'[20]

Along with this appeal to the young went a calculated attempt to present Reagan as a friend of the senior citizen. This required some clever manoeuvring since it often meant downplaying his opposition to New Deal reforms and social security programmes that benefited the old. In an attempt to make a distinction between good government assistance and bad, Reagan alleged that Brown had reduced old-age pensions while increasing welfare payments. The main thrust of his appeal to senior citizens, however, played upon their pride in America and their fears of moral decline. Reagan presented himself as the person who would rescue the past, appealing to the old to 'help us bring back what you feel America and California should be'.[21] Polls showed that the law-and-order issue ranked high among the concerns of the elderly, therefore Reagan's emphasis upon this problem resonated well with that constituency.

Black people were essentially written off by the Reagan campaign: the team decided that any effort in their direction would be wasted. Overtures were, however, directed toward Hispanics, a community always more conservative in outlook. In April 1965, Reagan received a letter from Phil Saenz, publisher of the *Mexican American*, urging him to run for governor. 'I am confident that Mexican-American voters can be encouraged to support you,' he wrote, 'although 95% of them are Democrats. This ethnic group is susceptible to influence if the approach is right.'[22] Intrigued by this possibility, Spencer-Roberts brought in Dr Francisco Bravo to devise a special appeal. Bravo formed the Mexican-American Democrats for Reagan Committee, which produced pamphlets attacking Brown and organized events to showcase Reagan as a true friend of the community. Bravo's literature questioned the knee-jerk support that Mexican-Americans had traditionally given Democrats: 'We have been taken for granted for *too* long.'[23] In the Spanish-language periodical *El Grito*, Bravo published an article entitled 'La hora de la decisión' ('The hour of decision'), in which he urged Hispanics to register and to support Reagan. He also devised the 'Ya Basta' ('Enough Already') campaign, which suggested that a change of government would be economically beneficial. He insisted that Reagan, a friend of the working man, would protect Hispanics' jobs. Campaign literature, bumper stickers and lapel badges were printed in Spanish.

In line with this appeal, Reagan pointedly criticized the federal government's cancellation of the Bracero programme, which stopped the practice (established in 1942) of allowing Mexican labourers to cross the border to work on farms. This cancellation had caused chaos in the agricultural community, with the harvest disrupted because of a severe shortage of pickers. Reagan's stance, originally designed to please farm owners who wanted cheap labour, also delighted Hispanic residents eager for family members to join them. Reagan's glamour was also used to considerable effect. Pamphlets featured photographs of him with Hispanic leaders or volunteers, dubbed 'Reaganistas'. Each piece of literature invariably included a photo of Reagan with his wife and children, a calculated appeal to the importance the community placed upon family. During Cinco de Mayo celebrations in 1966, Reagan, wearing traditional Mexican ceremonial clothing and large sombrero, rode his horse in a parade. The effort seemed to work. 'Our people like a guy with style,' William Orozco, a Reagan field representative in Los Angeles, explained.

A Mexican-American might wear a dirty shirt but he doesn't want to vote for a guy with one. When Reagan came to East Los Angeles, they saw this big, good-looking guy, a beautiful dresser, with that flashing smile and that great handshake. How could Pat Brown compete with that? Pat kept calling them 'You people', and saying how much the Democrats were doing for them. He bored the hell out of everybody.[24]

While Reagan's devotion to the community was rather contrived and the imagery superficial and cynical, the campaign succeeded. 'We did a lot of work in the Mexican-American community,' Roberts recalled. 'We managed to get almost 25 percent of the Mexican-American vote who were very unhappy with Brown over a lot of things.'[25] That indicates the campaign's priorities: a huge effort was worthwhile if 25 per cent of Hispanic voters switched sides. Since no amount of effort would have had even a fraction of that effect on blacks, they were ignored.

By far the largest effort was directed toward coaxing whites whose natural loyalty was to the Democrats but whose disenchantment with the party was growing. In order to woo these voters, the team had to find out where they lived and what their concerns were. This is where computers came to the rescue: in particular, a state-of-the-art Precinct Index Priority System. PIPS comprised a computer program that processed census data to predict voting intentions in specific neighbourhoods. The system allowed a candidate to analyse the demographic profile of a precinct, the better to shape the messages targeted at it. For example, if an area was packed with married white couples of retirement age whose profile suggested they were worried about crime or the Rumford Act, those issues could be stressed when volunteers visited. The system also gave Reagan a good indication of the areas most susceptible to his message by building a profile of the swing voter. In tandem with PIPS, the campaign used what Spencer called 'thought-leader research', which involved identifying the people of influence in an area (businessmen, politicians, religious leaders, etc.) and interviewing them to find out the important issues and to gauge their reaction to Reagan.

PIPS was developed by Vince Barabba, a business student at UCLA. Disenchanted with academia, Barabba took his ideas to Spencer, who helped him form a company called Datamatics. 'Stu', Barabba explained, 'is a very street-smart person, [he] knew there were better ways of doing what he wanted to do. He looked for reasonably bright young people to help him do his job better.'[26] Supported by Spencer, Barabba merged his work with that of two sociologists who had devised a model called Social Area Analysis, which used census data on class and family composition to profile neighbourhoods. Barabba mapped this data onto precincts, by feeding it into a rented IBM 1401. This became PIPS, which was used to good effect in two Los Angeles city council elections in 1965. He explained:

> The goal of Precinct Index Priority System … is to help campaign strategists find areas containing citizens most likely to vote for their candidate. P.I.P.S. highlights the relative priority (or strength) of the areas in question on the basis of the facts and information which political judgment indicates will be important. P.I.P.S. can help to organize political judgment, to place evidence behind political judgment, and to develop a factual check of political judgment.[27]

The evidence collected went beyond the usual material on age, income, ethnicity, etc. and included more specific data like the number of girls registered in Brownies, Scouts and Senior Scouts – 'it was the strategists' opinion that families placing their daughters in such organizations would be more likely to have ambitions and hopes that would … make them vote Republican.'[28]

Barabba's system synthesized census data into three main indices. 'One was an economic index, one was a family relationship index, and the other was an ethnic index,' he explained. 'This tool allowed us to go into a community and tell its power structure a lot more about the community, at the small-area level, than they had ever seen before. They were used to looking at the aggregate.'[29] After crunching the numbers, Barabba realized that PIPS would be especially useful in targeting swing voters. As he later explained, 'There were enough Republicans to get you close, but if you got every Republican out there you [still] could never win. So you had to get swing voters.' PIPS allowed the campaign to target middle-aged white union members who might benefit from Reagan's policies – the cohort later known as Reagan Democrats. 'Everyone had classified union workers all the same,' Barabba explained.[30] That was a mistake. PIPS gave Reagan the ability to mine a promising seam of worker discontent.

Spencer objected to allegations that PIPS was a sinister new development dreamt up by manipulative social scientists. 'This is not new,' he insisted. 'Precinct index priority was another form of targeting. All the politicians talk about targeting ... It's very important, but you know they were targeting in Roman days. They've always targeted.' The real difference was that targeting became more accurate when computers became available. Echoing Barabba, Spencer confirmed that the Reagan campaign was enthusiastic about PIPS because: 'we could simulate a campaign or build a campaign to the point where we knew what a Reagan voter would be. We took age, housing costs, income, ethnicity, labor union membership, and applied that to past voting patterns and some other things, whatever we could steal off of census data.'[31]

Once the swing voters were identified through PIPS, the campaign team would then persuade those voters to switch sides. This was done by canvassing, direct mail or by having Reagan visit the area. All these methods of persuasion had been used in previous campaigns, but seldom with such surgical efficiency. Thus, despite the use of computers, this was still primarily a grassroots effort, old-fashioned in its reliance upon techniques calculated to foster individual contact. Even when television was used, the same goal of forging a bond between candidate and voter was paramount. Television, Nofziger explained, offered Reagan the opportunity to project 'a kind of a picture of himself he wishe[d] to give to the people'.[32] When Reagan visited an area that had been identified for targeting by PIPS, the media would be alerted beforehand, thus spreading the word even wider through what was essentially free advertising.

The campaign also produced paid advertisements, but did not spend profligately in this area. Spencer reckoned that the total budget did not exceed $1 million. 'It was all pretty canned TV spots and stuff.'[33] He claimed that television in those days was 'nothing but radio with a face', but that seems more an indication of his prejudice than of the potential of the medium.[34] Reagan ads were simple camera talks, primitive in presentation. He would first be shown in long shot, then in medium shot, then finally in close-up when the crux of his message was delivered. Ernest Rose and Douglas Fuchs, who analysed 60 of these ads, concluded that they were like 'a page out of the early history of television, with [their] reliance upon the on-screen commentator format ... [They were], however, lacking in any of the humor and spontaneity which were the saving graces of that TV era.'[35] This might seem strange from a candidate who grew up in Hollywood. Rose and Fuchs eventually concluded that 'It is almost as if the films were intentionally bumbling and naïve; that their awkwardness was calculated to make Reagan seem less like an actor candidate than a "common ordinary citizen".'[36] Fred Dutton, one of Brown's senior advisers, agreed that primitive ads probably reflected 'a conscious decision ... by Reagan and his staff that he did not want to look like too much the movie actor with too polished a technique'.[37]

A similar understated approach was evident in the handling of the press. Not long after Reagan's declaration, Nofziger was hired as press secretary. Finding a suitable person was not easy since Spencer and Roberts wanted someone with Republican sympathies who was familiar with the national press. As Nofziger quipped, 'It's kind of hard to find Republican reporters in Washington.' Salvatori and Tuttle persuaded Jim Copley, publisher of the *San Diego Union*, to give Nofziger leave of absence and then coaxed the reporter with a salary double what he was then earning. In truth, Copley, a rabid conservative, did not need much persuading, since he desperately wanted Brown defeated. Nofziger at first turned down the offer on the grounds that he was unqualified. Spencer and Roberts didn't seem to care. A deal was finalized on 4 February 1966 and Nofziger joined the campaign on 1 March. It is nevertheless significant that the campaign did not hire a full-time press secretary until nearly two months after Reagan's formal declaration and more than a year after he started his quest for the governorship.

Nofziger was a walking cliché: an overweight, cigar-smoking, rough-talking reporter whose fondness for fast food and doughnuts was evident by the stains on his crumpled tie. He did not at first know what was expected of him, and the campaign managers did little to enlighten him. One of his duties was research, a remit similar to that of Kenneth Holden and Stanley Plog, who were brought on board around the same time. The overlap of duties was never clarified, nor was the chain of command. 'We had some very good researchers,' Nofziger reflected. 'We would sit down together, when I would be back in town, and we would work on position papers and issues.' His research responsibilities were, however, mainly supervisory. A more obvious and time-consuming duty was to act as a front man liaising with reporters in order to get Reagan's message out. This was obviously important, but not something Nofziger did well, primarily because he lacked the staff to do it properly.

'We were very limited ... in the press-p.r. area. I would never want to campaign that way again.'[38]

'As I look back on it ... there was much that a press operation should have done that it didn't do,' Nofziger explained. 'The job of the press secretary in the first Reagan campaign was unlike that of any press secretary I have seen before or since.' Under normal circumstances, research and PR might have been the extent of Nofziger's duties, but the nature of the campaign and the peculiarities of the candidate widened his role. Because Reagan was inexperienced, he needed a full-time minder. 'I was the guy who travelled with the candidate ... It was Reagan and me on the road ... sitting there making policy decisions ... in the back seat of a car.'[39] He had to be ever alert to potential catastrophe. 'I was often accused of thrusting my ample belly between the candidate and the reporter,' Nofziger recalled. 'I plead guilty. Most candidates have a compulsive urge to answer a question. It was my job ... to keep the candidate and the campaign on track. Otherwise the other guy wins.'[40] Confusion arises because, as will be seen, Plog and Holden claimed that they performed the same task at exactly the same time. The weight of evidence, however, supports Nofziger's greater influence. Reagan, in fact, had a difficult time remembering what Plog and Holden actually did during the campaign.

'In this business,' Nofziger added, 'if you're halfway competent and if you have halfway the confidence of the man you're working for, [you become] not so much a mechanic as a spokesman.' This meant an exponential increase in his role:

> Anybody can put on a press conference if you tell them what ought to be done. You can find a lot of people to write a press release. You can find a lot of people to do research and even to write speeches. But you've got to be careful that the spokesman for the candidate or the officeholder is somebody who understands how far he can go and who understands what he can say on behalf of the person he works for. [He has to]

understand when he is speaking for himself and not for the candidate, and understand when he should be on the record or off the record, and all those kinds of things.[41]

Nofziger often felt overwhelmed: 'We were out there pretty much alone.' As Reagan came to rely more heavily on him, he became 'an advisor and ... a person helping [to] make policy ... it was different because most candidates in major campaigns have more people around them like that when they are on the road. Our entourage was ... very small.'[42] In retrospect, he was not particularly impressed with his performance. 'I had no experience in this area, and frankly ... in many respects I was a lousy press secretary ... But the world is filled with lousy press secretaries. I was not alone.'[43] The press operation contrasted sharply with the otherwise competent management of the campaign. 'As I look back at ... what we might have done if they'd given me just a couple more people, I kind of weep.'[44] His own deficiencies nevertheless convinced Nofziger that Reagan was an exceptional candidate. 'Let me repeat. We won that election for one reason, and that's Reagan.'[45] In other words, the press secretary did not need to be perfect since Nofziger's inadequacies were more than compensated by the candidate's brilliance.

According to Nofziger, once the campaign was in full swing the press began to treat Reagan 'as well as they treat anybody else. You can always go pick an isolated case where a guy wrote something that wasn't so ... But I don't know of any reporters who really consciously set out to get him.'[46] Spencer agreed: 'Ronald Reagan doesn't realize how kind they were to him ... Number one, it was because he was forward and honest, and number two, they were in awe of him. They were in awe of Ronald Reagan the actor.'[47] The favourable reaction was all the more surprising given that Reagan did not actively court journalists. Most politicians use journalists as conduits to the people. Reagan, in contrast, preferred to communicate directly with the people through Q&A sessions. In time, Nofziger adjusted to that preference, cutting down on press conferences in favour of Q&A sessions with the public.

Reagan never felt comfortable around journalists. 'He's ... not the kind of a guy who buddies up easily to other people, especially people whose job puts them a little at odds with him.' Most politicians know how to court the press and many consider the booze-fuelled bonhomie an enjoyable aspect of the job. 'Ron was not a part of the system,' Spencer admitted. 'We have a political establishment in this state ... It's people like me, it's the press people ... it's the officeholders; it's the pols. Ron wasn't a part of that; he was an intruder.'[48] Nofziger agreed that Reagan 'is not a guy who sits around at the bar, and drinks with the boys and plays poker with the boys, and that sort of thing. You'd never find him at Frank Fat's in Sacramento, or anything like that.'[49] Journalists found him aloof, but not sufficiently so that he alienated them. 'The media was very kind,' Spencer admitted. 'They could have destroyed him, but they were fair ... they could have gone out on a vendetta and decided, we are not going to let ... this actor become governor.'[50]

In San Diego, the notoriously right-wing Copley papers were firmly on Reagan's side. The *Sacramento Bee*, the most left-wing mainstream paper in the state, was predictably dismissive, so much so that it over-egged the pudding. It could not mention Reagan without prefacing his name with 'the ultra-conservative Republican', or with references to Goldwater or the Birchers.[51] Between those two extremes, most papers allowed Reagan the opportunity to earn their respect. The *Los Angeles Times*, for instance, went through the motions of neutrality and then eventually backed him. This was important since endorsement seemed to be earned, rather than partisan. Reagan benefited enormously from the fact that most minor papers in the state were Republican in outlook. Small-town editors were thrilled with a candidate who embodied small-town values. As for the larger papers, Nofziger concluded that most 'supported Reagan because they felt that Pat Brown had run his course and was not a particularly good governor, and that Reagan offered something new and vigorous, and would be more pro-business, and more conservative in his spending.'[52]

Reagan earned the respect of journalists because he proved so good at defending himself in front of them. Weinberger attributed this to how well he responded to coaching:

> We used to brief him before press conferences ... Obviously, the rule was to think up as many difficult, disconcerting, and hostile questions as we could to see what sort of responses he would make. If he said he didn't know anything about that, we would talk a little bit about the subject matter. He would get it into his memory, and then he would go out. Most of these questions would come up in the press conference, and he was just absolute – photographic. He could repeat proposed answers, almost word for word.[53]

Reagan was never daunted by encounters with the press, which in turn made him seem confident, authoritative and natural. 'He liked the give and take,' Weinberger reflected. 'He was very, very good at it. The general comment at the end of [a] press conference was ... "We never laid a glove on him."'[54] 'The thing that stayed in my craw forever', Cristina recalled, 'was, he won't panic in front of a bunch of media people.'[55] Plog witnessed how the opposition tried to engineer situations designed to embarrass Reagan. 'But he ... always kept his cool ... The voting public began to say, "Hey, this guy's pretty cool, isn't he, man?"'[56]

Reagan's coolness eventually became an issue. Hostile critics speculated that the slick image camouflaged a weak candidate. A few days after his declaration on 6 January, the *Riverside Press* called him 'the polished product of the Spencer-Roberts public relations agency and the McCann-Erickson ... advertising agency', while criticizing his campaign for being 'formal, splashy, and expensive', as if this was something new to California.[57] The *New York Times* described the declaration speech as a 'dramatic and carefully rehearsed television entry into the race'.[58] The paper, significantly, sent its Hollywood reporter to cover the story. 'Estimates are that Reagan's debut cost at least $50,000,' Sydney Kossen wrote in the *San Francisco Chronicle*, failing to point out that the amount was hardly exorbitant.[59] The *Sacramento Bee* highlighted the views of Paul Posner, Los Angeles County Democratic chairman, who argued that Reagan's 'pre-taped script was written by professional image changers and staged by theatrical experts. It was their job to hide the real Ronald Reagan ... They put words of moderation in his mouth and right amount of make-up on his face.'[60] The paper never abandoned that line of argument. After his primary victory in June, Reagan was still being criticized for a campaign 'lifted from the Madison Avenue boys who sell merchandise by the attractiveness of the package'.[61] As late as September 1966, the journalist Drew Pearson was still recycling this line, arguing that Reagan had been 'groomed'. He was 'ruddy and rugged of face, but faceless on issues'.[62]

Spencer and Roberts were sensitive to this criticism, but could do little about it because the problem arose precisely because Reagan was so good at presentation. He memorized minute detail and delivered it with perfect cadence. He played fast and loose with statistics, but somehow made his fibs sound believable. For instance, in his declaration speech, he claimed that 'The unemployment rate is almost 40 percent higher than the rest of the nation.' While this was technically true, what it actually meant was that the jobless figure was 5.6 per cent in California and 4.2 per cent across the nation.[63] In any case, unemployment was higher than normal precisely because the downtrodden still saw the state as a land of opportunity. On another occasion he stated that anyone coming to California could get welfare within 21 days. That was not remotely true. The 21 days was the period between application for welfare

*Vietnam*

and the payment of the first cheque. The applicant still had to prove residence in the state for five of the previous nine years. Perhaps because Reagan was not yet seen as a politician, he could get away with tricks of this sort. The performance wasn't always perfect, but didn't need to be. Occasional gaffes demonstrated that Reagan was not a perfect mannequin designed by advertisers.

One of these gaffes illustrates the difference in outlook between press and people in a populist campaign. During the summer of 1965, when Reagan was still testing the waters, discussion often turned to Vietnam. This was particularly so because, in May, ground troops had been deployed for the first time, sparking significant protest at Berkeley. Reagan took umbrage with students who objected to the war. As he recalled:

> I said, 'Well, isn't it strange that people are able to do legally what amounts to giving comfort and aid to the enemy. They'd be charged with treason if this was a declared war.' I said, 'It's a war to the fellows that are fighting it and getting shot.' Of course, in saying that one of the press men said, 'Well, should it be?' And I said, 'Why not? Why couldn't we solve this whole matter of how to handle the actual interference with the war effort – not just people disagreeing with it, but the actual interference – by declaring war?'

The response sounded exactly like Goldwater. It was also astoundingly ignorant, since it justified a declaration of war purely on domestic political grounds, ignoring the implications for Cold War relations. Probing this weakness, journalists pressed Reagan on what should be done in Vietnam. He replied:

> You know, look, it's ridiculous that our young men are dying in a war with a country whose whole gross national product is less than the industrial output of Cleveland, Ohio … If we could get this over with – if we would simply go in there and do it,

good Lord, we've got the strength to level North Vietnam, pave it, paint stripes on it, and make a parking lot out of it.[64]

According to Nofziger, this gaffe 'came up to haunt him a time or two'.[65] While it is certainly true that the press got considerable mileage out of it during the campaign (and since), Reagan was more interested in impressing voters than journalists. The comment undoubtedly annoyed liberals, but Reagan didn't want to impress them. Far from being a mistake, the remark seems instead to have been calculated to appeal to that constituency of voters who were frustrated at America's inability to impose its will in Vietnam and, at the same time, appalled at the protests. Reagan was talking directly to his favourite constituency – the voter who wanted to 'kick ass' in Vietnam. As he once confessed, 'If I am getting my message across to a truck driver, then I know I am delivering my message effectively.'[66] On these occasions, he was expressing white, working-class logic – truck driver logic – very effectively. His remarks on Vietnam were calculated to appeal to voters in Southern California who saw the war in simple terms: they wanted America to get aggressive and were not bothered by consequences. Many of them worked in defence industries and were therefore likely to gain financially from an escalation.

Controversial opinions were often delivered through jokes, the better to disown them if they proved contentious. 'I was only joking' became his preferred escape route when cornered. Telling a joke was easier back then, before political correctness. Thus, when asked about emerging African nations, he remarked that when those countries 'have a man to lunch, they really have him to lunch'.[67] In similar fashion, Reagan attacked anti-war protesters: 'One group of militants were carrying signs that said "Make Love Not War". The only trouble was they didn't look like they were capable of doing either. Their hair was cut like Tarzan, they acted like Jane, and they smelled like Cheetah.'[68] Reagan made the line seem impromptu. In truth, it was probably carefully crafted for truck drivers – a perfect combination of humour, derision and outrage. The press might occasionally have objected to Reagan's style, but what mattered most was that he was talking to the people he needed in order to win.

# 5
# Those Boys from BASICO

Stanley Plog and Kenneth Holden first met Reagan at his home in Pacific Palisades in early 1966. The meeting had been arranged so that the three men could explore whether there was scope for working together. After pleasantries were exchanged, they explained what they could do for him. They asked Reagan what sources of information he was using to prepare himself for speeches and press conferences. Without replying, Reagan got up and left the room. About a minute later, he returned with a shoebox stuffed with newspaper clippings. He explained how he would cut stories that piqued his interest out of newspapers and would store them in the box. As he spoke, bits of paper fell to the floor. For Plog and Holden, that little box seemed ominously symbolic, an indication of just how much needed to be done to brief Reagan on the issues in this campaign.

Little incidents often carry big importance. Except for the fact that this one might never have occurred.

While Reagan tested the waters for a gubernatorial campaign, Californians wrestled with the question of whether an actor could make a good governor. The aversion to actors was, in truth, a desperate attempt to deny the obvious: since politics is often pretence, actors have a natural advantage. It was precisely the actor's ability to play a part that aroused suspicions. The 'just an actor' line became a favourite tactic for those frustrated by Reagan's polished presentation. Thus, the columnist Arthur Hoppe argued that, if stage presence, personality and dramatic ability were sufficient qualifications for office, why not run Lassie for governor?[1] In some circles, the word 'actor' became a metaphor for shallow or stupid. To some, Reagan's candidacy seemed an indicator of just how low the Republican Party had sunk. 'The Republican Party isn't bankrupt,' an *Esquire* journalist quipped, 'or isn't that bankrupt that it has to turn to Liberace for leadership.'[2] In actuality, there was nothing particularly new about the phenomenon of the actor-politician, since George Murphy had successfully completed the journey from Hollywood to the US Senate in 1964. Murphy was described as 'a new breed of public office holder, generated in the strange politics of the nation's most populous state – the smooth performer who knows every trick of the mass media'.[3] Wading into the debate, the *Boston Herald* argued that 'There is no reason to sneer at actors who enter politics.' The voters should nevertheless beware of bad actors. 'Ronald Reagan ... was never a good actor,' the paper warned. 'His stock-in-trade was surface charm with no substance underneath. And because he has displayed the same fluffy qualities on the campaign trail, it is highly unlikely that he will ever be a good politician.'[4]

That issue of substance remained stubbornly prominent during the first few months of 1966. While Reagan's acting past provided many advantages, it also produced one significant disadvantage: it is often carelessly assumed that actors speak from scripts, do not possess thoughts of their own. Reagan therefore had repeatedly to prove that he had knowledge, principles and convictions – a test that ordinary politicians did not have to undergo to the same rigorous extent. Since hindsight tells us that he became one of the most successful politicians in American history, logic suggests that he acquired substance, or a convincing facsimile thereof. Two questions then arise: how and when did this happen?

According to Holden and Plog, it occurred over three days in Malibu in early February 1966 when they worked their magic. An interviewer once asked Plog what effect he had had on the making of the Great Communicator. 'A lot,' Plog replied. 'He probably would not have made it. That may sound like a self-congratulatory statement. It is not.'[5]

Plog and Holden, partners in the Behavior Science Corporation (BASICO), were hired by the campaign in early 1966. Despite all that has been written about Reagan, confusion still exists over what they actually did. Lou Cannon, who has published extensively on the gubernatorial years, discounted their impact, despite acknowledging that BASICO personnel shadowed Reagan throughout the campaign.[6] Herbert Baus and William Ross, who managed Brown's campaign, felt that the employment of BASICO was a 'major innovation' in campaign management, 'of clinical interest as a breakthrough in political technology'.[7] That seems gross exaggeration, perhaps encouraged by the fact that the authors spent too much time talking to Plog. As for Reagan himself, he neglected to mention Plog or Holden in his memoirs and, when interviewed in 1986, could not recall what they did.[8] The most extensive analysis of BASICO's role (albeit just five pages) comes in Garry Wills's biography of Reagan, in which he argues that Plog and Holden pioneered 'behavior engineering' in American political campaigns.[9] Wills believes that they 'retool[ed] Reagan ... coaching him on all points of matter and manner'.[10] Elsewhere, he claims that 'In his very first campaign for public office, Reagan made so many mistakes that [BASICO] ... was hired to program him.'[11] The words 'behavior engineering', 'retooled' and 'program' intentionally convey sinister, Orwellian designs. Wills clearly thinks that Reagan underwent a makeover all the more disturbing because psychologists crafted it.

Wills probably developed this line of reasoning by reading Baus and Ross. According to them, BASICO, with a staff of 32 psychologists, sociologists and political scientists, 'contributed … a package including clinical psychology, practical behavioral analysis, creative interpretation of public opinion research, plain but inspired fact-finding, and other neo-modern trappings'.[12] This might explain why admirers of Reagan have ignored BASICO. In other words, the firm's contribution might seem unpalatable, since it undermines the 'Great Communicator' myth. To credit two 'shrinks' with shaping Reagan tarnishes the lustre of his remarkable victory in 1966 and his subsequent campaign prowess. More fundamentally, recognition given to BASICO contradicts widely held assumptions that Reagan was a natural – a politician born, not made. Thus, hagiographers reject the notion that, early in his political career, Reagan needed to be taught communication skills. Recall that, during the 1966 campaign, Reagan made a virtue of his neophyte status. 'I am not a politician,' he repeatedly insisted.[13] How ironic, then, if this noble amateur was rewired by a couple of expensive shrinks.

Another explanation for the tendency to ignore Plog and Holden lies in the discord that existed within the campaign. Stated simply, the young men from BASICO despised Spencer and Roberts, who in turn judged Plog and Holden rank amateurs with no understanding of strategy. Spencer later claimed that BASICO was dismissed in late 1965 – in other words, long before they were actually hired. Somewhat more charitable, Roberts accepted that Plog and Holden contributed to the campaign, but that their access to Reagan was carefully restricted. In contrast, Plog insisted that either he, Holden or their colleague Jim Gibson stood by Reagan's side 'every waking moment', even following him into the toilet.[14] (As evidence, they boasted their intimate knowledge that Reagan preferred trousers fastened with buttons rather than a zipper because he was deathly afraid of the latter falling down.) Since the evidence suggests that Plog and Holden did play a role in the campaign, one suspects a virulent case of professional pique on the part of Spencer and Roberts. Yet why such a prestigious pair should be jealous of mere minions remains a mystery. Then again, antipathy can make men do strange things. For their part, Plog and Holden doubted the commitment of Spencer and Roberts and insisted that Reagan won in spite of the firm's inept guidance. Holden in fact thought that the firm was intentionally trying to sabotage the campaign.

Confusion is compounded by the manifold inconsistencies in Plog and Holden's testimony. The most charitable conclusion would be that they simply forgot what actually happened during the campaign. A less charitable conclusion would be to label them fantasists. Some historians (including Wills) have relied uncritically on a short interview Plog gave in 1981 which is excessively self-congratulatory.[15] While they were eager to tell their story (indeed too eager, as this author discovered), there are risks associated with their account, mainly because they did not react well to neglect. Their assessment of their own importance stands in inverse proportion to the disregard shown them.[16] While their story must be approached with caution, it nevertheless remains that their absence from studies of the election leaves a gap in our understanding of how the campaign was managed.

'[Reagan] knew zero about California when we came in,' Plog later claimed. 'I mean zero.'[17] He and Holden were shocked at Reagan's lack of understanding of California politics. It seemed to them that he was running for president, not governor. He had concentrated his attention on affairs in Washington, and seemed to think that examples of bureaucracy and mismanagement could be applied equally to Sacramento. Spencer admitted that 'at that point in time Reagan didn't understand government.'[18] He figured that the fault arose because Reagan was essentially running for president and had little interest in the minutiae of state government. Communism 'was *the* issue that drove Reagan', even though it was not relevant to state politics. Spencer was not, however, particularly bothered by Reagan's long-term aspirations, nor by his focus. 'He had to start somewhere. You usually don't start out running for President. He ran for Governor.'[19]

To Spencer and Roberts, Reagan was a work in progress. They accepted that, if his candidacy took root, he would have to undergo an intensive education. Throughout 1965, they were always worried 'of him being asked a question and he'd make something up'.[20] As Roberts explained:

> he came on to this thing with probably the same kind of knowledge that you or I would have of government, not being directly involved to the point that we need to know a lot about an issue ... And so he had a need, since he was not a politician really, to get boned up enough so that people wouldn't be unhappy with him over that point, which could be devastating for somebody who's a movie actor ... People might think, 'Well, [he's] not too bright, another movie actor.'[21]

Spencer and Roberts remained confident that they could fix this problem because Reagan seemed so manageable – if they told him he needed to learn the essentials of state politics, he would do so. They also had no doubts about his ability to absorb what he was taught. 'It wouldn't have worked at all if he wasn't a good learner and a good reader. He's a voracious reader ... he's a constant learner.'[22]

The firm first brought in Assemblyman Charles Conrad to tutor Reagan on the intricacies of state government. As a former actor and the premier parliamentarian in the state legislature, Conrad was particularly appropriate.

> Charlie was one of the really knowledgeable people concerning the laws of the legislature, how it functions, the rules and also the guidelines and restrictions of the governor's office, what they could and couldn't do. In other words, he was a valuable person in teaching Reagan ... all the mechanical things of the powers

of the governor, the powers of the executive, the powers of the legislat[ure] ... and so forth.[23]

Conrad came to Reagan's home twice a week for these lessons. 'It was so great because both actors could talk at the same level about things I didn't know anything about,' Spencer recalled.

> The rapport was there between them. Charlie would say, 'Okay Ron, we have a bill here, Bill 1A. We want to get that bill through the process,' and he'd say, 'This is how we get it through the process.' ... I'm sure he bored Reagan to death, but he started to get an understanding that when there is a bill introduced, this is the process of what it's going to go through before it gets to him, before he can do what he wants to do and be Governor ... Charlie was very, very helpful. We used to call it Politics 1A.[24]

While Conrad could help with the mechanics of government, he was less useful when it came to coaching Reagan on issues. Here, a different set of experts was needed to provide background on the problems affecting the state. 'We tried to get some ... experts in those areas, such as water, agriculture, and whatever the problems were in California.' This was all part of a long-term plan of trying to work out what Reagan knew, what he needed to know, and how the issues of the day might be grafted onto his overall philosophy. There was, the partners felt, no reason to rush this process. Experts would be brought in 'to sit down with Ronald Reagan and talk ... and he would listen ... We tried to present both sides of the issue so that he would get an idea of what position he might want to take.'[25]

The other side of the Spencer-Roberts strategy was to make a virtue of Reagan's inexperience. His ignorance was proof that he was not a politician. By being 'honest and saying, "I'm not a professional pol," it worked,' Spencer explained. 'It even worked on the cynical media that was covering him.'[26] His lack of experience meant that he did not have to shoulder the baggage of a political past. 'As a virgin in the field,' the columnist Abe Melinkoff argued, 'Mr. Reagan has never made a wrong appointment. He has never raised anybody's taxes or spent a penny of them. He may not have had a chance to make political friends. But he hasn't lost any, either. How can he lose?'[27] Baus and Ross concurred that 'inexperience possesses some of the same advantages for a candidate on his way to high office that virginity has for a bride on her way to the altar.'[28] Furthermore, the 'citizen-politician' tag was an adroit method of camouflaging his ignorance in the early stages of the campaign. In other words, a well-informed candidate was not actually a high priority at this stage. As Roberts explained: 'Most people don't like politicians. If Reagan appeared a little uncertain, people would say, "Well, he's not a professional."'[29] Had he been able to speak with authority he would not have been able to carry off the neophyte role so convincingly. In the same way, by not talking about specifics, Reagan could hide the sharp edges of his radicalism. Rather than being pinned down on his policies and their consequences, he could instead offer reassuring platitudes. Vagueness was a clever way of dodging the extremism problem.

This strategy worked well at first, but, after Reagan formally entered the race on 4 January 1966, voters and journalists began to demand substance to back up his style. Substance was certainly lacking in his declaration, which sounded awfully like 'The Speech':

> California's problems are our problems ... it won't matter if the sky is bigger and bluer out here if you can't see it for smog. And all our elbow room and open space won't mean much if the unsolved problems are higher than the hills ... Our problems are many, but our capacity for solving them is limitless.[30]

The *Bee* compared the effect to that of 'a bowl of mush hitting a tub of lard'.[31] While that was typical of the paper, more worrying were complaints about Reagan's thin grasp of the issues. He claimed, for instance, that 15 per cent of California residents were on welfare, when the real number was closer to 5 per cent.[32] Even more fundamental was the following criticism from the *Bee*:

> Reagan acted as if he did not understand the duties of the governorship. He complained about federal and state laws as if he would have the power to change them if he occupied the governor's mansion. He lamented the growth of federal government and many of the welfare and racial programs it has adopted as if he could veto acts of the United States Congress.[33]

While everyone expected the *Bee* to oppose Reagan, this comment carried a worrying ring of truth. Reagan's ignorance was ceasing to seem a virtue.

With the campaign now official, the knives were out. 'This candidacy is no more impressive than it was when it was first a matter of rumor and humor,' one editorial complained on 11 January.[34] Watching from afar, the *Washington Post-Intelligencer* derided a Reagan appearance on *Meet the Press* a few days after his declaration:

> Ronald Reagan ... proved he might be able to portray a politician, as an actor, but also that every actor needs a good script – which he did not have ... Equipped with little more than great sincerity and some vague clichés about believing in individual freedom, Reagan proved unequal to coping with the questions he was asked and the stimulating half-hour pointed up that, for politicians, there is no substitute for practical experience.[35]

None of this seriously troubled Spencer and Roberts since the press seldom pays attention to a non-entity. The volume of vitriol was proof that Reagan was being taken seriously. Not all supporters, however, shared that aplomb. In some quarters, panic set in, especially when gaffes began to roll in like waves on Malibu. One prominent Republican, initially supportive of Reagan's candidacy, told the *Chronicle*: 'Now that I have talked with Ronnie, I am amazed at how little he knows about state government.'[36] In what was clearly meant to be an epitaph, the *Chronicle* remarked: 'In all charity ... if Mr. Reagan's gallant performance as an amateur politician who decides to run for governor remained unconvincing, it was, in the final analysis, not his fault. It was simply a flagrant example of miscasting.'[37]

The criticism began to worry Tuttle and Salvatori. They feared that the qualities that made Reagan so appealing – his wit and charm – were being overshadowed by his ignorance of state politics. While the jibes came primarily from the liberal press, they still seemed disturbingly apposite. Plog recalled how Tuttle and Salvatori eventually 'said no more to this. "If he's going after it he's going to have a professional campaign. We're going to get some good research background for him."'[38] Roberts understood the need for research, and fully intended to address it, but did not share the urgency. The firm was already in the process of lining up a research team when Tuttle and Salvatori forced one upon them.

Salvatori approached Parkinson and the political analyst Robert Krueger for advice. They both recommended Plog, who had earlier worked for Krueger. The recommendation made little sense, since Plog and Holden were hardly more experienced in government than was Reagan. While employed at UCLA, they had formed University Consultants, Inc. to provide psychological services to school districts in the Los Angeles area. They then renamed the company BASICO and began offering human resource evaluations to a variety of clients. While their expertise had some political applications, they had no campaign experience and were not, strictly speaking, a political-research firm. Young, brash and intelligent, they possessed a formidable self-belief which camouflaged a rather lean curriculum vitae. They talked their way into a contract covering the primary period, at a fee of $20,000. The fact that they were hired was an implied criticism of the campaign management. Spencer and Roberts resented this intrusion, but had to live with it.

Spencer and Roberts understood that, when it came to issues, a delicate relationship had to be cultivated. While Reagan clearly needed educating, he had still to be left to form his own opinions. 'We just said, "Look Ron, all the issue stuff is your bag",' Roberts recalled. 'You just tell us how you want it, and we'll give it to you as quickly and solidly as we can. You make up your own mind ... Once a decision is made, then we'll sit with you and say, "Okay, now, which of these issue positions ... should we stress the most?"'[39] Roberts insisted that they never put words into Reagan's mouth:

> The ultimate decision rests with the candidate as to what he wants to do. If you try to force decisions down candidates that they neither believe nor want, all you succeed in doing is getting them in trouble because they'll forget it as soon as they've done it. Then when it comes up again at the press conference a week later, they can't remember because it wasn't in their head and their heart.[40]

The partners understood that what mattered were not the issues themselves, but their presentation – what is today called spin. Poor delivery had destroyed Goldwater. This made the research role all the more complicated, since the suppliers of information had to be sensitive to the campaign strategy. They could not, for instance, advise Reagan to emphasize an issue in a manner contrary to that strategy. This is where the clash with BASICO arose.

The operations manual for the Southern California Reagan for Governor Committee described a vague remit: BASICO would 'put into the hands of our Candidate and his supporters the materials which they will need to wage a winning Campaign'.[41] Plog and Holden interpreted this widely, Spencer and Roberts narrowly. The latter tried desperately to limit BASICO's influence. According to Roberts, Plog and Holden were used 'strictly to do the research on issues, and for no other reason'.[42] What is confusing about this arrangement is that two highly trained and expensive psychologists were deployed as researchers and news analysts, something an able team of graduate students could have done. One suspects that Spencer and Roberts were obliged to use Plog and Holden, but did not actually want them to perform the services for which they were most experienced, namely psychological profiling, or what Wills calls 'behavior engineering'. That expertise seemed irrelevant or at least redundant. 'Bill and I didn't understand it,' Spencer recalled. Worse still, Reagan didn't understand what Plog and Holden were proposing. 'They were honest guys, they were maybe on the cutting edge of some kind of research, but the users didn't know how to use it, so there was no reason to screw around with it.'[43]

Spencer was referring to the fact that BASICO offered its own version of PIPS, a method of targeting swing voters. The firm, however, preferred to go with Barabba, with whom they had already worked.

> I have to be honest with you ... Any time you come up with a program of this nature, a scientific behavioral program, and try to apply it to the political process, the big question is how do I move it from the theoretical to the practical? We couldn't do that with what [BASICO] were giving us ... Reagan didn't know what they were talking about and he had no interest in what they were talking about.[44]

This explains why Plog and Holden were never allowed to do the work for which they had the most expertise. 'We were saying, "Is this a tool we can use?",' Spencer recalled. 'We couldn't see how to translate it. They were asking for a lot of money so we decided that our resources were better spent in other ways ... It just wasn't working from our standpoint.'[45]

A further clash arose over differences in outlook – specifically what Plog and Holden mistakenly interpreted as a lack of commitment from Spencer and Roberts. They could not understand the dispassionate detachment of professionals. As Reagan rightly observed, 'Spencer and Roberts ... don't really have a high regard for candidates. They kind of think of them as a horse in the stall, and they'll take them out and run 'em when they think they should be run.'[46] They were hired guns, professionals confident in their ability to win elections. For this reason, they resented intrusion by passionate amateurs like Plog or Holden. To them, passion was the enemy of efficient management, as the Goldwater campaign had revealed. Plog and Holden were ideologues – the self-confessed 'true believers' – who accepted the Reagan assignment because they believed zealously in his radical conservatism. 'We were there for Reagan,' Holden wrote, 'and if we were the only ones who were, that was fine with us. We would go to the wall for him ... If he went down in flames, well, [we] would go down in flames, too.'[47] They had much in common with the fanatics who had caused so many problems in 1962 and 1964, men who abhorred compromise. They quite simply did not understand professional campaign management. 'Roberts perplexed us,' Holden admitted. 'He was supposed to be the campaign manager. He was the designated representative of the team that was supposed to manage the campaign of Ronald Reagan. From where we sat, we didn't see any management happening.'[48]

Plog and Holden made two demands before agreeing to work for Reagan. First, they insisted that they would report only to Tuttle and Salvatori, a condition made because they doubted the commitment of Spencer and Roberts to the candidate. They also insisted that they should have three days alone with

Reagan in order to get a sense of the man. These sessions would be conducted at a secret location, with no interference. Spencer and Roberts could only grumble when Tuttle and Salvatori agreed to these demands.

Before starting work, Plog and Holden attended a dinner speech by Reagan in Inglewood, California in order to get a sense of their new assignment. What they witnessed disturbed them. Reagan simply recycled 'The Speech', a performance that could have been delivered in Delaware without raising an eyebrow. Reagan railed against Washington bureaucracy, his intention apparently being to tar Sacramento with the same brush. He then told a story about federal bureaucrats spending long hours in acrimonious debate about what to call toilets, in order to remove the stigma attached to that name. The story, like the vast majority of the speech, was entertaining but had nothing to do with California. Plog and Holden came to the conclusion that the candidate was abysmally ill-prepared for his new role. What is interesting about their reaction is that they were shocked not only by the content but also by the presentation, in particular Reagan's response to questions from the audience. That reaction contradicts that of almost every other observer up to that point. The standard refrain was that Reagan was a smooth communicator of vague generalities. Yet, Plog and Holden decided that without a crash course on California politics *and* remedial training in presentation skills, Reagan was doomed.

Their assumptions about poor management were confirmed during that first meeting with Reagan at his home in Pacific Palisades. The shoebox incident might or might not have occurred, but what is important is that Plog and Holden came to the immediate conclusion that Reagan was badly briefed because Spencer and Roberts had little commitment to his campaign. Like superheroes flying to the rescue, they assumed control of the situation. Reagan was, in truth, apprehensive. Over the previous year, he had pilloried the University of California

(UC) on the student unrest issue, attacking the 'liberal bias' of academics. He feared that it might seem hypocritical that he was now conspiring with two university psychologists whose expertise threatened to undermine his populist, non-politician image. Despite these apprehensions, Reagan offered his customary warm smile and gracious manner. It was at this point that Plog and Holden formed an impression they would cherish for the rest of their lives. Reagan's famous charm convinced them that a special bond had been forged. 'He liked the cut of our sails and we liked the cut of his,' Holden said.[49] This reaction mirrored that of thousands of others who met Reagan during his lifetime, and assumed from his response that they had acquired a new best friend.

The fact that the political beliefs of the three men were basically in harmony fostered a good working relationship, yet exactly how good is difficult to gauge. He did not appreciate being dictated to, nor was he as ignorant as they claimed. 'Usually I accepted anything ... as a recommendation by someone, but if it didn't meet with what I thought was my own belief, I didn't accept it.'[50] The two psychologists were struck by Reagan's lack of guile and his naïve trust, yet they were perhaps the naïve ones, misinterpreting his abundant charm for genuine intimacy. Confidence (of which they had plenty) has the power to blind. One suspects they did not notice what the more cynical Nofziger observed. 'It's a funny thing about Ronald Reagan,' he once remarked.

> You sit there, you know him, and I spent a lot of time with him ... and I always felt ... that there was a kind of a veil between him and the rest of the world. You could never really get in next to him.
>
> I finally decided, after he became governor and time had gone by, that what you saw was what you got. That you had, in fact, the real Ronald Reagan. That he had become a little aloof, a little careful because, as an actor, with all the publicity, and people

after you, you have to guard your private life very carefully if you are going to maintain a private life. I think that he just naturally had built a kind of a fence between him and the outside world.[51]

'There's a wall around him,' Nancy confirmed. 'He lets me come closer than anyone else, but there are times when even I feel that barrier.'[52]

Reagan hated conflict – it was his mission to be loved. 'He had a great desire to get along with people,' Weinberger recalled. 'He always said he liked to leave them laughing.'[53] Shortly after taking on the Reagan account, Spencer was warned by a colleague that he would have to fire a lot of people because 'Ron ... has never fired anybody in his life.' He soon discovered just how appropriate that advice was. 'Reagan hated personnel problems. He hated to see differences of opinion among his staff. His line was, "Come on, boys. Go out and settle this and then come back."'[54] All this suggests that Plog and Holden probably completely misunderstood their relationship with Reagan. They convinced themselves that they were emotionally closer to him than any of his other aides, yet, if this was indeed true, his inability to recall their contribution when interviewed in 1979 seems strange. Their time with Reagan was perhaps too short or too beguiling for them to discover that he treated almost everyone exactly like he treated them.

During that first meeting, Plog and Holden discussed how they would approach political research. They would equip Reagan with the facts necessary to shield him from hostile journalists. In order to do this, they explained, it was first necessary to probe his ideology. 'The purpose was to just question ... him, challenge him on his beliefs, and everything, and also learn ... how he takes in information so that we knew how to give him the information back.'[55] They would then provide him with information that harmonized with his beliefs, which would be like neatly packaged ammunition, ready to be used at any moment. They would also write position papers on issues as they arose, to help Reagan present an informed, consistent point of view, in easily digestible form.

When asked about ideology, Reagan revealed that he was an avid reader of eighteenth- and nineteenth-century political philosophy. His favourite philosopher was Frédéric Bastiat, whom he quoted in casual conversation. Plog and Holden were immediately smitten. 'If you take Reagan's position on most things, you'll find a great amount of consistency, because he has fundamental beliefs,' Plog later reflected. 'These are based on many Revolutionary times and early constitutional writers, about the nature and concept of democracy.'[56] They were impressed also by his integrity: he seemed unwilling to alter his position in order to court majority opinion. This impression contrasts sharply with that of Spencer and Roberts, who were struck by Reagan's pragmatism and flexibility. Indeed, he had already shown his willingness to tone down his radical conservatism in order to decouple himself from Goldwater. As was mentioned in the last chapter, within days of his meeting with Plog and Holden, Reagan told a Young Republican gathering: 'It is wrong to fly off the cliff with all flags flying. It is wrong to believe that you would rather be right than win.'[57] Clearly, Plog and Holden had become ensnared by Reagan's charm and by his innate ability to say precisely what listeners wanted to hear.

The two psychologists were also deeply impressed with Reagan's ability to express complicated ideology in simple language. Plog did not consider this 'dumbing down': 'Now the question is, is he getting to the heart or is he being simplistic? OK, if you remember that this guy has a very integrated political philosophy ... then a lot of things flow out of that philosophy and come as easy statements. These may seem simplistic answers but they are not necessarily.' Suitably entranced, Plog and Holden left the Pacific Palisades meeting excited about their assignment, but worried about the magnitude of their task. 'We wondered how we could turn him around and bring him up to date on complex state issues,' Plog recalled. 'Was there sufficient money in the contract to hire enough people to do the job, and would he be able to learn a vast amount of information from us in a short period of time?'[58] These concerns contrast sharply with the confidence felt by Weinberger, Spencer, Roberts and others, all of whom had already grown accustomed to Reagan's ability to absorb information quickly and effectively. Despite all the praise that had been heaped upon Reagan by this stage, Plog and Holden somehow felt that a major transformation was necessary in order to make him electable. By failing to recognize the progress already made, not to mention the innate skills of the man, they effectively set themselves up as the architects of the Great Communicator.

Plog and Holden had insisted that the three-day session with Reagan had to take place somewhere free of distractions. A beach house in Malibu belonging to a friend of Reagan's was found. On their first day, they probed Reagan about his beliefs. He explained how he had once been a loyal Democrat and union supporter but had grown disenchanted with the left. His move rightward had brought accusations of betrayal. He insisted that he was not a turncoat, that his heartfelt beliefs had remained consistent throughout his life. The only thing that had changed was his realization that those beliefs were actually conservative ideas. He then talked about how government restricts freedom and opportunity. Playing devil's advocate, Plog and Holden cross-examined him. They were impressed with his answers and the way his core philosophy did not waver. He seemed to them a man of principle, not a candidate who would tailor his policies to the political wind. Plog and Holden had found their political deity, a man who expressed their conservatism in perfect cadence. They would henceforth worship the man. While their estimation of Reagan's intellectual sophistication is open to doubt, it is immaterial to an assessment of BASICO's role. What is relevant is that, on that day, Reagan had demonstrated some important political skills. His performance under cross-examination suggested that he would stand up well to hostile reporters. His skill for memorizing complex passages and reciting them with passion (an actor's talent) indicated that, given the right material, the problems apparent in Inglewood could be corrected. It didn't matter that Reagan had already demonstrated these skills to Spencer, Roberts, Nofziger, Weinberger and scores of others, since Plog and Holden were intent upon reinventing the wheel and stamping it with the BASICO trademark.

The three days in Malibu followed a set pattern. The men arrived early in the morning and quickly got down to work. They toiled solidly until noon, ordering lunch from a local deli. Over lunch, Reagan would entertain his handlers with show business anecdotes. They then worked until about 6 p.m., when everyone went home. Over the course of those three days, Plog and Holden discovered a 'positive candidate speaking out positively on conservative issues'.[59] That was important since, in the past, conservative candidates like Goldwater had come across as pessimistic and threatening. They wanted Reagan to present conservatism as an upbeat ideology of progress, not regression. Again, this was nothing new, since it was essentially what Reagan had been doing since his first day with GE. They nevertheless convinced themselves that the idea was a revelation for him and that, as a result, a connection was made that was qualitatively different to that which he enjoyed with his other handlers. It seemed to them that a special relationship had been forged, that they alone understood Reagan and that he appreciated their empathy.

'We looked at the campaign as a problem in human behavior, a very complex problem,' Holden recalled.[60] He and Plog discovered what others already knew: Reagan was a quick learner who could process information efficiently, as long as it was presented in manageable chunks. His mind would, however, wander in long-winded briefings and he hated reading lengthy reports. They chose to stick to the familiar by giving him cue cards. Again, they took credit for the idea, apparently unaware that he had used cards during his GE tours, not to mention in Hollywood. They used 5" x 8" index cards printed front and back. These were ordered according to topic, keyhole punched and inserted into binders. Eventually, seven binders, or 'black books', were compiled, each indexed so that information could be accessed quickly. 'We had everything filed out and cross-referenced,' Plog recalled. 'It was a nice little system, almost like a small library.'[61] Reagan was urged to memorize the material, since, if he was caught consulting cards, it would encourage criticism that he was reading someone else's script.

Plog and Holden went on to explain that they would not only personally direct his research, they would also accompany him to campaign events and coach him on handling journalists. They then turned to delivery, in particular their feeling that Reagan was over-answering questions. Long-winded answers, they warned, increased the risk of gaffes and gave journalists more material to pull out of context. The key, they explained, was to have answers prepared for almost any question. They claim credit for teaching Reagan the art of the soundbite, though they did not call it that. This seems unlikely, given that his ability to craft pithy one-liners was one of the attributes that had made him such an attractive candidate in the first place. They also recalled telling Reagan that, if confronted with a difficult question, he should immediately move the discussion into an area more to his taste – he should dodge questions and try to make vague answers sound meaningful. Again, since those skills had already attracted the attention of hostile journalists, it is difficult to believe that Plog and Holden were the originators.

Plog felt that Spencer and Roberts were worried that Reagan, an unintelligent neophyte, would destroy himself with glib, ill-informed remarks. The firm seemed intent on hiding Reagan and limiting opportunities for him to speak his mind. There was some truth to that allegation, as Nofziger confirmed:

It was easy to see that Reagan had never inspired any great feeling of confidence in Bill Roberts. Bill was a good day-to-day campaign manager, as good as anyone I've ever known, maybe better. But like a lot of moderate Republicans he looked on Reagan as a not very smart right-wing actor. The Reagan campaign was a job to Bill Roberts, a job that paid well, and if he and Stu pulled off a victory, a job that presaged many more jobs in the future.[62]

Plog and Holden objected to what seemed a very defensive strategy and instead insisted that Reagan should get aggressive, that he should state his opinions without qualification or spin. They felt sure that, after the three days in Malibu, a change occurred in Reagan's approach and they credited themselves with the transformation. They insist that they encouraged Reagan to be himself, to state his beliefs, as forthrightly as possible, on the assumption that his avuncular manner would sweeten his radical views. As will be seen in subsequent chapters, this caused friction within the campaign team, particularly when they tried to take Reagan in a direction different to that his campaign managers had charted. Spencer and Roberts assumed that BASICO's role was only to supply information, not to coach Reagan. Plog insists that because he and Holden had complete confidence in Reagan they felt secure in stretching their remit.

'The mercenaries Spencer and Roberts had all but given up,' Holden later reflected. 'They saw Reagan's race for the governorship as a short-term gig. They were in the game for the long haul, and they couldn't let an imperfect candidate drag them down.'[63] Holden warned his partner that 'they really don't expect to win with this candidate and I have a feeling that they wouldn't be too disappointed if he didn't.' As with other right-wing zealots, they were suspicious of the firm's earlier dealings with Rockefeller, which convinced them that their commitment to Reagan could not be genuine. 'They didn't think of Reagan in great-man terms,' Holden felt.[64]

They were convinced that he couldn't be unleashed in a full-blown, full-throated political campaign. He would scramble the facts, become a joke, make them all a laughingstock. And they would forever be tarred with the reputation of being the smart guys who had thrown it all away backing a no-win conservative candidate. It would ruin them with the Rockefeller Republicans. They would be on the losing side of history.[65]

On another occasion, Holden offered a completely different scenario. Sniffing a conspiracy, he decided that scuppering Reagan's chances was part of a cunning plan by Spencer and Roberts to court party moderates and, at the same time, destroy the conservative movement once and for all. That scenario ignored the fact that Spencer and Roberts had already represented plenty of right-wingers, including Rousselot.

These absurd accusations indicate just how deep was the emotional commitment of the boys from BASICO. Emotion clouded rationality. The journalist Jack McDowell, who worked for Reagan's 1970 re-election, reflected on what happens when pragmatists clash with ideologues in a campaign:

> I have always regarded [Spencer and Roberts] and others as professionals, and I try to regard myself as one ... A professional doesn't permit himself to get emotional in political things. That is for the volunteers, and they are essential to every campaign. It's up to the professional ... to see that that energy and force is enhanced and put to good use. But deliver me from any zealots running around our ... office. No way!
>
> If they're real zealots, they seem unable to become pragmatic technicians as members of a professional team must. If they do get into this business, no matter what they're hired to do, they seem to want to become campaign managers and create strategy. They are less able to recognize that their candidate can commit errors that must be met head-on.[66]

McDowell's description perfectly fits Plog and Holden. Unrepentant ideologues, they did not appreciate that for some people politics was just a job – serving a candidate did not require emotional commitment. An ideologue might wish to sabotage a campaign by disrupting it from within, but a professional would never do so. 'We are mercenaries,' Roberts once admitted.[67] A mercenary would never sabotage a campaign, for the simple reason that it's his bread and butter. Spencer realized that Reagan was a gamble, but one that might pay off handsomely. This was the biggest campaign his firm had ever handled. 'I think Bill and I were the only two people that had a lot on the line professionally,' he recalled.[68] Had the gamble gone bust, scorn would have been heaped upon the firm. Plog and Holden invested their emotions, Spencer and Roberts their careers.

The two psychologists left Malibu confident that much had been achieved. They were convinced that they could turn Reagan into a winner and equally certain of their own indispensability. The candidate, they recalled, seemed to change before their very eyes – he was more confident and well informed, gave shorter answers and was prepared to speak his mind. There is probably some truth to this contention. Previously, he had appealed to voters because he didn't seem like a politician. That facet remained attractive, but, after his formal declaration, his audiences began wanting specifics. A solid knowledge of the issues added a new dimension to his candidacy. Plog felt that journalists and the general public noticed the change and responded positively. While there is no doubt that Reagan became an even more formidable candidate after his knowledge of the issues improved, it is difficult to believe that Plog and Holden were alone responsible for this transformation.

The most noticeable change came in Reagan's performance in question-and-answer sessions. The Q&A format offered him the opportunity to answer the doubts of his critics. As he recalled:

Stu Spencer and Bill Roberts called me, very upset, had a new problem ... They told me that Brown was beginning to make headway with a campaign thing in which he was saying, 'Well, remember, he's an actor. Sure he makes a good speech—' because my speeches were being, I guess, effective. And he said, 'But remember, as an actor, he's used to learning lines. Who writes those speeches?'

Reagan told his handlers: 'Well, it won't do any good for me to get up and say, "I write my own speeches in the campaign." They expect me to say that, even though it's true.' He proposed instead a shorter speech followed by open questions. 'Somebody may think that someone else wrote that short speech, but they'll have to know that nobody could write the answers to those questions.'

Spencer and Roberts were at first 'a little discomfited', Reagan admitted. 'I know that they must have lost sleep thinking, "What's he going to say?"'[69] Reagan nevertheless insisted. Weinberger was amazed at the effect: 'when [they] ... moved away from the rehearsed questions or ... into more detail, he was always ready ... He had an enormous ability to articulate what a very large number of men and women felt and thought and didn't articulate very well themselves.'[70] Once the tactic proved effective, Spencer and Roberts claimed provenance for it. 'Every place that Ronald Reagan gave a speech,' Spencer recalled,

> we'd go to a Q&A format, because that was our way of saying, 'Hey this guy's got a brain – he just gave you a speech, but he also can do these things.' And they'd ask him questions. If he handled the questions well, people would walk out of the room saying, 'The man had some smarts.'[71]

Roberts boasted that the technique was specifically designed to 'disarm the public and make them feel that he did know what he was talking about, and he had some knowledge of the issues'.[72]

McDowell remembered how the press pool came to realize that Reagan was 'not dumb'. 'Really the thing that drove that home was under Q&A. He would throw back sensible answers ... I thought, "This guy isn't so stupid. He's handling these pretty well." I began to realize he was a quick learner and that he must have some IQ, or he wouldn't be able to do it.'[73] He sensed a turning point: 'I'm covering this campaign and the election, and this campaign is taking a turn. I'm seeing this nobody, political nobody ... becoming a real challenge to the incumbent.'[74] *Newsweek* took a similar view: 'Late last spring, the former movie actor's campaign began to click. The strained, defensive look disappeared. His off-the-cuff remarks stopped getting him into trouble, and he finally learned to roll with the punchy questions of hostile reporters.'[75] Carl Greenberg, political correspondent of the *Los Angeles Times*, was deeply impressed:

> Having watched many a political professional with years of experience squirm under sometimes deft cross examination, and often get the shakes even at the stupid questions ... I thought Reagan did as well if not better than a lot of them ... He was adroit in fielding questions, he has the ability to grasp what is being asked and by and large put on as good a performance as the old-timers in the business.[76]

Another reporter concluded that Reagan's secret weapon was his 'facility for acquiring instant expertise on state questions that allows him to speak with far more apparent authority than his critics would give him ... He is creating a far stronger image of knowledgeability than his opponents would like.'[77]

The Q&A performances forced a change of tack from the Brown camp. Reagan was now accused of intentionally dumbing down politics. The governor's hatchet man Bob Coate, Democratic state chairman, argued that Reagan was too cowardly to face a grilling from journalists – 'who ask intelligent questions'. The allegation was not only wrong (Reagan relished sessions with journalists), but stupid given its implied insult to 'the people'. 'Obviously Mr Coate doesn't believe in the people's ability to ask intelligent questions,' Reagan retorted. He insisted that he was 'taking his case to the people', who, he maintained, were fully aware of the failures of the Brown administration. 'I think Coate's lack of confidence in the people is typical of this administration which is characterized by its belief that the people lack the capacity for self-government.'[78] Reagan's mention of 'the people' four times in three sentences was not accidental.

In 2013, Holden published *The Making of the Great Communicator*, a slim memoir long on grandiose self-promotion. The message is clear from the title: 'It was Plog and Holden who kept Reagan afloat when almost everyone else was ready to jump ship,' the author claims in his book. 'It had all come together in Malibu.'[79] He and Plog felt that their contribution to the campaign was never properly recognized. They insisted that, in Malibu, a special relationship was formed that had an immense impact upon the campaign. 'Like a thoroughbred reacting to a gentle touch, he would go where we were going before we had to tell him. He seemed to know before we did. It was as if he were waiting for us.'[80] They both insisted that they had single-handedly turned the campaign around. Without their contribution, Reagan would have failed. Furthermore, if he had failed in 1966, he would not have been elected president in 1980. Hey presto, two obscure psychologists gave Americans their favourite president.

A vast body of evidence suggests otherwise. Reagan had been encouraged to run precisely because of his outstanding communication skills, as demonstrated during the GE years. While his performance did improve noticeably in the early months of 1966, that is not surprising given his initial unfamiliarity with state politics. His improvement probably owes more to natural abilities than to the guidance he received from specific individuals. Spencer had no doubt where credit was due:

> [Reagan] was the best communicator I've seen in my political life and that starts with Roosevelt, who was good. That's how good I think he was. Secondly, and a very interesting point in terms of communication, Ronald Reagan wrote all his own speeches when he ran for Governor. I say to this day, he's the best speechwriter I've ever seen ... He also had the style to use the new medium of the time, television. There are lots of people that are good on the stump speaking, but they can't translate it to television.[81]

Nofziger agreed with Spencer. He insisted that the only person responsible for Reagan winning was Reagan himself. 'He'd have won without Spencer-Roberts, Lyn Nofziger, or my mother ... The state was ready for a change, and he turned people on. He turned people on that year like nobody I have ever seen before or since.'[82]

'There was only one Ronald Reagan', wrote Holden, 'and only one miracle moment in Malibu.'[83] In an attempt to buttress their claims of indispensability, Plog and Holden were fond of quoting a note Reagan sent after the election.

> I want you to know how much I enjoyed our relationship, and how grateful I am to both of you for all that you did. I know that my homework on all your good findings was a major factor in what finally happened. I would have been lost without the sound facts and material which you provided. I hope our paths will cross many times in the future, and again I want you to know how deeply grateful I am.[84]

One should not make too much of the above note; one suspects he wrote similar ones to the scores of people who helped during the campaign. Reagan was an expert at synthetic sincerity, both in person and in writing. He had a talent for convincing everyone that he was a best friend. 'He has a lot of emotion and a very good false front, which is protective more than anything else,' his brother recalled.

He'd be the most generous and gracious listener in the world ... [Those who met him would] go out saying, 'we've really got him on the hook. Now all that we've got to do is tighten up the line.' At the same time that he's going out saying, 'I don't know who they think they are fooling.'[85]

Perhaps more revealing than the above note was a remark made in 1979, when Reagan was asked about BASICO's contribution: 'I can't remember an awful lot about it. But it was true what the columnists were saying ... that I did not know anything about the organization of state government, the problems and what would be the issues.' When the interviewer pressed him on the black binders, Reagan replied: 'I have to tell you I have very little memory of that.'[86] In that interview, he was effusive about Spencer and Roberts, but did not mention Plog or Holden at all.

On their final day in Malibu, Reagan apparently told Plog and Holden that he was worried about how the people might interpret the presence of two psychologists at his side. Those worries were well founded since it was always unlikely that any observer, faced with the presence of two shrinks at Reagan's side, would conclude that they were simply innocent collectors of information. Faced with a choice between the sinister and the mundane, most people preferred the former. Eugene Wyman, the Democratic national committee man in California, accused Plog and Holden of 'fiendishly rooting out the hidden fear and prejudice of the people to manipulate the masses'.[87] The *Saturday Evening Post* complained of a 'newfangled, scientifically enhanced' style of campaigning, thanks to BASICO. According to the *Sacramento Bee*, Brown complained that '[Reagan] meets every week with a little committee headed by two behavioural scientists.' The expertise of these 'vile sounding fellows', the governor argued, is 'digging into the minds of people and finding out their anxieties. The technique is to find out what people are afraid of and then exploit this fear by warning that it could happen to them unless they vote for him.'[88] Critics of Reagan have echoed that line, citing BASICO as a harbinger of an ominous trend toward precinct profiling and negative campaigning. In fact, they were simply gatherers of information. Every campaign staff has a team of people who do precisely that.

In assessing the role of Plog and Holden, one should bear in mind their inexperience. Reagan was their first and only political client. In contrast, Spencer-Roberts had already managed 40 political campaigns, with victories in 34 of them.[89] Given the significant disparity in experience, it is possible that they simply did not understand what Spencer and Roberts were trying to do. In particular, they might not have appreciated the 'long game' of campaign strategy, with the result that they found the firm's tactics suspicious. This perhaps explains why Reagan was their last campaign. If their achievements had been as brilliant as they subsequently claimed, aspiring politicians would surely have come knocking. 'I don't know of anything they did afterwards,' Spencer remarked, rather acidly. 'They were dead in the water.'[90] They certainly felt slighted, which might explain their subsequent obsession with rewriting history. 'Basically it hurt,' Plog confessed. 'We purposely stayed in the background very quietly – that's the way we wanted to be – and as a result we got no publicity and so very little identity with the campaign.'[91] Holden insisted that Spencer, who benefited greatly from his association with Reagan, 'owes us more than he'll ever acknowledge'.[92] They claimed that they were never interested in working for other clients because they knew they would never find one as ideologically committed as Reagan. If that is true, it speaks volumes about their limitations. When Reagan ran for re-election in 1970, no one phoned BASICO. The explanation might be simple: they were over-qualified for the tasks they performed in 1966. Why hire psychologists to cut press clippings?

Plog and Holden contributed to the success of Reagan's campaign, but not in the manner usually assumed. Their role was confined to providing the research Reagan needed to sound well informed, and did not involve the sinister 'behavior engineering' with which they are sometimes credited.[93] While their claims that they 'made' the Great Communicator are fantasy, it remains that Spencer's attempts to erase them from the historical record seem petty. Reagan was formidable by himself but, armed with BASICO's research, he became even more so. Reagan probably benefited from the interplay of these two radically different firms. BASICO provided the commitment necessary to keep Reagan informed. Spencer-Roberts provided the professional detachment essential to see the big picture. Each firm compensated for faults in the other.

As will be seen, the important issue regarding Plog and Holden is not what they did, but what they were prevented from doing. They were right-wing zealots who adored Reagan, but had little understanding of the need to package him in order to widen his appeal. They did not understand that an election is an exercise in marketing. Spencer-Roberts camouflaged Reagan's extremism, a process Plog and Holden considered unnecessary. Left to their own devices, these two men might have done a lot of damage. Zealots do not make good campaign managers. Adoration clouded their judgement and rendered them blind to the safe road to success.

# 6

# The Great Pretender

When Reagan announced his candidacy for the governorship of California on 4 January 1966, he attacked the superficiality of politics. 'Modern political dialogue isn't based on legitimate debate anymore,' he argued. 'There's a great deal of false image-making and an effort made not to dispute the views you really hold, but to invent some and hang them on you with the hope the false image will appear real.'[1]

The statement sounded sincere, because Reagan made it so. It carries heavy irony, given the clever image-making Reagan required in order to win. In November 1964, he seemed a Goldwater extremist. By the time of the election in 1966, he had become something altogether different. His handlers tried hard to make sure that the views he really held did not come to the surface. His success owed a great deal to his image-makers, but also to his ability to pretend.

Manipulating images was essential in order to heal the rifts that plagued the Republican Party in California. The arguments between Shell and Nixon, and Rockefeller and Goldwater had cleaved the party. Hatred followed labels; enemies were easily defined. Reagan brought harmony by managing to be all things to all men. James Hall witnessed this magic early in the campaign. He was at first sceptical about Reagan's candidacy, fearing that he might be what his critics claimed – a dumb actor, and an extremist to boot. Then Hall witnessed him in person:

> Reagan came through San Diego … and one of the appearances was a garden party … at which he fielded questions from the crowd. It was a Republican crowd with a mix of conservatives and liberals, and each side was throwing the hardest pitches they could, and he was doing a great job of fielding these questions. He was not coming down strictly on the right-wing side nor was he pandering to the liberals. He was responding in what I considered to be a very, very politic way, and it was at that point that I concluded that this guy had great political talent.

Hall was impressed by Reagan's unique ability to deal with the internecine strife between the Goldwater and Rockefeller groups. 'A lot of politicians were falling by the wayside because of that. They couldn't handle the internal dissension that existed in the Republican party at that time. But Reagan did a good job of it.'[2]

Reagan the Peacemaker contrasted sharply with George Christopher, an addict of ill-will. Interviewed on 28 September 1965, Christopher came across as the epitome of pessimism and rancour. When asked if left and right could settle their differences in time for the election, he replied:

> I don't know if they can or not. I've had many of the extreme rightists tell me that they won't vote for a moderate candidate, but they do expect the moderate thinking Republicans to vote for an extreme rightist candidate, should he win the nomination. I try to tell them that this is not a one-way street … [There] has to be unity based on a coalition of effort on both sides.[3]

Christopher was a man with a long memory and a fondness for throwing stones. Asked whether he would be willing to head a ticket in which Reagan ran as lieutenant governor, he stated that there was 'not the remotest possibility of that' and stressed that the party must select a candidate 'not tainted with extremist philosophies'.[4] Had the party been populated entirely with people like Christopher, Brown would easily have won a third term.

Into the fracas rode a mild-mannered gynaecologist named Gaylord Parkinson, who had recently become party chairman. 'My role', he recalled, 'was to pull the party together and to convince both sides ... that they need each other and a lot of Democrats to win anything here in the state. I was able to kind of knock a few heads together and produce some sort of semblance of order.'[5] The task was like 'walking on eggs'.[6] That's an understatement. It was more like conducting business in a pond full of piranhas.

Parkinson respectfully pretended neutrality, in order to make it seem like he was putting the party before any individual candidate. 'I think that's the major function of the state officers, to strengthen the party,' he explained. 'I felt very strongly that I ... could not take a stand for any candidate for the primary.'[7] While he dutifully maintained that illusion, his actions mainly benefited Reagan. Roberts felt that Parkinson was 'behind the scenes very much pro-Reagan'.[8]

In previous elections, Republican candidates had freely attacked one another in a vicious and personal way, thus doing the Democrats an enormous favour. As a solution, Parkinson proposed the 'Eleventh Commandment' – 'Thou shall not speak ill of any Republican.' The idea was the brainchild of Bob Walker, a San Diego lawyer and party activist, who was determined that 1966 would not be a repeat of 1964. He proposed it to Parkinson in early September 1965. Parkinson at first thought it impracticable but was eventually persuaded to give it a try. 'The Eleventh Commandment was so vital,' Walker felt. 'To come along in '66 and to say in effect, "We've got to cut out this nonsense, you're going to have to quit attacking each other in such a brutal way, if you're ever going to win anything."'[9]

The Eleventh Commandment took effect just when Christopher and Reagan supporters were gearing up for a bloody brawl. At the Republican Convention in September 1965, Parkinson urged 'all elements to pull together ... In other words, concentrate on the Democrats, even in the primary. Show how you are better able to beat the Democrats than anybody ... In that way you will win our primary.'[10] While the commandment was presented as a noble, non-partisan gesture, it was nothing of the sort. 'It was not done with any grand thoughts in mind,' Roberts admitted. 'It was designed and put together for a very narrow, selfish interest of ours, and that was to keep from having a big battle in the party.' He elaborated:

> we needed it, because we felt that we were in the lead, and we didn't want any divisiveness in the party, and [we thought] this might go a long way toward avoiding a big party fight, a fight philosophical ... in nature, with Christopher representing the more liberal Republicans and Reagan representing the more conservative. We wanted to avoid a 1964 ... [which] was a blood bath.[11]

Nofziger confirmed that the 'Eleventh Commandment' was intended 'to keep the other side in the primary from attacking Reagan, because ... Reagan was ahead. Therefore, if we could keep these people from going on the attack, you could render them impotent.' Reagan was the obvious beneficiary since his lack of experience and links with extremists rendered him especially vulnerable. Parkinson was fully aware of this. '"Parky" ... was supposed to be neutral, but was nevertheless very quietly on our side,' Nofziger confessed.[12] Roberts agreed: 'The "Eleventh Commandment" was probably the best thing Parkinson accomplished. That was done with our approval.'[13]

The arrangement allowed Reagan to pretend to be above the fray, a man running for the good of the party who would respect whatever Republicans decided. As he told a gathering of journalists in late March 1966, each Republican candidate should campaign against Brown, not one another, in order to discover who would pose the most serious cha[...] Democrats. 'Any one of us might turn out to be [...] and if [Christopher] does, all the rest of us shou... camp, trying to get him elected.'[14] Reporters, however, remained sceptical, judging this a cynical attempt to suppress debate. Their annoyance was understandable, given that harmony is seldom newsworthy. Parkinson replied that he was only trying to ensure that debate remained relevant and constructive:

> I said, 'You can discuss any issue you want and you can discuss any personality you want and as long as you are telling the truth about somebody. If a man was married three times and wasn't divorced, I mean that's your right to say that. We don't want to cover that [fact] over.'
> All I wanted to suppress was the innuendos and the slurs ... It was not so much in the party as among candidates ... I don't think the public wants that ... I don't think the candidates should stoop to that.[15]

The beauty of the Eleventh Commandment was that it allowed Reagan, an outsider with an extremist past, to cast himself as a consensus politician and loyal party man. Immediately after it was proposed, he enthusiastically welcomed the commandment, and promised to abide by it. Equally predictably, Christopher angrily rejected the idea since he had most to lose. 'That's perfectly silly!' he shouted. 'I'm not going to be quiet. If I see something I want to criticize about Ronald Reagan, I'll criticize him.'[16] As a result, Christopher seemed, in contrast to Reagan, petty and vindictive – too much like a politician.

When asked about the Eleventh Commandment, Christopher said: 'We should not disparage wantonly and recklessly any fellow Republican ... but this is not a popularity contest' – a clear admission that he desperately wanted to disparage Reagan.[17] Pressed by journalists, he joked that he wasn't going to abide by the Eleventh Commandment because he had enough trouble with the first ten. (Christopher's jokes were never as funny as he seemed to think.) '[It was] perfectly his choice to do what he wanted,' Parkinson remarked.[18] That was theoretically true, but, in reality, he was damned if he did and damned if he didn't. If he obeyed the rules, he was criticized for his weak challenge to Reagan, but, when he did speak out, he was castigated for breaking the commandment. 'They had the so-called "Eleventh Commandment" which they concocted for specific reasons, and if you dared open your mouth against somebody you were ostracized. But they nevertheless condemned me, and blasted me, and did certain things to me by indirection from various other insidious areas. I was a little helpless.'[19] 'I had a large part to do with holding Mr. Christopher down,' Parkinson later admitted.[20] Nofziger praised that contribution:

> The role he played was keeping the party neutral ... ready to join forces after the primary. 'Parky' ... understood that some things had to be done to build the party, and I think he clearly understood that Reagan was going to win this thing early on. So he did things quietly. He wasn't overt about it, and he didn't do anything particularly to hurt George Christopher. He just didn't do anything to help him. Really, by not helping George Christopher ... Parkinson pretty much helped assure a Reagan victory.[21]

Walker agreed that the Eleventh Commandment was crucial. 'From then on Christopher went downhill.'[22]

Reagan solved the ideological rift by running primarily as a personality rather than as an ideologue. This, Cristina felt, was immensely important to his success. 'You can espouse a philosophy until hell freezes over, but you're not going to get to first base. You've got to attach that philosophy to a person, or it just don't work.' Goldwater had appealed only to those who supported his ideals – the man himself was unpleasant. The opposite was true of Reagan: he could attract voters who were lukewarm on his beliefs. 'It's got to be a person,'

Cristina insisted. 'Even those who disagree with him may like something else about the man. They think he's direct, they think he's honest, they think that integrity just blooms out of him ... They translate all those things to something that they can be for. And it may not be ... [his] philosophy.'[23] Brown agreed. 'You can be brilliant, you can have all those qualities, but you've got to have electability,' he argued. 'I think Reagan's a boob, but he's electable. He's a guy that makes a good impression on people. They like him. He's able to soften that hard image he has.'[24] Parkinson credited Spencer and Roberts with this softening. 'I used to marvel at how he was being handled ... The packaging was a big part of the man. There's no question about the image that he portrayed and he did masterfully. He did beautifully.'[25]

Shortly after the declaration speech, Roberts and Spencer described their role to James Perry of the *National Observer*. They were confident by that stage that most of the party faithful had come to accept that Reagan was not an extremist.

> [His] position has been clarified with the party hierarchy. He has tended to give the impression he is a sensible man, that he has compassion and that he's not just some kind of character from outer space. Now it's our job to do that same kind of clarifying for the general public.[26]

Nofziger insists that the makeover concentrated on image, not principles:

> The ... policy on how to run the campaign was all Spencer-Roberts, and properly so ... The ... policy on where does the candidate stand and what are his beliefs and what are his views was all Ronald Reagan. And he took some tough stands. He took some stands that his own people didn't like, and he took some stands that I'm sure cost him votes, but he was very firm in his convictions.[27]

'[We] don't regard ourselves as overall policy makers in a campaign,' Roberts insisted. 'We do not try to totally dominate the campaign process. We are, in effect, a chief of staff, rather than policy makers.'[28]

What this revealed was the importance of the impression made. As long as Reagan pretended to be reasonable, and he was very good at that, he could still hold beliefs that were quite extremist. As Cristina explained, each observer managed to find something impressive in Reagan. He had the ability to absorb the hopes of voters and then reflect those hopes back in Technicolor. It is ironic that a campaign noted for image manipulation produced a candidate effusively praised for his honesty. This was important because the public craves authenticity. Reagan, despite the makeover, always seemed genuine. While he did not perhaps change his position in order to court votes, he always paid close attention to the impression he made. 'Reagan was versatile,' Christopher remarked in a comment that combined annoyance, envy and grudging admiration.[29] This versatility was only possible if the candidate himself was likeable. Otherwise, he would seem cynical, slimy, prepared to bend with the wind. 'He was so convincing in everything he said,' Cristina felt. 'I was thoroughly convinced that what he said, he meant.'[30] A Brown aide found this terribly frustrating: 'I disagree with almost everything he says, but, dammit, I can't help but feel that he is basically a nice guy.'[31]

Reagan created unity by ignoring dissension. Instead of pandering to those on one side or the other, he formed his own movement that appealed directly to the people. 'Ronald Reagan was his own candidate,' Parkinson admitted. 'He's always been his own man.'[32] This bothered Parkinson, who was keen to preserve the predominance of the party over the individual. On the other hand, he recognized that:

> It is basically the people who vote in the party, not the activists. You remember, only one percent of the Republican vote is an

activist ... The rest of them all they do is ... go to the polls ... If they don't like the way a candidate is conducting his campaign, they'll vote against him. Even ideology doesn't make that much difference. You've got to appeal to the reasonable, sensible electorate. The party that doesn't, that gets too far off to the left, or too far off to the right ... they're not going to get elected.[33]

Reagan's success inevitably weakened the party machine. 'One of my major complaints', Parkinson reflected, 'is that ... with a candidate like Mr. Reagan, not beholden to the Republican party whatsoever, he said and did just about what he wanted to.'[34] Robert Monagan felt that while Reagan might have superficially healed the divisions, the cost was high. 'One of the things that his tenure brought about was the destruction of the Republican party. He dismantled, in a sense, the Republican party and built the Reagan party. If you didn't belong to the Reagan team, then you were not in.'[35]

Reagan's handlers understood that if the party could be presented with a winner, internal disagreements would dissolve. The aim was to establish a groundswell of popular support so overwhelming that disgruntled moderates and right-wing zealots would be forced to jettison their animosities and climb on the bandwagon. The strategy worked precisely because Reagan was an outsider. Other than a few key speeches, his roots in politics did not run deep. He enjoyed the best of both worlds: though an outsider, he was still famous. 'Reagan at that time was looked upon as being a curiosity, a glamorous curiosity, having come out of his background in Hollywood and all,' William French Smith explained.

> I can remember that during that period *Life* Magazine ... ran an article on him. It wasn't a cover or anything like that, it was just a couple of pages. The other candidates ... were highly irritated with *Life* Magazine that they would give this kind of publicity to a candidate, which was free publicity.[36]

'He had great name ID,' Spencer confirmed. 'He had an approval rating with women in 1965 of 93% ... That was purely based on the roles he played in the movies, the nice guy versus the bad guy.' That was a huge advantage for the campaign team. 'We didn't have to worry about spending money on name ID. They knew who he was. We just had to define him.'[37]

The definition the team settled on was 'citizen-politician', which perfectly encapsulated Reagan's own perceptions. He saw himself as a man of the people, committed to service, not tainted by politics. 'He was a citizen that was concerned and he was going to run for a job as a politician,' Spencer remarked. 'He was just one step ahead of the electorate, not twenty steps ahead of them in the political arena.' Citizen-politician 'came somewhere out of our long brainstorming sessions,' Spencer explained. 'We felt it was a strength to have somebody that had been out of the system ... We felt that that's what people wanted for a change, somebody that wasn't a bureaucrat or in the present system.'[38] Nofziger elaborated:

> What we were saying was that Pat Brown's a hack politician who has surrounded himself with hacks and cronies, and appointed political hacks to jobs. We're offering you a new approach which is a guy who's not a politician, but is a citizen coming in and saying, 'Okay, I've got to serve my state because it's been good to me, and we will come in with a citizen's approach to this. We will serve the citizens instead of the politicians.'
>
> It was a good, effective approach against a guy who had spent all his life in politics. What they were saying is, 'Ronald Reagan is innocent. He doesn't know anything about politics. He doesn't know anything about government. He doesn't know anything about running anything. He's never been there.'
>
> And we were saying, 'Well, the trouble with Pat Brown is that he's been governor too long.'[39]

The homespun image was reinforced by Nancy. 'In newspaper and television interviews it became clear that Nancy had a script as carefully crafted as Reagan's basic speech,' Lewis discovered. He noticed how she robotically repeated a carefully crafted script: 'she and Ronnie never dreamed about a political career; she never considered the governor's mansion let alone the White House; she and Ronnie are just folks who prefer the quiet life to the Hollywood round.'[40]

The citizen-politician label turned weakness into strength. As Reagan told a crowd at the University of Southern California:

> I am not a politician. I am an ordinary citizen with a deep-seated belief that much of what troubles us has been brought about by politicians and it's high time more ordinary citizens brought the fresh air of common sense thinking to bear on these problems. It's time now for dreamers, practical dreamers, willing to re-implement the original dream which became this nation.[41]

It was the perfect populist sermon. Critics who disparaged Reagan's inexperience played into his hands by underlining the fact that he was not one of the Sacramento mob. When Christopher and Brown boasted of their experience, that merely confirmed their establishment credentials. Weinberger found it fascinating that, in 1966, the public 'didn't want all that much experience ... they were tired of experienced people. They wanted something fresh and new.'[42] The other side of the coin was to stress that Brown *was* a politician, with all the negative baggage that carried. Reagan claimed, for instance, that Brown was 'aided by his well-oiled and heavily financed machine' – a somewhat ironic charge. This tactic completely wrong-footed the Brown camp. 'Of course, we were surprised,' Kline recalled, 'we didn't understand that the public wanted non-politicians.'[43]

'The man who currently has the job has more experience than anyone,' Reagan quipped. 'That's why I am running.'[44]

Politicians, so the argument went, thrived on government. Thus, the citizen-politician theme harmonized perfectly with a campaign geared toward downsizing government and setting the people free. Brown was baffled: 'he was stupid and his statements were illogical ... he was a person running to be the head of a government to make government work and he was like an atheist being elected pope. He didn't believe in government.'[45] That was precisely the point. As Reagan argued, only a non-politician could be trusted to bring government under control, since a politician by definition was an insider who worshipped the institution. 'The fact that I hadn't held political office became a plus, not a minus. He [Pat Brown] was running on his experience, and I turned it around and kept saying, "Look, if you want an experienced politician, re-elect Pat Brown."'[46] When polled on the governor's weak points, voters consistently listed 'he has been in office too long' and 'he is too much of a politician' at the top.[47]

Citizen-politician was, however, simply a label, not a programme. The voters wanted to know what Reagan would do. Policy developed as the campaign gained momentum. 'You don't sit down and hatch it up,' Smith explained. 'It just develops. There wasn't very much discussion ... I suppose the blueprint [was] ... "the speech" ... that so many people were subscribing to. In other words, its time had come, after all the years since Roosevelt.'[48] Over time, 'The Speech' morphed into 'The Creative Society', a vague plan of action. The New Deal would be rolled back, setting the people free to use their creative instincts. 'You're always looking for a theme,' Spencer explained. 'Sometimes you can't find one and you fake one and it comes out phony ... You're better off just to ignore it and go without a theme. Sometimes they just fall right into your lap.' That was the case with the Creative Society. 'The Great Society, which was Lyndon Johnson's, was going on at the time. Everybody liked it conceptually, but it didn't work out. We were taking advantage of the society aspect, not the great.

We put creative into the society.'[49] Using the word 'society' in a manifesto was a clever way of camouflaging the every-man-for-himself individualism that was the usual Republican fare.

Plog typically insisted that 'the Creative Society came from us.'[50] In fact, the idea emerged long before they were hired. While BASICO had some input in the later stages, the concept itself does not reflect well on their influence, since it oozed ambiguity – precisely what Plog and Holden abhorred. The idea was actually the brainchild of Reverend W. S. McBirnie, who suggested it to Reagan on 30 November 1965.[51] McBirnie's contribution is interesting given that he was a bona fide member of the loony right who spouted Welch's conspiracy theories and deeply admired Billy James Hargis, founder of the anti-Catholic, anti-Semitic Christian Crusade. None of this prevented him from attending key planning sessions early in the campaign. 'It is going to take a program which fires the imagination of the voters in order to overcome your lack of governmental experience,' McBirnie advised. Reagan needed 'a definite *program* which would stamp you as electable. You certainly have all the other attributes of the successful candidate – but ... now is the time to come forth with your program – *specifically*.'[52] That word 'specifically' seems to have been used rather loosely, since the Creative Society was painfully short on specifics.

Reagan took McBirnie's Creative Society idea and explained it in his own words: 'there is present within the incredibly rich human resources of California the dynamic solution to every old or new problem we face. The task of a state government ... is to creatively discover, enlist, and mobilize those human resources.'[53] Small was beautiful: local government was better than state, and state better than federal. Bureaucracy at all levels had to be reduced in order to set the people free to look after themselves. Government, Reagan argued, 'is like a baby. It is an alimentary canal with a tremendous appetite at one end and no sense of responsibility at the other.'[54] A position paper elaborated:

Paternalistic government can solve many problems for the people; but the inexorable price it must extract is power over them, ever increasing power at the cost of ever decreasing individual freedom. The Creative Society idea is that the government shall lead and encourage the people to participate in a partnership to solve their own problems, as close to home as possible.[55]

In a letter to a supporter, Reagan described how government might act in a Creative Society:

The state government would turn to the industrial community and ask for a committee created by them to evolve a plan, including suggestions as to how government could cooperate in order to stimulate industry and improve the business climate, so that industry could provide the jobs we need.

The government would then do whatever it could to remove roadblocks such as regressive taxes, excessive record keeping, etc., plus such stimulants as might be practical. For example a tax incentive or rebate for companies that would put into operation on-the-job training programs.[56]

McBirnie was eventually banished after his Bircher links and marital infidelity were exposed in the press, but his idea continued to thrive.[57] The Creative Society gave Reagan the opportunity to present conservatism in a positive way. 'I can remember [McBirnie] suggesting not to fall into a trap of being always against, but to make sure that I was offering positive alternatives.'[58] Granted, this was achieved by being purposefully vague; at no time did Reagan reveal precisely what practical measures he would implement. Republicans nevertheless welcomed what seemed a profound departure from the strident negativity of Goldwater and the hysteria of the Birchers. 'We felt that the creative society and citizen politician just fell into our lap,' Spencer explained. 'Everything fit. It all worked with the media. It worked with the candidate. It worked with the press people.'[59]

As the Creative Society demonstrated, Reagan was far too upbeat to be a Bircher. While most voters were convinced by his denial of membership, critics still believed that there was mileage to be gained from the Bircher connection. According to Spencer, 'It was the first problem that Reagan had to face.'[60] That problem refused to go away, in large part because Reagan would not condemn the Society. As he explained, 'if someone – I don't care what he believes – comes and says to me, "I'm going to vote for you because I agree with the things that you're saying", well, I'm not going to tell him I don't want his vote.'[61] That explanation was honest but insufficiently robust, especially after Birchers began arguing that Brown was a Soviet stooge intent on making California the first communist state in the Union. Nor did it help when Reagan admitted that he had considerable sympathy with a lot of what Birchers advocated. 'I have always felt that Mr. Welch took some factual material and drew some wrong conclusions with it,' he tried to explain.[62] Sentiments like this, when combined with the Rousselot and McBirnie connections, made Reagan vulnerable.

In the summer of 1965, Spencer discussed with Rousselot the best way to spin his relationship with Reagan. Rousselot, keen to help, promised: 'I'll do whatever you want. I'll be for you or against you, whatever helps the most.' Unfortunately, while Spencer was mulling the matter over, Reagan, at a coffee hour in Monterey, described Rousselot as a 'terrific fellow' and quipped that he had agreed to do 'anything from calling me names in public to endorsement – whatever we want'.[63] As was his habit, he had responded to a difficult situation by joking. Unfortunately, no one thought the Birchers funny. The moderate Jane Alexander, sensing an opportunity, leaked the quip to the press, thus encouraging journalists to conclude that Reagan was bargaining with Birchers. 'Reagan was naïve,' Spencer admitted. 'He didn't realize that what he said to 15 women in Monterey ... could be leaked to the *San Francisco Examiner*. He ... didn't think that people were evil enough to leak. He didn't know that reporters had plants.'[64]

The papers jumped on the story. Carl Greenberg of the *Los Angeles Times* returned to it repeatedly over the following week. The deal, argued the *Beverly Hills Courier*, 'is the quintessence of political chicanery, betokening an absolute cynicism and a willingness to mislead and deceive the electorate that is wholly shameful ... By any yardstick, Reagan must be found fatally lacking in the moral judgement required of a public official.'[65] The Reagan camp did not respond, in part because the story was essentially true. What is interesting about this incident is that, despite all the negative publicity, Reagan still did not see the sense in denouncing the Birchers. He repeatedly insisted that an entire group should not be condemned simply because of a few lunatic extremists. Several months later, he apologized to Rousselot in typical tone:

> I want you to know how sorry I am if my attempt to get a laugh caused you any embarrassment. I solemnly pledge that from now on I'll only tell dirty stories suitable for male company, and thus there will be no chance of Jane Alexander having anything to quote.[66]

Reagan's determination to remain on friendly terms with Birchers caused endless trouble for his campaign team. Eventually, aides were mobilized at party gatherings to form a protective ring around him, in order to keep Birchers at a distance so that no compromising photos could be taken.

Spencer finally decided that the Bircher issue needed to be settled once and for all. 'We did not want it to get a life of its own. We didn't want to have to be on the defensive and point out that he wasn't a Bircher.'[67] A statement, released on 24 September 1965, cleverly distanced Reagan from the Society: 'I have never been and am not now a member of the John Birch Society, nor do I have any intention of ever becoming a member.' He condemned the Society's 'lunatic fringe' and, for the first time, openly repudiated Welch for his attacks on Eisenhower. The statement was not, however, a complete condemnation, since Reagan still took care to point out that the FBI had not labelled the Society subversive. Then came the sentence that would be his mantra for the rest of the campaign: 'It would be my intention if I seek public office, to seek the support of individuals by persuading them of my philosophy, not by accepting theirs.'[68] Spencer thought that statement perfect. 'After that, we weren't defensive about it and we never had to be.'[69] Indeed, Brown credited Reagan with 'a much cleverer answer than Nixon who repudiated it'.[70] That did not stop Brown's camp from attempting to revive the issue periodically over the following year, but it did ensure that these attacks were consistently ineffective. As Spencer explained, whenever the issue was raised again, Reagan simply replied: 'I've answered that and if you care to have me enlarge upon it, here's a written piece of paper to be handed out to you when we leave the room. Now let's get on to the major issues of this campaign.'[71]

The Bircher issue nevertheless required considerable agility. Potential supporters often demanded that a total repudiation was the essential prerequisite to their backing Reagan. He refused to provide what was demanded, but did emphasize his objections to the Society. That then alienated those on the far right. 'I was shocked at your recent repudiation of the John Birch Society,' Mrs H. Albright wrote in response to the September 1965 statement. 'Especially since you did not at the same time mention any disinclination to accept the votes of the murderous Black Muslims or the Communist-ridden NAACP.'[72] Typical of the extremist hard-liners was a complaint from Josephine Powell Beaty of the Defenders of the American Constitution. She berated Reagan for his lack of ideological purity. 'How naïve can you be?' she wrote. 'No matter how "liberal" you may try to appear, no liberal will ever vote for you.

You *had* considerable backing from Conservatives but I wonder if they are not becoming disenchanted with your "new" look.'[73] In a bizarre twist, he argued with Birchers over the intensity of his anti-communism. On one occasion, he boasted that communists had threatened to kill him while he was president of the Screen Actors Guild and that he had to 'live for the better part of a year with a police guard for my family as a result of communist threats against me. I will match my record for fighting, not talking about, Communism with anyone you care to name.'[74]

Meanwhile Reagan's opponents, frustrated at being unable to profit from the Bircher issue, tried instead the Goldwater card. A political cartoon showed a demonic Goldwater directing Reagan offstage: 'Perfect, Ronald ... enter stage right.'[75] 'Reagan is a good candidate', wrote Marianne Means in the *Chronicle*, 'if you don't bother to listen to what he says ... He's just a bit player in a continuing Goldwater script.'[76] The attacks were incessant, but mostly ineffective. Parkinson felt that 'his reasonableness and his humor' allowed Reagan to duck the flak:

> His candor, I think, was a big element with the press. He never came across as being as much of an extremist as Goldwater was. He was very careful to do that. Mainly, of course, it was by Spencer and Roberts, who had been running liberal candidates since they'd been doing the business. They themselves deep down were liberals. They felt they had a winner and so they moderated a lot of the things that he [Reagan] might have accepted without question.[77]

'This is my campaign,' Reagan insisted in early February. 'Goldwater is not running it. I want the voters to listen ... to what I have to say and how I stand on the issues and then make up their own minds what is the Reagan image.' That was a poor choice of words, but the voters still found it convincing. Spencer admitted that, in policy terms, Reagan and Goldwater had an overwhelming expression of opinion as bigotry. 'Instead of bowing and saying whatever the people have said is the ultimate wisdom,' Champion reflected, 'Pat said ... it was a vote for bigotry.' While that was an entirely fair statement, 'you don't win elections on it ... that pushed Pat, in the minds of a lot of voters, out of the middle where they were, and further to the left.'[84]

Despite the explosive racial connotations, Reagan saw no reason to prevaricate on the Rumford issue. Hale Champion, a Brown aide, was astonished at his ability to pull this off without suffering adverse consequences. 'He didn't try to fudge ... on the Rumford Act ... what clearly came through out of that discussion was that he really was fundamentally where he'd always been.'[85] He based his opposition on freedom, not race. Rumford, he argued, was the perfect example of a 'government usurping rights it didn't have'.[86] A briefing paper argued that the 14th Amendment to the American Constitution 'has a built-in antagonism between liberty and equality. Accordingly, it is reasonable to conclude that *private* discrimination does not come within the prohibitory authority of the 14th amendment.'[87] Reagan took that briefing and turned it into homespun logic:

> This is a pretty important point in the constitution, and it was part of what made us rebel against England, the right of the individual. As a matter of fact, I once said, 'If somebody in Santa Monica wants to say that he will only rent to members of the Rotary Club who have freckles and red hair isn't that his right with his property, if he's foolish enough to want to do that?'[88]

The statement hinges on the word 'foolish'. Discrimination, Reagan essentially argued, was foolish, but it was not the responsibility of government to legislate against fools. As Spencer explained:

> Ronald Reagan was not anti-minority. He is almost a libertarian in beliefs. He thinks we should be able to work these things out

> without the government encroaching on … individual choice … He's not against a black person living in a neighborhood, but he thinks that somebody has the right to sell their house to who they want to. That's sort of a basic Reagan philosophy.[89]

Reagan was certain in his own mind that his position was not racist. He repeatedly insisted upon his unequivocal 'opposition to prejudice and bigotry'. Those who judged his position racist were, he felt, guilty of an unfortunate 'misunderstanding'.[90]

Whenever Reagan was challenged on this issue, he would drift into an anecdote about Franklin 'Burgie' Burghardt, one of two black players on his Eureka College football team.

> I was raised to detest bigotry and prejudice, long before there was any talk of the civil rights movement … In college, I played football beside a [black] fellow in the line who still to this day is one of my dearest friends. We fought and bled together in a day … when you played both ways, offense and defense. Ours was a little school. We usually played schools much larger, so you really did bleed. You didn't have anybody to take your place. You spent most of the sixty minutes in there.

The story was true. On one occasion in 1930 when Eureka was on the road, the two black players were denied entry to a whites-only hotel. The coach suggested they could sleep on the bus, but Reagan decided to take them to his parents' home nearby. The story, however, also reveals the limits of Reagan's understanding of the racial problem. While he had sympathy for individual blacks who suffered the effects of racism, he did not have empathy for how legislation affected the black community as a whole. He later admitted that he had misunderstood how blacks interpreted his stand against the Rumford Act. 'Later, after I became governor,' he recalled, 'after meetings all over the state with members of the minority community, I realized the symbolism of the Rumford Act …

and how much it meant morale-wise to them, I frankly said no. I changed my mind.'[91]

'I don't think that Proposition 14 was essentially an anti-black vote,' Brown later admitted. 'It was part of the revolt against too many governmental controls.'[92] That might have been true, but the fact remained that Reagan's position also appealed to racists in California, of whom there were many. 'Don't ask me about civil rights,' one woman told a reporter who enquired about her position on Rumford. 'I don't want to talk about it. If I had a gun, I'd kill every nigger on this block.'[93] Reagan did not understand the encouragement he gave to bigotry despite receiving, during the campaign, hundreds of letters from overt racists who clearly thought he was their champion. 'I hope you are against open housing,' Evelyn Anderson wrote to Reagan. 'I don't think Negroes and whites should mix. The Negroes have pushed the whites out of neighborhood after neighborhood ... Now we must take a stand.'[94] Another correspondent warned Reagan of the 'forthcoming Negro revolution' and urged him to 'send them to Africa'.[95] The most bizarre letter came from Jack Barron, who sought Reagan's support for introducing a new baseball bat which would supposedly stop black domination of the game, itself a communist conspiracy. 'Prove to Russia and China that you can do this and the *wars will end*,' he promised.[96] Bertram Coffey, a veteran of the California Democratic Committee, concluded that race was enormously important in the 1966 election. He felt that, over the course of the campaign, Brown came to be identified as a 'nigger lover' and he paid the cost of that assumption. 'These terms were used, and we wince at those words, but they were used. It was played very well by Reagan.'[97]

Reagan managed, quite remarkably, to turn opposition to civil rights into a vote-winner. This sort of success was common in the Deep South, but it should not theoretically have been possible in California. Brown recalled his frustration at having to defend what seemed a cast-iron moral principle:

> I felt very badly that my good works were not appreciated but I knew that I was going to lose in the campaign [for Rumford]. I could sense it, you could feel it ... When people would ask me ... whether I believed in fair housing and I would say, 'Yes, certainly I believe. You can't have any discrimination in housing', I'd see even the union people walk away from me ... I mean there's no such thing as a liberal when it comes to black and white relationships. They're just negative about it, that's all there is to it.[98]

Opposition to Rumford allowed Reagan to invade traditionally Democratic constituencies and thus to redefine loyalties in the state. Worried by black unrest, white workers were desperate for someone to defend them. As Means commented in the *Examiner:*

> The riots in Watts and San Francisco have intensified the fear of lower and middle income whites that they will lose their jobs and their houses to Negroes ... All the political signs point to massive defections to Reagan among normally Democratic ranks of labor, in the past the hard core of Gov. Brown's strength.[99]

Champion recalled polls that confounded the Brown team:

> The most striking thing I saw during all of those polls during that period of time is that whereas 90 percent or more of the blacks in California thought Brown had done and would do more for them, more than 50 percent of the whites interviewed thought Reagan would do more for blacks.
> Yes! What was good for the black community, in effect, in the view of a lot of whites, was to have somebody like Reagan ... what it was saying to us was that Pat was almost totally identified with the blacks in the minds of a majority of white Californians, and that they thought that the blacks would be better off with somebody like Reagan.[100]

In the wake of urban riots, these findings were very significant. Whites equated Brown with well-meaning legislation that did not actually improve the fortunes of the black community, nor make the state a safer place. Whites assumed they knew what was best for blacks.

The Watts riot changed the rules of discourse in the civil rights debate. Northern whites had found it difficult to criticize black protesters when they campaigned non-violently behind Martin Luther King. When the protests turned violent, however, a different reaction became possible. Los Angeles Police Chief William Parker blamed the civil rights movement for encouraging blacks to believe that 'you don't have to obey the law if you think it's unjust' – a direct reference to King's 'Letter from a Birmingham Jail'. Parker went on to remark that the escalation of violence had occurred because 'someone threw a rock and, like monkeys in a zoo, they all started throwing rocks.'[101] He warned that pretty soon decent folks would find those monkeys on their doorsteps, a reaction that brought 40,000 letters of support.

'The whites thought ... there would be a different kind of atmosphere if Reagan were governor,' Champion admitted.[102] An electrician remarked:

> I've had enough of this. These people burn and loot and get people killed in their riots, and then we turn around and give them money. They don't want to work, they can't do anything for California, they just lie there, waiting for another excuse to throw a brick. I'm a Democrat, but I'm voting for Reagan. Brown has coddled these people too much.[103]

'Brown has practically ruined the state,' one woman argued. 'He has a nice home but he lets the Negroes come right next to you.'[104] Writing in the *New York Post*, Pete Hamill claimed that, in this election, 'The not-so-secret issue is race.' He quoted a Hollywood screenwriter who offered an interesting observation:

> People will have a real opportunity to indulge their prejudices. They know that neither Brown nor Reagan is going to blow up the world, the way they had to figure with Goldwater. So they're going for Reagan because of the race issue, and telling themselves it's for other reasons altogether.[105]

Without personally crossing the line into racism, Reagan managed to encourage a racist backlash. 'I thought it was a very smart campaign,' Champion remarked. 'He played on [racial fears] but he did not say anything outright. It was a triumph of manner and style. It's the thing I think Reagan is best at – appearing to be reasonable while reaching, in almost jocular style, for those emotions.'[106] In his declaration speech, for instance, he warned: 'Every day the jungle draws a little closer. Our city streets are jungle paths after dark, with more crimes of violence than New York, Pennsylvania, and Massachusetts combined.'[107] He left it to his listeners to interpret the jungle metaphor in the way they wished. By this means, Reagan gave succour to racists while hiding behind the pretence of principle.

The efforts to define Reagan were enormously successful. The 'citizen-politician' label, the Creative Society idea, the opposition to Rumford and the adroit handling of the Bircher issue were all designed to broaden Reagan's appeal. While it is true that he moved closer to the centre of the political spectrum, he did so by taking the right with him. Conservative extremists were still able to find much that they liked about Reagan, a trick that neither Nixon nor Rockefeller had managed. At the same time, by appearing to move to the centre, Reagan made Brown look ever more left wing, at a time when the left was suffering, particularly in California. This allowed Reagan to make serious inroads into Democratic support by appealing to white working-class voters annoyed by civil rights legislation and the expansion of welfare. 'He turned out to be not just a guy who could deliver one speech,' Champion reflected, 'but a guy who … understands that you don't need to appear threatening …

you can take very conservative attitudes if you don't behave like a thundering conservative, which he didn't.'[108]

As a result of this alchemy, the definition of what constituted a Republican became blurred, much to Reagan's benefit. 'No way of knowing how many voted for him [from] each party,' Parkinson recalled, 'but I will tell you that there were an awful lot of people who voted for him who were not organized Republicans.'[109] Parkinson might have regretted the effect Reagan's efforts had upon the Republican Party machine, but to the ordinary voter it seemed that the party was suddenly united and electable – something that had seemed impossible just two years earlier. This transformation owed everything to pretence. Liberal journalists watched in frustration at the success of the makeover. 'In the world of drama, an actor has no ties with his old roles,' warned C. K. McClatchy in the *Sacramento Bee*. 'The only one that counts is the present one. But this is not the case in politics. It is not possible for a politician to change his political coloration in the way an actor changes his role.'[110] That warning was endlessly repeated precisely because Reagan was proving it untrue.

# 7

# Drowning in Milk

During the primary campaign, George Christopher and Ronald Reagan often found themselves on the same podium in what was essentially an informal debate. On one of these occasions, several thousand people crowded into an auditorium in Southern California. Reagan had the floor first and, in response to a question on how he would control government spending and reduce taxes, announced his intention to impose an immediate across-the-board budget cut of 10 per cent. 'Any business can deduct ten percent if they try hard enough, so why can't we do it?'[1] The crowd erupted in approval. No one asked Reagan about feasibility.

Christopher then came to the microphone. Not surprisingly, his first questioner asked whether he, too, would impose a large cut. He tried patiently to explain that cutting the budget was not as simple as Reagan suggested. 'My experience in government tells me that you just can't do this automatically, cut ten percent. You have to work, number one, through the elimination of duplications but through the process of attrition. You don't fill jobs as they become vacant.'[2] That was not the answer the crowd wanted. From every corner of the auditorium came a chorus of boos. Christopher realized that he was in for a hard evening.

Like every populist, Reagan peddled simplicities. His easy solutions and grandiose promises sounded wonderful during the campaign, though most were impossible to carry out in the real world. Christopher responded to these facile statements with the wisdom that comes of long political experience and the knowledge that answers are never easy. That was the only weapon in his armoury, yet it was not very useful in the battle he chose to fight. One of his main pamphlets, for instance, had the single word 'EXPERIENCE' on the front page. This would have been a completely reasonable point to stress in any other campaign. In this one, however, it backfired, since Reagan was successfully arguing that, in politics, experience was the same as culpability. Those who knew the system were guilty of perpetuating the system.

Christopher never came to terms with how politics in California had changed so quickly and dramatically. He still believed that the politician's role was to educate the voters on the complex issues facing their state. That, however, was not what most voters demanded. They wanted a candidate who would respond viscerally to their gut emotions. In this sense, Christopher could not compete with Reagan, who entertained the voters by giving mellifluous voice to their crude passion. 'There was no depth ... to what he said,' Christopher complained, 'you need more than clichés and you need more than rainbows at both ends of the room to really make a good administration.'[3] Christopher never specifically mentioned the phrase 'dumbing down', but that is precisely what he meant. The phenomenon was particularly acute in Southern California, Reagan territory. Newly arrived voters were generally of low educational attainment and therefore more susceptible to simplistic logic, or at least ill-equipped to question it. 'Despite my experience in politics I encountered difficulties that I didn't anticipate down in Los Angeles, San Diego, Orange Counties,' Christopher recalled.[4] It was like campaigning on Mars.

Steeped in the sensibilities of the old California Republican Party, Christopher had steadfastly insisted that a moderate offered the only hope of beating Brown in 1966. For that reason, he was certain that the nomination should go to Kuchel and did not at first take seriously Reagan's chances, dismissing him as a Goldwater extremist. Kuchel, however, recognized the threat Reagan posed and decided not to risk embarrassment. 'Kuchel's decision created havoc in the Republican ranks,' a journalist remarked. 'They suddenly realized that they had only one candidate, actor Ronald Reagan.'[5] Keen to avert what he saw as a disaster, Christopher threw his hat into the ring. 'I didn't believe – frankly, I just didn't feel that Mr. Reagan was qualified to be governor ... I looked around to see who was going to run and thought that if only Mr. Reagan was going to run, well, that we needed somebody with some governmental experience.'[6] He was convinced that his declaration would return the party to its senses.

Poor Christopher simply didn't get it. He was an earnest man who took his politics seriously but lacked the ability to adjust to the world in which he now lived. He could not compete in a contest in which personality figured so large. '[Reagan] had the charisma of standing on a podium and sweeping you off your feet,' he recalled with more than a touch of envy.

> He was very adroit. For instance, every time we'd meet ... and there were other candidates present, and they would put us in line for a photograph, the same thing happened. As soon as the photographer was ready to snap the picture, Reagan would put up his hand like this [raises forefinger into the air] and make it appear that all of us were deferring to him and looking to him for advice. Well, this was the actor's ability to steal the scene.[7]

Reagan was an actor; Christopher an accountant. Reagan had Hollywood good looks; Christopher looked like one of those potatoes that resemble a human face. Reagan could reel off wonderful anecdotes of his acting days; Christopher could recount how many parking garages he had built in San

Francisco. In an election heavy on glamour, Christopher never had a chance.

Reagan did not, however, always have things his way. On 6 March 1966, the three Republican candidates – Christopher, Reagan and William Penn Patrick – appeared at the California Negro Republican Assembly in Santa Monica. 'We knew Ron wasn't going to get anywhere with Negroes,' Spencer admitted, 'but he had to go anyway because it would look bad if he stayed away'.[8] To make matters worse, Reagan was suffering from an illness that made him tired and irritable. Midway through the event, a black delegate declared: 'It grieves me when a leading Republican candidate says the Civil Rights Act is a bad piece of legislation.'[9] Reagan had earlier stated that he would have voted against the act, which he called a 'grandstand stunt'.[10] He tried to explain that he supported the spirit of the legislation but still felt it badly devised. Patrick and Christopher, jumping on the opportunity, tried to make Reagan sound racist. 'This was one of the times that the "Eleventh Commandment" got a little eroded, and they were painting me as a bigot,' Reagan recalled.[11] 'George really started hammering Reagan,' Spencer explained. 'That was a test. Ronald Reagan had never been hammered before. He'd never been hit.'[12] Patrick eventually made the closest thing to an outright accusation of racism. When Reagan rose to reply, he was incandescent with rage. 'I resented it. Finally, I blew my top,' he later admitted. He responded, as usual, with an anecdote:

> I told a little incident that ... a black friend of mine had told it to me. And unfortunately, being angry and all, it's an incident that I have difficulty telling without my voice breaking ... This friend ... was telling me of his experience in a park with his three-year-old son on a hot summer day, thirsty. This was in the South, his little boy was crying and wanting a drink. How did he explain to him that he was not allowed to drink out of those fountains? ... I ... said that my dream was that never again would anyone

in this land ever have to tell their child that they couldn't have something because they were different.[13]

It's difficult to tell a homespun homily while angry. Thrown off his stride, Reagan failed to achieve his customary gravity, sounding instead insincere. His frustration eventually boiled over. 'I resent the implication that there is any bigotry in my nature,' he spat.[14] He then wadded up his programme, threw it on the floor and muttered something about 'those sons of bitches'. He was referring to Christopher and Patrick, but some observers thought he was cursing his black hosts.[15]

'He came off that stage steaming, cussing and steaming,' Spencer recalled. 'A couple of press guys picked it up. They're running around, grabbing me and the others, trying to get confirmation of the exact verbiage. I said, "What are you talking about? I didn't hear anything."'[16] Reagan, meanwhile, had stormed out of the building, followed closely by Nofziger and Holden. 'I walked down the aisle with him and he was muttering profanities,' Nofziger recalled. 'I said, "Shut up, Ron, shut up."' Nofziger told him to go home and cool off while they decided what to do.

At this point, recollections diverge. Nofziger maintained that he went back into the hall and put out the fire, as press officers do. 'I talked to people, and they understood that he wasn't upset at the blacks, he was upset at what ... [Patrick and Christopher] had said, and they all said, "You'd better have him come back."'[17] Nofziger then went to Reagan's house and convinced him to return. He did so, tempers cooled, and the storm passed.

Holden's version is distinctly different. 'Roberts and Nofziger were letting their man crash and burn.'[18] He claimed that Nofziger told Reagan to go home and stay there. 'I knew he had to return ... If his departure stood, it would be jumped on by the opposition press as a rejection of the black community and a confirmation of all the negative appellations hurled at him.'

He phoned Reagan at home, got a busy signal, and told the telephone operator 'in a voice somewhere between a scream and a plea ... that this was an emergency ... and ordered her to break into the call'.[19] He then urged Reagan to return immediately. Roberts and Nofziger, who had arrived at that moment, allegedly told him to stay put. Reagan confronted his handlers and accused them of not trusting him. He then followed Holden's advice, went back to the meeting, and spent three hours answering questions and received a standing ovation.

Or so Holden claims. He concluded that he had personally saved Reagan's career. If Reagan had not returned to that meeting, the inevitable storm in the press the next day would have destroyed his candidacy. Reagan would not have become governor. If he had failed in 1966, he would not have become president. A molehill became a mountain: the chain of consequence leads inevitably to 1989 and the collapse of communism, an event that Plog and Holden attribute entirely to Reagan. In other words, if not for Holden's faith in Reagan on that day in March 1966, America would still be stuck in the Cold War.[20]

In fact, the matter did not blow over as quickly as Holden and Nofziger remembered. Interviewed after the event, Christopher offered $5,000 to anyone who could find incontrovertible evidence that he had called Reagan a bigot. In perhaps his best remark of the campaign he called Reagan 'a temperamentally and emotionally upset candidate whose sole escape from problems is to dash hysterically to his dressing room'.[21] The press, delighted to find a chink in Reagan's formidable armour, used the incident both as an example of his vulnerability on the race issue and of his inability to control his temper. Polls a few days later showed that Reagan's lead over Christopher had slipped to single digits, from 13 to 8 per cent. Salvatori, always inclined to panic, tried to persuade Goodwin Knight to enter the race. After considerable effort, Nofziger persuaded Salvatori to get back on the bandwagon. Reagan, meanwhile, struggled to come up with a credible explanation for his behaviour. He first offered the preposterous claim that he had left because he thought the meeting was over. Eventually, however, he resorted to blaming his opponents:

> The other candidates ... seemed unable to answer the questions without demagogic inferences that I was a racist or bigot. There is no single thing I detest more in others than bigotry and to have this charge directed at me was more than I felt I had to take. I have traveled up and down the state urging party unity and shall continue to do so even though I seem to be the only candidate who feels it is important. But this doesn't include remaining silent when my integrity and sincerity are attacked.[22]

In the *Chronicle*, Sydney Kossen called the incident 'rare melodrama':

> It was the actor's most memorable unrehearsed performance since he entered the contest for Governor ... Many political pros think Reagan blew it. Along with his tears of anger, the actor shed a great deal of dignity ... Now his campaign may, in the phrase of the market analysts, bottom out ... He will find it difficult to erase the impression that his performance in Santa Monica last weekend was not just absurd but frightening.[23]

Seven weeks later, the *Bee* was still recycling the story and speculating on unease in the Reagan camp: 'If [he] could hit the canvas so early in the game, they wondered if their boy had a glass jaw.'[24] Journalists were nearly unanimous that Reagan had brought catastrophe on himself. Playing on the title of his autobiography, the Pulitzer Prize-winning cartoonist Paul Conrad drew a decapitated Reagan with his head under his arm, the caption reading: 'Where's the rest of me?'[25] Reagan was so incensed by the cartoon that he decided to call Buffie

Chandler, owner of the *Los Angeles Times* and demand that Conrad be fired. Nofziger, ever vigilant, grabbed the phone and talked Reagan out of making an ass of himself.[26]

Reagan eventually turned the incident to his advantage. In subsequent Q&A sessions, if the matter arose, he responded with a stock line. 'I'm not a politician. Maybe they have ground rules that say you don't get mad. But I think sometimes things are said about you that make you mad. I got mad.'[27] That seemed to work. 'I would get applause, for simply saying that.'[28] Pro-Reagan papers loved that explanation. 'It's possible that Reagan's image as a "nice guy" needed a little humanizing,' argued the *Oakland Tribune*. 'Even nice guys get mad occasionally, don't we?'[29] Reagan's critics were again frustrated at his annoying ability to turn straw into gold.

Spencer was predictably astute in his analysis of the incident. He felt that Christopher intentionally baited Reagan because he 'finally realized about four or five months into the campaign that he's in trouble'. Reagan over-reacted because he wasn't accustomed to dirty politics. 'It really threw him out of whack,' Spencer recalled. 'He got obsessed about this thing. I kept saying, "This isn't the last. As long as you're ahead you're going to get hit again and again and again." He started to adjust to it, but he never liked it.' Over the long term, Reagan managed to profit from the abuse thrown his way. As Christopher fell further behind, his tactics grew nastier. 'Basically it played into Reagan's hands in the sense that the rougher George Christopher became, the more the public realized this guy's behind and is panicking. He's attacking this real nice guy ... It really backfired on George.' The mud never stuck to Reagan's Teflon exterior. 'You could go down in flames attacking him ... Reagan was bound to get elected.'[30]

Brown shared Christopher's assumption that Reagan's inexperience would eventually defeat him. An assistant sent to scout Reagan in 1965 reported that: 'He will fall apart when he gets attacked from the floor and is asked leading questions, hounded and the like.'[31] Once formed, that judgement never faltered and became the guiding philosophy of Brown's campaign. Like a mantra, Brown kept repeating the actor line because he refused to believe that an actor could beat him. 'While I was working for this state, as district attorney, attorney general and, for the last eight years as governor, what was ... [Reagan] doing? Well, he was making movies like *Girls' Night Out* and *Bedtime for Bonzo*. Can you imagine turning over this great state to that actor?'[32] From this notion came Brown's decision to target Christopher. 'We felt that Christopher would be a stronger candidate,' he recalled. 'Reagan and I were running almost neck and neck where Christopher was ahead of me 13 or 14 percent.'[33] The press mostly agreed. 'Even with his pancake make-up and his cordon of Hollywood flacks,' the *Chronicle* commented, 'Reagan will have a well nigh impossible task in attracting a winning share of the 4,850,000 votes of the State's registered Democrats ... Christopher can capture this necessary share to win.'[34]

Brown decided to help Reagan defeat Christopher, thus leaving the weaker Republican in the field. James Mills recalled a meeting of prominent Democrats in early 1966 when this strategy was debated:

> Pat was saying ... that he wanted to do all he could to make sure that Ronald Reagan was nominated because he didn't think people would vote for an actor for governor ... We told him that we thought he was making a very grave error, that we thought Ronald Reagan would be a tremendous candidate and would be very hard for him to handle and would probably win.[35]

Manning Post, a party fundraiser, did not mince his words:

> Pat, you don't really understand. You've got advisors around who tell you what you want to hear. Now stop and analyze it ... Reagan has always been a good guy ... He's been the Boy

Scout troop leader, the choir guy in the church, the husband, the family man ... He's the guy with the white hat. He's the Shirley Temple of the male set. This sonofabitch is going to beat the shit out of you ... because the first thing you've got to have in politics is recognition, that's what you pay all the money for. All this shit for recognition. You take an actor who had the image of a good guy; man, you can't overcome it. You just can't make him a bad guy anymore.[36]

Brown ignored these warnings and his closest advisers backed him. 'We thought Christopher was ... more dangerous,' Champion explained. 'He could occupy the middle against Pat and push Pat to being a too liberal Democrat.' They were certain that this was a contest of ideology, not personality:

> all of us, the Governor included, made a wrong calculation: that George Christopher would be a tougher candidate than Reagan or at least would be harder to handle. That was made in the traditional context of California politics which was that ... somebody who could occupy the center would have liberal Republican support (or if you were a Republican, would have major Democratic support) and that fringe candidates or people who were viewed as fringe candidates ... were usually the losers.[37]

'We knew that the only chance Brown had of winning re-election was if he was up against some utter non-entity,' Kline later confessed. That seemed to be Reagan. By this logic, it made sense to concentrate fire on Christopher. 'We were conventional thinkers,' Kline admitted. 'The people want to elect to high office those politicians who are qualified for high office. George Christopher was qualified ... Ronald Reagan was a movie actor with no public experience and a right-winger to boot.'[38]

It is easy, in hindsight, to condemn the decision, but polls consistently suggested that Christopher was indeed the greater threat. At the end of January, Reagan led Christopher by nearly

7 per cent. When their strength relative to Brown was measured, however, Christopher led the governor by close to 9 per cent, while Reagan trailed by 4 per cent. 'It is ... possible that the Republican Party could nominate the weaker candidate,' the widely respected pollster Mervin Field predicted on 16 February. He concluded that: 'Christopher's good showing against Brown stems from his ability to hold almost four out of five Republicans and to raid the Democratic Party ranks for 23 percent of their members' votes. Reagan holds slightly fewer Republicans and does less well among Democrats.'[39] This trend continued throughout the primary campaign. At the end of March, Christopher's lead over Brown was 15.6 per cent, while Reagan led by just 0.2 per cent. Three weeks before the primary, Christopher led Brown by 20 per cent, while Reagan's advantage was just 3 per cent. Field came to the conclusion that the Republicans were about to make a big mistake. He pointed out that a Republican, in order to win, 'can lose only 10% of the Republican support, and ... must also pick up better than 20% of the Democratic vote'. He concluded that 'Christopher, rather than Reagan, has a much better chance of achieving those levels of support come November.'[40]

Bagley came to the same conclusion. On 15 April 1966, he and his fellow Assemblymen George Milias and Alan Pattee, all moderates, urged Reagan to abandon his campaign. Citing the most recent Field polls, they urged him to 'withdraw from the Gubernatorial race and from this point forward devote all of your talent, energy and financial resources to the Christopher campaign ... We again repeat our sincere and overriding desire for a Republican victory in November.'[41] Reagan ignored the polls and never responded to Bagley's demand. He never doubted his ability to beat Brown.

'They were bad polls,' Nofziger claimed, 'and I said so all that time'.[42] Plog put the discrepancies down to a reluctance among voters to admit that they liked Reagan. He found a marked difference between oral polls taken on the street and anonymous ones using a confidential ballot. Nofziger got the same impression, but less scientifically. 'I travelled constantly with Reagan during that period. I would come back and say, "Look, we're just going to beat the heck out of these guys." ... All my friends back here were saying, "You're out of your mind."'[43] He felt that the pollsters never did tune in to the real mood of the electorate. 'All of a sudden it came down to late May, and those poll takers were out there scrambling around, trying to make their polls catch up with what was happening, and they never did.' Nofziger had never experienced a race like this one. 'Of all the campaigns that I have been in, and all the campaigns I've watched, the one where there was a guy clearly winning and clearly widening the gap was Ronald Reagan's ... There was just no question in my mind.'[44]

Having decided to target Christopher, the Brown team took to the task with gusto. In 1938, Christopher, who owned a chain of dairies, had been arrested in Marin County for tampering with milk by adding water and failing to obey price controls. Brown knew about the arrest because his law firm had handled the case and his brother Harold had acted as defence attorney. In addition, Fred Bagshaw, director of public works in the Brown administration, was related to the Marin County DA Al Bagshaw, who had prosecuted Christopher. Through these connections, Brown got hold of the case file and fed it to the muckraking journalist Drew Pearson, a Brown supporter. At press conferences in Los Angeles and San Francisco, Pearson described Christopher's crimes as if they had happened the week before and were capital offences. He handed out blown-up copies of Christopher's mugshot, complete with the crime case number printed underneath. That photo was then made into an unofficial campaign handbill showing Christopher with the single word 'WANTED' below. Clever use was made of the famous Olympia Beer slogan: 'Drink Christopher milk. It's the water.' Pearson was like a pit bull, at one point quoting former governor Goodwin Knight who, in 1962, said that Christopher's criminal record 'is the worst I have ever seen' from a candidate running for office.[45] The forlorn Christopher made matters worse when, in his best gaffe of the campaign, he promised that 'if I am elected, I will restore moral turpitude.'[46]

Controversy, like a Coke can, could be recycled. As the *Los Angeles Times* remarked: 'To a vast array of voters, the milk story was something new. If they had heard it before, it was so long ago they had forgotten it.'[47] The damage done to Christopher was immense. 'At that point George Christopher was thirty-six [per cent] and Ronald Reagan was thirty-nine in the Field poll,' Bagley recalled. 'From that point, Christopher went down ten points because of the diabolical Democratic attempt to get rid of [him].'[48] As Brown recalled: 'His polls went down. I think Reagan would have beaten him anyway, but Reagan slaughtered him in the Republican campaign.'[49] Christopher accepted that the material leaked to Pearson was true, but argued that it was irrelevant. 'In San Francisco the case was understood. But down south they could never understand it.' In addition, 'This violation was a misdemeanor ... not a felony, although my opponents ... construed it as a felony.' In retrospect, he felt that the incident demonstrated that modern politics was headed for the swamp. While behaviour of this sort from a Democrat did not surprise him, he felt betrayed by Reagan, who did not defend him. 'Brown used it, but Reagan didn't discourage it either.'[50] In truth, the pot was calling the kettle black. As the incident in Santa Monica had shown, Christopher was not lily-white, though the milk issue revealed that he was a great deal more vulnerable to the rough stuff than Reagan ever was.

Champion was unapologetic. 'The polls showed that Christopher was creeping up on Reagan quite successfully ... It's easy to see how at that time you would have thought that Christopher was going to probably be the one to fight.' He insisted that 'we did play a role in ... a smear campaign ... no question', but was adamant that 'we did ... nothing ... out of line.' The tactic had wide support within the Brown camp. 'Everybody ... knew what was going on, including the Governor.' A few colleagues thought it tactically unwise, 'but I don't think there was any basic disagreement that we were more concerned about Christopher than we were about Reagan. I don't think there was any basic feeling that what we were saying about Christopher was unfair or untrue.'[51] He insisted that the story needed to be told because it had a bearing on Christopher's fitness to govern. The problem with mudslinging, however, is that it leaves everyone dirty. The *Chronicle*, usually supportive of Brown, condemned 'the terrified Governor's ... tactic to excavate this dung heap of ancient and inconsequential charges in order to confuse Southern California voters who may never have heard of them before'.[52]

'I never wanted to bring it up', Bradley said, 'because I never thought Christopher was a threat. But I used to say that campaign policy depended on whose day off it was.'[53] In the end, the tactic backfired badly because it put paid to any hope of attracting moderate Republican support. Brown had always assumed that, if Reagan did win the primary, a significant chunk of Christopher supporters would switch to the Democrats. 'This destroyed all that,' Bradley discovered. 'We had planned ... to form a committee of Republicans for Brown that would really have some substance to it ... We never did get those people ... They just sort of stayed out.'[54] Champion agreed that it was a 'major miscalculation'. He concluded that, 'had Christopher lost and had we not been involved in that ... Christopher and his people would have supported Pat and Pat would have had the election.' While that seems far-fetched, there is no doubt that Brown's dirty tricks did persuade many moderates who might have switched sides to stay put. As Champion noted, 'Reagan played that very well ... played on the theme of Republican unity and this is the chance to win.'[55]

Up to the eve of the election Christopher kept repeating, 'I am the only Republican that can win in November.'[56] The polls had once supported that view, but now suggested otherwise. He kept shouting smear, but could not escape the fact that he had actually committed a crime. Leaving that aside, he was yesterday's man. His urbane style, once his greatest strength, looked decidedly old-fashioned in the glaring lights of television. For Reagan, on the other hand, the camera lights were a grow lamp. Peggy Whedon, producer of ABC's *Issues and Answers*, marvelled at how Reagan thrived on television. 'He was extremely poised, extremely charming. When the little red light goes on, everyone else freezes. Something happens. They get dry in the throat. Reagan knows what the little red light means.'[57] Christopher's campaign was also a mess. 'I had terrible management,' he admitted. 'I had no money.'[58] One particular incident illustrates perfectly the gulf between the two candidates. On the eve of the primary, Reagan appeared on television in a short, five-minute film cleverly drawn from his best campaign appearances. The spot was nothing more than a reiteration of soundbites from the black books, but it was slickly presented and mercifully short, which meant that it did not interrupt regular programming. Christopher, in contrast, used unedited and long-winded footage of his speeches in a fifteen-minute programme which cut into Johnny Carson's *Tonight Show*. Given a choice, most voters preferred Carson to Christopher. In the television age, they wanted bite-sized politics.

On the following day, 7 June 1966, Reagan annihilated Christopher by a margin of more than two to one: 1,417,623 votes to 675,683. He took 54 out of 58 California counties, thus demonstrating that his appeal was not limited to the south. Christopher had failed to develop a statewide campaign, assuming instead that his credentials as a moderate would be enough to sway sufficient support in his direction. The Reagan team had, in contrast, meticulously organized at precinct level, so that no voter was ignored. An army of volunteers spread the Reagan message and then made sure that potential supporters voted on election day. The non-politician showed his seasoned opponents how modern campaigns were supposed to be run.

# 8

# 'What Are You Going to Do About Berkeley?'

On 3 March 1965, at the corner of Bancroft and Telegraph in Berkeley, John Thompson sat down on a bench and paused to watch the crowds pass. Feeling bored, he decided it might be fun to get arrested. He took a piece of plain lined paper, folded it in half, then took a red felt pen and wrote a single word in capital letters – 'FUCK'. He held the paper up and waited to see what would happen.

His little gesture changed the course of California politics. Thompson inadvertently gave Ronald Reagan the perfect gift, an issue that superbly encapsulated the main themes of his populist campaign. His four-letter rebellion sparked a moral outrage that would propel Reagan to the statehouse.

Thompson had left New York a few months earlier searching for excitement amidst the Bay Area dissonance. The previous autumn, the Free Speech Movement (FSM) had thrown the Berkeley campus into turmoil and, in so doing, kicked off a nationwide student protest movement. For activist students around the country, Berkeley was Mecca. Thompson wasn't remotely political, nor was he a student, but he couldn't resist Berkeley's allure. 'Walking the streets in the days of the Free Speech Movement got you higher than a handfulla bennies,' he recalled. He was a wannabe poet in need of inspiration: 'I wanted to be a writer, but thought I had nothing to write about, so in my search for experience I took LSD, speed, downers and smoked pot, hitched all over the state of California, and later, had sex with any woman that would look twice at me.'[1] In short, Thompson was an ass.

His puerile act set loose a typical Berkeley uproar. On seeing the little sign with the single bad word, a big guy with a crew cut, bulging muscles and no neck started shouting at Thompson for insulting his girlfriend, who wasn't anywhere near. He ripped up the sign and threatened to break Thompson's neck if he persisted with his obscene gesture. Ignoring the hulk, Thompson made another sign. The next to object was a policeman. He argued with Thompson for a while, then arrested him for indecency and carted him off to jail. The entire 'demonstration' lasted less than half an hour.

The arrest of a student protester (even if he wasn't a student and there was no protest) was like a red rag to the activist community in the East Bay. Many were delighted at the prospect of a new issue over which to demonstrate. Within days, Thompson was heralded (or lambasted) as the founder of the Filthy Speech Movement. He and six friends styled themselves the Filthy Seven. Before long, signs advertised a 'Fuck Rally', while collections were made for a 'Fuck Defense Fund'. One prankster thought it would be fun to read *Lady Chatterley's Lover* to a police patrolman. The cop failed to see the humour. Another arrest.

In order to understand the impact of Thompson's stunt, it is essential to go back four years to a commencement speech Governor Brown gave at the University of Santa Clara. In that speech, he paid innocent homage to student protesters:

> Here is an honorable source of college spirit; here is a worthy, unifying and organizing principle for your whole campus life. I say: thank God for the spectacle of students picketing ... for students protesting and freedom-riding, for students listening

to society's dissidents, for students going out into the fields with our migratory workers, and marching off to jail with our segregated Negroes. At last we're getting somewhere. The colleges have become boot camps for citizenship – and citizen-leaders are marching out of them. For a while, it will be hard on us as administrators. Some students are going to be wrong, and some people will want to deny them the right to make mistakes. Administrators will have to wade through the angry letters and colleges will lose some donations. We Governors will have to face indignant caravans and elected officials bent on dictating to state college faculties. But let us stand up for our students and be proud of them. If America is still on the way up, it will welcome this new, impatient, critical crop of young gadflies. It will be fearful only of the complacent and passive.[2]

Speaking that day was Brown the person, not the politician. The speech is proof that he was a good and decent man who had an awkward habit of following his heart instead of his head. Unfortunately, by 1965, those gadflies had turned into a storm of locusts. Brown's noble words would forever haunt him.

The governor's liberal values could not withstand the intense pressure exerted by the FSM during the autumn of 1964. The leaders of that group – Mario Savio, Jack Weinberg and others – had spent the summer of 1964 working for the civil rights movement, attempting to register black voters in Mississippi – what came to be known as Freedom Summer. On their return to Berkeley that autumn, they discovered that the university had, in the interim, banned political campaigning within the boundaries of the campus. The irony of fighting for basic freedoms in the South only to be denied them at Berkeley proved impossible for Savio and company to ignore. From that seed, a nationwide student protest movement grew, helped by the rumblings from Vietnam.

Savio and Weinberg should have been heroes in Brown's eyes. The FSM was doing precisely what he had encouraged in

1961. Unfortunately, the people of California were not inclined to be as tolerant as their governor. The protests, they decided, were contemptuous, immoral, even treasonous. Brown could not ignore the storms of outrage. He had to be a politician, not a person – follow his head, not his heart. At first, he toed a careful line, arguing that it was up to the universities to handle campus disturbances in the way they saw fit. He feared that interference by the governor's office might be interpreted as an assault upon academic freedom. That was a typically liberal response and also one that was legally and intellectually sound. But these were no ordinary protests, nor ordinary times. The energy, endurance, determination and numerical strength of the FSM proved more than a match for the university's policing powers. As a result, Brown was forced to abandon his scruples on 3 December 1964. On that day, he approved a request by Alameda County District Attorney Edwin Meese to send police onto the campus to restore order. Meese's request had been buttressed by bogus allegations that the students were destroying public property. That gave Brown the justification he needed to bypass the university's own policing and disciplinary mechanisms. The university administration did not ask for outside help and did not want it, fearing (rightly so) that it would inflame the situation.

Brown's actions permanently changed the nature of the Berkeley problem and the state's involvement in it. Eight hundred arrests were made, each of them applauded by those outside the ivory tower. The governor's office received over 4,500 messages in response to the action, with 80 per cent praising Brown's decision. A typical message read: 'We appreciate and approve your stand. We have tried to raise our children in an old-fashioned way. We deplore the lack of respect for authority shown in a tax-supported university.'[3] Those three short sentences carried a huge weight of political meaning. Clearly, repressing freedom was a vote-winner: taxpayers trumped intellectuals. While Brown must have welcomed notes of support, their implications were ominous. He had walked into a trap, since the public would henceforth expect an aggressive response by the governor's office to *every* instance of unrest. Furthermore, as the radical journal *Ramparts* commented:

> By invading the university, Brown said to Californians, in effect, that student demonstrators are the kind of people you send cops after; and by failing to exert his leadership ... Brown allows Californians – and other Americans – to regard Berkeley as a symbol of wild-eyed political irresponsibility and sexual license, instead of one of the great intellectual assets of America.[4]

Brown had unintentionally embroiled himself in an anti-intellectual crusade that he could never win. He had inadvertently transformed the Berkeley problem from one about civil liberties and academic freedom into one about morality. While the governor derived short-term gain from his assertion of authority, it was Reagan who would benefit from this transformation. Berkeley was the perfect issue for the citizen-politician's populist crusade.

While the public enjoyed watching long-haired student protesters getting clubbed by police, the mass arrest of the FSM was not a spectacle that could easily be repeated. The students were clever; they knew precisely how to court attention without bringing down the heavy hand of the law. In any case, the autonomy of the university was still sacred: Brown had to give campus officials the chance to deal with problems in their own way. He could not invade every time a student held up a picket sign, even if that was precisely what the public demanded. The issue was complicated further when the university sensibly decided to grant the students rights that were constitutionally theirs. Protesting on campus became legal. FSM claimed a victory and, on campus at least, those arrested became martyrs to a noble cause.

The FSM had not bothered to define what it meant by free speech, because the issue seemed pedantic amidst life-changing events like civil rights and the Vietnam War. Thompson, however, forced the FSM to consider definitions, a dangerous task. Some radical activists took the view that all speech should be protected, a principle they were eager to defend at the barricades. Unfortunately, that meant backing Thompson, who was, by common consent, an attention-seeking jerk. One activist, Lee Felsenstein, was furious that a single prankster now threatened all that the FSM had achieved. 'My feeling on the Filthy Speech Movement was, "Oh, shit! These guys are ruining it for everybody!"' He felt that Thompson and his friends 'should be taken up a dark alley and have the shit beaten out of them'.[5]

Thompson's action transformed what had been dignified protest into a circus spectacle. His actions demonstrate a universal truth, namely that the greatest weakness of student protest is that it is conducted by students, who are prone to immature, unpredictable, attention-seeking behaviour. His was not the only puerile stunt to take place at Berkeley in 1965, but, coming as it did so close to the FSM victory, and connected as it was to the contentious issues of free speech and morality, the effect was catastrophic. Just when the student movement had achieved a notable victory, Thompson dragged it into the gutter. Those, like Reagan, who peddled horror stories about radical revolution now had an easily identifiable monster.

After much agonizing, the FSM executive released a statement a week after Thompson's arrest:

> Only in the recent controversy over 'obscene' words can students be said not to have acted responsibly. The FSM did not initiate or support this controversy. We regret both that the students involved acted in an unfortunate manner and that the police and some administrators chose to escalate the issue and endanger campus peace rather than permit student interest in the subject

to wane. The problem is now in the courts, where it belongs. Any disciplinary action by the University will be directly contrary to the principles we supported last semester.[6]

Though carefully worded, the statement was unlikely to deter the hounds baying for the FSM's blood. Savio wanted simply to ignore the problem, in order to underline FSM's non-involvement. His colleagues, however, convinced him that the issue had to be confronted given the group's commitment to the sanctity of free speech. As Weinberg argued, 'We fought for free speech, we didn't fight for *responsible* free speech.'[7] Savio reluctantly agreed that if speech was to be free, all speech had to be free. 'My position was that we should take a stand on the issue of due process,' he recalled. He realized, however, that he had walked into a trap. 'The issue seemed too abstract to people. People didn't want to associate themselves with the problem of obscenity.'[8] For the mild-mannered Savio, this was cruel irony. A few months earlier, he had taken his shoes off before standing on a police car during a protest outside Sproul Hall, because he did not want to damage the car. He was arguably the most dignified, earnest and mature of all Sixties student protesters. Yet here he was, having to defend a stupid gesture by an immature punk.

A week after Thompson's prank, UC President Clark Kerr and Acting Chancellor Martin Meyerson both resigned when the Board of Regents put pressure on them to expel members of the Filthy Speech Movement. The regents, in typical knee-jerk fashion, had failed to take into account that, in truth, there was no such movement and Thompson, who was not a student, was untouchable. Since the governor was an ex-officio member of the Board of Regents, the tremors from Thompson's act now rumbled towards Sacramento. Brown was caught in the worst of all possible worlds: in an election year, he got blamed for the unrest but could do little to prevent it. When the Filthy Speech crisis erupted, he frantically went into damage control, attempting to direct all blame toward Thompson and his fellow pranksters. That was an entirely appropriate response, but not one likely to impress the public. 'I think it is a terrible shame', he remarked, 'that a few thoughtless troublemakers can hurt the reputation of the greatest University in the world and cause this brilliant president and hard-working chancellor to resign.'[9] Kerr and Meyerson were eventually persuaded to withdraw their resignations, but they could not wash away the ugly stain that the incident left on their reputations. Kerr decried the 'continuing and destructive degradation of freedom into license',[10] but his critics (of whom there were many) saw a man determined to defend obscenity on campus. As Savio understood, the ordinary citizen of California had little patience with the nuances of law.

Enter Reagan. He had already spoken out against the 'lawlessness' on the Berkeley campus, but had to be careful because the FSM protests had been remarkably good-tempered and the issue – free speech – was sacred to most Americans. The principle of academic freedom also militated against political interference. As Spencer recalled, 'the university system was almost an untouchable.'[11] Thompson changed that in an instant: suddenly making it open season on student protesters and university administrators. The problem, Reagan was now able to argue,

> began a year ago when so-called 'free speech advocates', who in truth have no appreciation of freedom, were allowed to assault and humiliate an officer of the law. This was the moment when the ringleaders should have been taken by the scruff of the neck and thrown off the campus permanently.[12]

That was precisely the response the public wanted to hear, even though it was nonsense. The issue was perfect for Reagan because it harmonized so well with the populist themes of his campaign, namely law and order, strong leadership, sensible taxation, traditional values and morality. Ironically, Savio and his friends revered the same Enlightenment thinkers that Reagan worshipped, the difference being that, when they referred to Jefferson, Locke or Paine, they actually understood what they meant. That was the benefit of a good education.

The issue was perfect also because Reagan was free to say what he liked, without having to act upon his bluster. As Roberts remarked, student unrest:

> probably ... served a major purpose in getting the average electorate together and out to the polls, and wanting to do something. In other words, civil unrest is never really a happy situation. Those who were not involved, which represent the majority of the public, wanted somebody who was going to deal with it a little more aggressively and strongly. So I think that ... helped Ronald Reagan quite a bit.[13]

The university, a public institution financed by taxpayers' money, was particularly susceptible to Reagan's diatribe. He argued that Kerr and Meyerson, as public servants, were failing in their duty to the taxpayers and in their responsibility to provide a good education to the vast majority of students who did not indulge in protest. Reagan understood that the best way to get a truck driver angry was to remind him that he was paying for Savio to read Proust.

Two months after the 'FUCK' episode, Berkeley students provided more fuel for Reagan's moral outrage. In May 1965, a 24-hour teach-in, organized by the Vietnam Day Committee (VDC), was proudly advertised as a carnival of protest. Savio had given way to the likes of Jerry Rubin, the self-confessed P. T. Barnum of student protest. His goal was to be 'fucking obnoxious', something he achieved in spades.[14] At this time, President Johnson's handling of the Vietnam crisis was still immensely popular, therefore protest of any sort was bound to annoy those who insisted on unquestioning support for the government in time of war. The VDC, however, thanks to its outrageous style, also managed to alienate those with misgivings about the war. The committee followed up Vietnam Day with a number of high-profile actions, including attempts to stop troop trains headed for the Oakland army base. The trains were never stopped, but dignified protest was dragged further into the gutter. A splinter group organized a blood drive for the Viet Cong, while others counselled students on clever ways to avoid the draft. Meanwhile, students exercised their freedom in other ways by overt experimentation with drugs and sex. Spencer and Roberts could not believe their luck.

The antics of the VDC and the Filthy Speech Movement allowed Reagan to tar all student protest with the same brush. The students' dogged campaigning on behalf of civil rights and freedom of speech could be ignored and Berkeley instead dismissed as a cesspool of youthful hedonism. When asked on *Meet the Press* whether he equated the Free Speech Movement with the Vietnam Day Committee and the Filthy Speech Movement, Reagan insisted that he did not, but then cleverly implied that he did. He argued that 'there seemed to be a great amalgam in some of the demonstrations of the various groups. Whether they were carrying on their own cause or not, it almost reached the point of demonstrating for demonstration's sake.'[15] In other words, expel the lot of them.

Student unrest had not figured prominently in Reagan's early planning sessions, before his actual declaration. Its importance was instead revealed while out on the stumps during Q&A sessions:

> Wherever I was in the state … mountain, desert, seashore, the situation at Berkeley and in the university came up. This is how this became an issue … When the hands would go up, the minute you opened the question period, the first question was [about] Berkeley, and you'd answer it. You'd see twenty hands then go down – that was their question. You knew that this was the number one thing on … people's minds.[16]

Even the question itself would get applause. 'If in '66 there was a buzz word ... it was Berkeley,' Fred Dutton, one of Brown's senior advisers, recalled. 'Berkeley, in our polls, was the most negative word you could mention.'[17]

Reagan insisted that 'the people' made student unrest into an issue. He merely responded to their clamour:

> the opposition tried to make out that I was persecuting the university for political purposes. I wasn't. I had never mentioned Berkeley as an incident, or as an issue, until those question and answer sessions ... I learned that the people of this state had a very, very deep and great pride in the university system. Because of that, they were very emotionally involved and disturbed with what was happening to what they thought was the great pride of California. My own position was born of the answers I gave to those questions.[18]

The talented populist knows how to respond to public outcry. 'We jumped on it as an issue,' Spencer confirmed. 'I think Reagan escalated it into an issue and it started showing up in the polls.'[19] Having gauged the level of public discontent, Reagan gave student unrest appropriate prominence in his declaration speech on 4 January 1966:

> Back at the turn of the century, we embarked on a master plan of education. It was a truly bi-partisan effort above political rivalry and differences. Its principal architects were a Democrat Assemblywoman and a Republican Assemblyman. Believing in that plan, Californians taxed themselves at a rate higher than any other American to build a great University. But it takes more than dollars and stately buildings, or do we no longer think it necessary to teach self-respect, self-discipline and respect for law and order? Will we allow a great University to be brought to its knees by a noisy, dissident minority? Will we meet their neurotic vulgarities with vacillation and weakness, or will we tell

those entrusted with administering the University we expect them to enforce a code based on decency, common sense and dedication to the high and noble purpose of the University?[20]

The rhetorical questions were essentially a call to arms. Reagan did not have to say precisely what he would do about the problem, since the public seemed satisfied with noise. 'There was an especially hysterical element in the psychology of southern California in the fall of '66,' Dutton felt. 'If you look at Reagan's TV spots or a recording of the speech he'd often give, it was his Berkeley references which always got the explicit, noisy reaction ... That was where the cutting edge of emotions were.'[21]

Reagan illustrated perfectly the American people's confusion about the meaning of freedom. 'We stand on the only island of freedom left in the world,' he told the Detroit Economic Club in typically apocalyptic tone. 'There is no place to run. If we fail, we face telling our children and our children's children what it was we found more precious than freedom.'[22] The Creative Society was supposed to set people free. The steadily expanding federal government was presented as a constant threat to freedom. Yet Reagan's concept of freedom was based on emotion, not law. He, like most Americans, did not think seriously about definitions or parameters. The idea that the free state should encourage and uphold nonconformity was abhorrent to him. It was so much easier to talk about how wonderful it was to be free than to explain what it meant. 'Governments don't produce freedom,' he argued. 'People have to take freedom from government and continually struggle to keep it.'[23] Reagan didn't seem to notice that the students were doing precisely that. He sensed no contradiction in placing limits on freedom in what was supposed to be a free society. 'Certain bench rules' had to be observed, he insisted when questioned on ABC's *Issues and Answers*. Chief among them was 'the right to privacy'. If a protester in a public place uses obscene language, 'I have no right to tell him he can't use that language. I do have a right to tell him that he can lower his voice because my family shouldn't have to listen to it.' Reagan had cleverly reduced a very big and complicated issue into a very simple and personal one, an affront to decency that everyone could understand.[24]

Small incidents were given exaggerated importance. For instance, a VDC-sponsored dance on the Berkeley campus provided Reagan with the perfect opportunity to moralize:

> The hall was entirely dark except for the light from two movie screens. On these screens the nude torsos of men and women were portrayed, from time to time, in suggestive positions and movements. Three rock and roll bands played simultaneously. The smell of marijuana was thick throughout the hall. There were signs that some of those present had taken dope. There were indications of other happenings which cannot be mentioned.[25]

That last sentence was a clever rhetorical device. It encouraged listeners to indulge their wildest imagination while allowing Reagan to emphasize his personal purity. He loved to preach from the edge of depravity's swamp. On another occasion he referred to 'sexual orgies ... so vile I cannot describe it to you'.[26] The decadence, he implied, was too deep for decent people even to imagine.

Whether by conspiracy or accident, the dance caught the attention of the California Senate Sub-Committee on Un-American Activities:

> According to reports obtained from law-enforcement officers the sweet, acrid odor of marijuana pervaded the area, many of the dancers were obviously intoxicated, and there was evidence of nausea in the lavatories, halls and other portions of the premises. Young people were, according to one official report, 'seen standing against the walls or lying on the floors and steps in a dazed condition, with glazed eyes consistent with a condition

of being under the influence of narcotics'. Sexual misconduct was blatant.[27]

Clearly, the committee members had never been to a campus party, or had conveniently forgotten the ritual. Mundane misbehaviour was elevated into a serious threat to social order, probably inspired by communist agents who lurked on campus. The committee promised that it would uncover 'how a minority of Communist leaders managed to bring this great institution to its knees'.[28] This alarmed Kerr and Roger Heyns (the Berkeley chancellor), both of whom suspected a calculated effort to besmirch the reputation of the university. Heyns, in particular, questioned where the committee got its information. 'The report ... presents an account which purports to be based on official law enforcement reports ... It is unclear what these sources might be.'[29]

The committee report, regardless of its reliability or provenance, provided more grist for Reagan's mill. 'A small minority of beatniks, radicals and filthy speech advocates have brought shame to ... a great University,' he claimed. They had sheltered under the umbrella of academic freedom. 'What in heaven's name does "academic freedom" have to do with rioting, with anarchy, with attempts to destroy the primary purpose of the University which is to educate our young people?'[30] In fact, academic freedom had nothing to do with students protesting or staging a controversial dance. Yet Reagan insisted that it was the root cause of campus anarchy. He intentionally confused the issues of academic freedom and freedom of speech, using them interchangeably, in order to ensnare a larger group of culprits. Thus, speaking in San Jose on 2 April 1966, he argued that academic freedom 'stops short of vulgarity and obscenity forced upon those that don't want to hear it and ... freedom of speech, when some Americans are fighting and dying for their country, must stop short of lending comfort and aid to the enemy'.[31] By this means, Reagan was able to transform a single dance or a scribbled expletive into threats to domestic tranquillity and national security. Likewise, the blame was shifted from puerile students to incompetent administrators and, from there, to the governor's office. 'There is a leadership gap and morality and decency gap in Sacramento,' he shouted.[32]

Reagan realized that there was little to gain from merely lambasting militant students. If, however, those students were supported (or, better, 'indoctrinated') by radical (or, better, 'communist') professors, the problem was then magnified and his call for tough action would seem more appropriate. And if the radical professors sought shelter behind liberal concepts of academic freedom, the list of enemies would grow even longer. The UC administration could then be blamed for failing to 'enforce a code based on decency, common sense and dedication to the high and noble purpose of the University' and Brown castigated for his 'policy of appeasement'.[33] That word had enormous resonance for a generation of voters raised in the 1930s. Though Reagan was, quite clearly, using the university for his own political purposes, he did this under the guise of fighting political interference in campus affairs.

> I charge that there has been political interference which has resulted in the appeasement of campus malcontents and filthy-speech advocates under the pretense of preserving academic freedom. Actually this policy of appeasement has been dictated by political expedience in this election year in the hope of sweeping the problem under the rug. This will, of course, be denied.[34]

The message sounded appropriately grave but did not, under close examination, make any sense. That did not matter, since these statements were not supposed to be deconstructed – all they required to be effective was a sufficient number of apocalyptic buzzwords. Reagan suggested that the root cause of problems at the university was that it had become a training ground for socialists and communists. 'The so-called "New Left"', he argued, 'has used the University, even in the classrooms, as a political propaganda base with no pretense of allowing balanced discussion and divergent points of view.'[35]

Had Reagan's assault been confined to the New Left, its success would have been limited. His growth as a politician can be measured in the way he widened the issue into something more fundamental. When the FSM first erupted in the autumn of 1964, his instincts were to attack radicals as communist stooges. Yet such an attack appealed only to extremists. By presenting student unrest as, more importantly, a moral problem, Reagan rendered it general – political without being party-political. Working-class Democrats, in particular, found his moral condemnation appealing, especially given their resentment about paying for a state provision from which they derived no direct benefit. Student unrest was eventually turned into a symptom of comprehensive social decline:

> There isn't anything that we can't do, and that includes solving the one overriding issue of this campaign ... the issue besetting not only California, but also the nation ... the issue that overshadows and colors all others. It is the issue of simple morality. Who among us doesn't feel concern for the deterioration of old standards, the abandonment of principles time-tested and proven in our climb from the swamp to the stars? Today voices are raised urging change for change's sake. Individuals have privilege, but not responsibility. While some young Americans fight and die for their country, others send blood and money to the enemy, and what is, in truth, treason, is called their right to freedom of expression ... Is this the way we want it to be? We can change it. We can start a prairie fire that will sweep the nation and prove we are number one in more than size and crime and taxes. If this is a dream, it's a good dream, as big and golden as California itself.[36]

The tactic paid off handsomely. Reagan was inundated with letters praising his stand against moral decline. A typical note lauded him for the 'cleanness and decency' of his campaign and for 'return[ing] a semblance of honor and morality to government'. Continuing on that theme, it concluded: 'In your final speech at the S. F. Cow Palace you covered pretty thoroughly all the parts of our state administration which so sorely need to be corrected, particularly those that leave our children with no decent standards for living – welfare and our colleges – and hope that by correcting those we can lift the morals of some of the parents.'[37]

While the issue itself was widened, blame for it was carefully targeted – at Brown. Reagan's complaints about a 'leadership gap' had sufficient credibility to cause the governor serious problems. Dutton felt that while Reagan handled the Berkeley issue superbly, his success was compounded by the fact that Brown handled it so badly.

> Part of the problem ... was Pat's own personality trait of appearing to consult everybody, delaying and thus, sometimes unfairly, seeming weak and vacillating ... on Berkeley for example, he [at first] didn't want to do anything. He had certain sympathies, and he respected the university and got along well with President Clark Kerr. Then, when he was politically getting eaten up alive, particularly by the *San Francisco Examiner* and the more sensationalist media, he precipitously reacted the other way, really losing both groups.[38]

Brown's problems, Dutton felt, arose from the fact that he acted like a governor, not a politician. The governor in him could, in truth, do little about the Berkeley problem since the autonomy of the institution severely limited his power to interfere. Nevertheless, given the importance of this issue to the public in a visceral sense, it was essential to appear to do something. Brown had to act assertive, even if it was just an act.

He needed to shout. By the time Berkeley became a problem, he seemed to have lost the ability to synthesize a semblance of control. 'It's part of the art of politics and government,' Dutton concluded, 'and nobody does it terribly well over the long run of incumbency.'[39]

Reagan, on the other hand, was a master of ersatz authority. The technique often involved misleading the public with false statistics and exaggerated alarm. A press release on 9 September 1966 claimed:

> There has been a 20% drop in undergraduate applications. This will be denied, but only because the University has changed the cut-off date and allowed previously unqualified students to fill the vacancies. There has been a drop in qualified graduate students. Professors are leaving the University at a rate of three times as great as the normal turnover. There are reports, too, from recent graduates that employers are leery about hiring them because of the University's new reputation for radicalism.[40]

No evidence was given to support any of these bogus claims and none has subsequently been found. Watching from the sidelines, Champion marvelled at Reagan's ability to construct a political platform out of cardboard certainties:

> He seems so pleasant and reasonable and a little knowledgeable – knowledgeable in a cynical sense about how people are behaving, or his opponents are not but without being threatening, without denouncing. He's a walking, talking Reader's Digest including the use of statistics, which aren't particularly germane, which often are sort of factitious in character.
>
> They sound like great facts, as if they're very revealing, and they're really a bunch of junk. But they're awfully hard to deal with or to refute. And they give an impression.[41]

Roger Boas, an aide to Brown, recalled how Reagan's tactics caused immense frustration because to deny his allegations meant to side with the university, which did not look good: 'Reagan sort of sided with the ... billy club swingers at University of California when the riots took place. That seemed to drag the Democratic Party in head first and I had to speak for it. But the work seemed onerous, hard to control, hard to manage, and hard to target.'[42] Champion recalled a similar frustration. Reagan had only to mention events at Berkeley and he could inspire the reaction he desired. 'He didn't need to get indignant about them. They were enough to remind people of what they didn't like about the society and to make them feel that Brown was not doing a good job.'[43]

An internal UC investigation into the VDC dance concluded that 'there appears to have been several instances of genuinely unseemly behaviour ... but certainly not warranting the political outcry which ensued.'[44] Heyns regretted the way an entire university was tarred by the brush of a few miscreants. As he pointed out, Reagan conveniently ignored the fact that Berkeley had, despite the unrest, been voted the 'best balanced distinguished university in the country' by the American Council of Education in 1966, finishing ahead of Harvard, Princeton, Yale and Stanford.[45] That success was smothered by lurid stories of the misadventures of Berkeley radicals printed in the *San Francisco Examiner*, *Oakland Tribune* and *San Diego Union*. A forlorn editorial in the *Sacramento Bee* lamented how:

> the public has been saturated with the misadventures of the few at Berkeley. It has read of beatniks stumping the campus, of LSD parties, of promiscuity, even of the occasional Communist preachment by an infiltrator. It has become so concerned with the one that has strayed, so to speak, it has lost sight of the 90 and 9, the thousands of others – the rule, not the exception – who represent the real student body on the campus; the solid,

responsible core of young pursuing an education at one of the world's best-ranked schools.[46]

The paper warned that 'the public is looking for easy answers in all things, these days, and one of those easy answers is to burn down the house to flush out a few roaches.'[47]

Brown made a similar appeal. 'We have the best university in the United States,' he pleaded. 'We have the best administration and the only thing that can possibly hurt [it] is a political witch hunt.'[48] Yet the governor, under pressure from Reagan, still felt obliged to ask the regents to investigate the Berkeley problem. Before they could do so, however, Reagan lambasted the proposal as 'a straight cover-up. What kind of political nonsense is it to ask the Board of Regents to investigate a situation in which it may be involved?' Reagan promised instead that, if elected, he would appoint John McCone, the former CIA chief, to head a commission to investigate why 'the campus has become a rallying point for Communism and a center of sexual misconduct'. Since McCone had earlier headed an investigation into the Watts riots, this was Reagan's way of establishing equivalence. A group calling itself 'University Community for Brown' bitterly objected to this blatant scare-mongering:

> In Watts, a leaderless mob caused the loss of 37 lives, and of millions in property damage, with no apparent principle involved beyond anarchic protests; in Berkeley no lives were lost or threatened, no property was damaged, and the basic principle involved was that students might have the same rights on campus as off.[49]

The McCone idea came from Holden, who proposed it to Reagan without first clearing it with Spencer-Roberts. The latter considered it too aggressive, but, once released, it could not be retracted. In the same breath, Reagan vowed to implement a 'code of conduct that would force [faculty] to serve as examples of good behavior and decency for the young people in their charge'. Chancellors would be told 'that it is your job to administer the University properly and if you don't we will find someone who will'. At campuses across the state, these proposals sounded disturbingly close to the loyalty oath controversy that had rocked the university in the 1950s. When asked on 6 May 1966 whether he would fire Kerr, Reagan replied: 'If the facts bear it out, yes.'[50] It did not matter that a governor had no such powers. The tough talk, however spurious, served its purpose: it embarrassed Brown and enhanced Reagan's reputation as a man of action. His supporters cared little about the nuances of higher-education policy, what they wanted was a governor who would kick ass. Reagan had become the hero of taxpayers outraged by campus unrest. Yet that outrage was his creation.

Though the issue was handled well, it nevertheless exposed the fault lines between Spencer-Roberts and BASICO. Plog and Holden actually believed the rhetoric Reagan spouted; they were genuinely convinced that a communist conspiracy existed at Berkeley. A draft statement they prepared argued that academic freedom stopped short of action 'designed to embarrass our government's foreign policy or promote an alien ideology'. The final version, incorporated into a campaign pamphlet and undoubtedly vetted by Spencer and Roberts, toned down the message, referring instead to 'beatniks, and advocates of sexual orgies, drug usage and filthy speech', but not to communists.[51] The issue arose again when Dr Hardin Jones, Professor of Medical Physics at Berkeley, approached BASICO, explaining that he wanted to help Reagan become governor in order to save Berkeley from communists who were imposing their dogma on students. Jones told lurid stories of how incoming freshmen were subjected to brainwashing by communist graduate students intent on undermining parental good sense. Jones alleged that the problem started at the top since Kerr's wife was a 'card-carrying communist'.

Jones was a great physicist but a political lunatic. His febrile delusions nevertheless harmonized perfectly with what Plog and Holden wanted to believe. Convinced that they were on to a winner, they were fully prepared to launch a McCarthyite witch-hunt in the middle of a gubernatorial campaign. They proposed making a five-minute film on the Berkeley problem, to be shown on prime-time television. While film of rioting students rolled in the background, Reagan would present his plans for the university, flanked by Jones and other eminent professors. When the idea was presented to Spencer, he vetoed it in his customarily abrupt manner. The film was symptomatic of the aggressiveness BASICO encouraged and Spencer dreaded. Holden claimed that the film was never made. Spencer insisted that it was. 'I must tell you it was a hairy, hairy film. They didn't even talk to us.' As he recalled,

> We killed it. We sat and we looked at the thing and just turned to Holmes Tuttle and said, 'Hey, that's not going on the air.' I mean they had gotten some great clips from police libraries – it was a brutal show. We had that issue under control. Reagan was on the right side of that issue. We didn't have to go out and do wild things about it.
>   Pat Brown was the incumbent governor and ... had to pay the price for Berkeley, but these people wanted to overstate the case, and we wouldn't let them, and Reagan stuck with us.[52]

Spencer was right: there was no need for such a film. The students were doing a good job destroying Brown. When they demonstrated, his poll ratings plummeted. 'The university thing drove us nuts,' Kline recalled. 'It was just utterly strange. All these things happening around us and why couldn't they be controlled?'[53] As Champion understood, Reagan had only to raise the issue and then offer a dignified response and the voters would migrate toward him. Plog and Holden had trouble understanding that subtlety. After the film was killed, the obsessively suspicious Holden became even more convinced that Spencer and Roberts were trying to sabotage the campaign.

On 12 October, a BASICO memo advised that: 'If the disorders boil into public prominence again, before the election, on balance it would be good for our campaign.' There was, however, the danger that serious unrest would allow Brown to act tough, as he had in late 1964. The memo warned that 'there are indications [the issue] is being heated up just so Brown can kick a few people off the campus and be a hero to the uninformed public.' This seems unlikely given that Brown had, by this stage, decided that Berkeley was an embarrassment and the less attention paid to it the better. Plog and Holden nevertheless suggested that:

> Some prediction of these disorders before they happen and emphasis on Brown's ineptitude in dealing with higher education at Berkeley, and revelation that his statements that 'Nothing is wrong with Berkeley' are false, may put him in a defensive position so he cannot capitalise on action he may be forced to take in the next several weeks. Since Berkeley and Higher Education are one of the public's greatest concerns, Brown cannot be allowed to, at this late date, pre-empt the role of saving the University from the radicals and the dissidents.[54]

Heeding this advice, Reagan turned up the heat on the 18th by urging the Berkeley Student Non-Violent Coordinating Committee (SNCC) to cancel a meeting scheduled for 29 October, at which the black activist Stokely Carmichael was scheduled to speak. He also sent a telegram to Carmichael reminding him that 'It is imperative that our election November 8 be held in an atmosphere of calm and goodwill. Your appearance on the Berkeley campus so soon before the election will stir strong emotions and could possibly do damage to both parties.'[55] The messages to SNCC and to Carmichael were released to all the major California papers, which was precisely the intention:

Reagan was baiting an already angry bear. No self-respecting radical group would bow to this type of pressure, yet by going ahead with the rally SNCC essentially demonstrated that Reagan's alarm was justified. Brown justifiably complained that Reagan was being intentionally inflammatory. 'Carmichael and his black power friends ... don't want peaceful progress. They want panic in the streets and publicity, and Mr. Reagan serves their purpose by helping give them both.'[56]

During his speech on Vietnam Day, the activist Paul Krassner, editor of the *Realist*, warned the crowd not to get too carried away by the energy generated on a single day of protest: 'when I speak at a college and then I go away, I fly, and I look out. There's a lot of *them*. You know, [the ones] who really *like* Ed Sullivan. It's very frightening. I mean, they aren't the extremists.'[57] Reagan understood precisely what Krassner meant. In the minds of most Californians, the student protesters were the real extremists, a group of self-important kids addicted to sex, drugs and social disorder. The liberal establishment in California had long tolerated the excesses at the university because the good massively outweighed the bad. Berkeley's international reputation seemed, on balance, a huge credit to the state. For Reagan, however, that was not enough to excuse campus excesses. He was not interested in what outsiders thought about the state or the university. He was interested only in Krassner's '*them*'. A typical response came in a letter to the *Chronicle*. 'Hooray for Reagan,' Mrs Rose Black wrote.

> If students have a little tuition to pay, it would be that much less of their summer earnings that they'd have for spending on LSD, cigarettes, beer, gasoline and clothes which I can't afford (and my husband is a good provider). If Reagan can make so much sense without experience, just think how proficient he'd be with it.[58]

Clearly, Reagan was in perfect harmony with his target audience – the Ed Sullivan watchers.

Reagan's onslaught against Berkeley was two-pronged. It was, obviously, an attack upon Brown, whose weakness, it was claimed, had encouraged campus lawlessness. But it was also an attack on the California higher-education system and, as such, unashamedly anti-intellectual. The system had, he argued, failed the heavily burdened taxpayer who financed the universities and the parents who entrusted their children to these institutions. Reagan made a direct appeal to those voters who had not had the benefit of a university education and who resented funding students who seemed more interested in making trouble than in bettering themselves. When the university hit back by accusing Reagan of impinging academic freedom, this merely underlined the elitist nature of the ivory tower – how out of touch it was with Reagan's common people.

Reagan could say what he liked about campus unrest without having to demonstrate the logic or feasibility of his pronouncements. For this reason, there is little point in trying to find a consistent line in what he proposed. On the one hand he attacked academic freedom for encouraging the atmosphere of protest, yet he also promised to 'protect this indispensable freedom, a freedom, like the freedom of the press, that is the heritage and the right of free people'. He put forth proposals which, if implemented, would have constituted significant political interference into the university's affairs, whilst at the same time castigating Brown for 'injecting partisan politics into the running of the University'. As evidence, he cited the fact that Dutton was both a regent and Brown's campaign manager, which was a 'violation of Article IX, clause nine of the State Constitution'.[59] The statement was uttered with sufficient authority to ward off a challenge – he undoubtedly realized that his listeners would have no idea what Article IX, clause nine actually said, but would be impressed with a person who claimed to know. Once he became governor, those technicalities became important and he found that the aggressive action he had promised was neither legal nor appropriate. As Dutton explained, 'the person who had the responsibility – Pat – had to see the problem more in grays than his outside political critics. Pat had the grays and Reagan had the black and whites.'[60]

Brown's respect for the university and for the liberal principles it embodied inhibited his ability to act. 'He identified with it,' Dutton recalled. 'He had been a night law school student and had never gone to university. It was not only that he admired the university, it was something very big that he had missed.' Reagan, in contrast, had no warm feelings toward the University of California. The UC system was the breeding ground of those intellectual elites who used their intelligence to hoodwink the common man. He used words like 'brats', 'freaks' and 'kooks' when describing the protesters, in order to emphasize their alien nature. It was not the duty of the taxpayer, he argued, 'to subsidize intellectual curiosity'.[61]

As he was fond of saying, 'My idea of higher education is four years on a campus with red brick walls and you leave with a tear in your eye.'[62] He had attended Eureka College, a Christian-oriented liberal arts institution with a student population of just 187. For him, education was never about intellectual enrichment, but rather about personal advancement. He once told his fellow students that if he wasn't making $5,000 a year within five years of graduation, 'I'll consider these four years here wasted.'[63] His romantic view of higher education on the Eureka model clashed violently with the 'multi-versity' envisaged by Kerr: in other words, a world-class institution supplying cutting-edge research to corporate and government clients, while still managing to teach tens of thousands of students. During the campaign, however, it was discovered that Reagan had led a student strike at Eureka, organized in reaction to proposed budget cuts. When this contradiction was pointed out to him, he managed, in typical Reagan style, to turn it to his advantage. The action, he argued, was supported by all the students, the entire faculty and most of the administration:

we must have been right. What you call a strike is the students just simply stayed home from classes, but I could contrast that with beatnik picketing and the demonstrations and the unlawful conduct of these present demonstrations over outside issues not really dealing with the University to a responsible group that every day met and studied and kept up on their school work ... This is like comparing Castro's take-over of Cuba with the American Revolution.[64]

Reagan insisted that his action, far from disrupting the college, brought it closer together. It resulted in 'the most tightly knit groups ever to graduate from Eureka ... Campus spirit bloomed. A remarkably close bond with the faculty developed.'[65] Never mind that his description of events at Eureka, and in particular his alleged role in them, do not accord with the surviving evidence or the testimony of his fellow students. Reagan often confused history with allegory. Facts were mere nuisance when they got in the way of edifying myths.

Reagan could not understand, or pretended not to understand, why Berkeley could not be more like Eureka. This coloured his judgement, not only of the protesters, but also of the entire student body. 'If they had any pride in their own school,' he explained, 'they should have told the protesters "Stop demeaning our university." It bothered me. As I say, I had gone to a school where students used to feel a kind of responsibility for the institution, it was theirs.'[66] His folksy 1930s version of school spirit was completely inappropriate to a giant world-class university in the 1960s. Nevertheless, it resonated beautifully with those outside the campus who, like Reagan, considered student unrest a personal affront.

The issue of public higher education lends itself perfectly to a populist campaign because it is something paid for by the multitude but enjoyed by an elitist minority. The burden is tolerated if the investment seems to offer a reasonable return. In the mid-1960s, however, the dividends were difficult for many taxpayers to discern. Reagan cast himself as the people's protector, always putting their interests before those of the university. 'I think the Governor, as a member of the Board of Regents, has a little more responsibility just as a member of the Board,' he argued. 'I think he must feel that he is speaking on behalf of the electorate with 18 million people.'[67]

'Campus unrest at Berkeley was a great issue,' Spencer admitted. No other campaign topic attracted such a straightforward, non-complex and unanimous response. As Dutton recalled:

> the polls at the time and every study we had said the biggest single reactive word in California then was not 'blacks' or 'Watts' or 'Vietnam'. It was 'Berkeley'. Berkeley at that stage meant longhairs, drugs, lack of order or even tidiness, hostility, sit-ins, not just the Free Speech Movement and kids being dragged out of Sproul Hall.[68]

This made it easy for Reagan. Because student radicals were perceived to be dangerously left wing, Reagan, by opposing them, rendered his conservatism mainstream. In contrast, Brown, who felt obliged to defend the university against Reagan's onslaught, was revealed in the worst possible light. '[Brown] was getting politically eaten up alive, particularly by the *San Francisco Examiner* and the more sensationalist media,' Dutton recalled. He felt that Brown, in contrast to Reagan, 'just never, at an intuitive as well as explicit level, handled the Berkeley issue well in '66'.[69] John S. Galbraith, a university regent and Brown supporter, summed up perfectly what happened in this election: 'Reagan promised to clean up the University, and so that was the end of Brown.'[70]

As Dutton suggested, Berkeley was an emotive issue and Reagan was perfectly tuned to those emotions. More than any other issue in the campaign, this one belonged to him. 'I went to him one night,' Spencer recalled.

We were in Fresno or someplace, and I said, 'Ron, the way you keep talking about Berkeley doesn't even show up in the polling data.' He says, 'It's going to.' This shows you, this guy understood the communications and the power of media.

By God, he pounded it and pounded it. This was without a big TV ad campaign. This is just one guy running around the state of California kicking the hell out of the hippies in Berkeley. Pretty soon on the polling data, he had 7 points, 9 points, 10 points, 15 points, 20 points. You'd show him the data and he'd smile and start looking for that number. He'd say, 'What did I tell you?'[71]

The incident taught Spencer a simple lesson. It was all very well to organize a modern media campaign, full of focus groups, exploratory committees, PIPS, poll analysis, etc. All those things could help win elections, but it was still essential to have a candidate who understood the electorate on a visceral level. That was demonstrated perfectly in late July, when Reagan was speaking in Lakeport, California. On the stage with him was a Vietnam vet, the shrapnel scars on his face not yet healed. He clutched an American flag to his chest as he listened to Reagan speak about everything that was wonderful about America and everything that was horrible about Berkeley. When Reagan finished his speech, he crossed the stage, shook the young man's hand, then put his arm around him as the photographers snapped their photos. Was that a tiny tear in the corner of his eye? Perhaps. The scene perfectly encapsulated all the values Reagan had promised to uphold. When the photographers finished, the vet handed Reagan the flag and said: 'You go get yourself some of those Berkeley Cong, Mr. Reagan.'[72]

# 9

## 'Who Shot Lincoln?'

On 5 June, two days before the primary, the Reagan campaign staged a massive rally in Santa Ana. The event perfectly embodied the combination of organization and pizzazz apparent over the previous year. In true Hollywood style, it was billed as the biggest rally in the state's history. It did not disappoint. Four thousand spectators packed the hall, many in a state of near hysteria. An army of volunteers made certain that no detail was neglected. Reagan's celebrity friends warmed up the crowd. Reagan Girls paraded on stage in mini-skirts, managing to be both wholesome and erotic. The headline act was, of course, Reagan himself, who delivered, as promised, the major speech of the campaign. As a spectacle, it was perfect.

Brown held a rally in Los Angeles on the same day. It was a disaster. Only a few hundred spectators attended, which at least limited the embarrassment. Journalists played heavily on the difference between the two rallies. Coverage of Reagan's stressed the huge crowd, the carnival atmosphere, the razzmatazz. Reports of the Brown event told how arguments had broken out over who would speak. These rallies were the official start to the general election campaign, and, as such, an indication of what lay ahead. The contrast was stark.

During the primary campaign, Reagan had ignored the official Republican Party by building his own machine and appealing directly to the people. By this means, he had avoided the internecine warfare that had been so destructive in the past. Having won the nomination, he was now able to draw upon help from the official party. He could also speak at party events around the state as the official candidate. The reunion was, however, more important for what it symbolized than for what it gave Reagan. By proving that he was a winner, he rendered the party beholden to him, effectively forcing it to reunite behind him. 'We were able, for the first time', Parkinson recalled, 'to have a really combined Republican party, north and south, conservative and liberal. That, of course, is an absolute essential before you can get anybody elected.'[1] These efforts were not confined to the state. The Reagan team worked hard to bring prominent Republicans from across the nation on board, including Eisenhower. Support from the former president, still the respected voice of moderation, effectively neutered allegations of extremism.[2]

Reagan now presented himself as the Republican Messiah. On the night of the count, his handlers phoned prominent officials from the Christopher and Patrick campaigns and offered them jobs working in the general election. 'We were right out there in front asking ... people to join,' Spencer explained. While Christopher, still bitter, ignored the invitations, almost his entire staff immediately joined Reagan. 'I became an honorary chairman ... for the Reagan campaign,' Bagley recalled. He sat next to Reagan at a few press conferences. 'That was Bill Roberts and Stu Spencer trying to show that the moderates were supporting Reagan, and some of us were trying to show that we weren't as bad as the far right who would not participate when they lost.'[3] Spencer felt that it 'was the most cohesive situation after the primary I've seen in the state'. As he explained, 'It [happened] for two reasons: number one, is when you beat somebody badly, the other side decides, well, I better get on the bandwagon; secondly ... we spent a lot of time wooing them.'[4] Nofziger agreed, adding a third reason: 'there was more strongly than any time since that I can recall, a feeling that we had to go beat the incumbent. People really put aside differences.' The marriage was made easier because Reagan was so 'hard to hold a grudge against'.[5] Unity made the party, and Reagan, appear more centrist. 'We do have the party glued together,' Reagan told Murphy, 'if only we can keep the kooks quiet.'[6] Courting the centre meant taking a more aggressive line on extremism. Reagan's references to the Birchers consequently took on a harder edge. Though he still refused to condemn them outright, he was more adamant in distancing himself from this 'outside organization'. He insisted that he had 'no relationship with ... [the Society] whatsoever. I don't belong. I have no intention of joining. I've never sought its support, nor do I intend to seek its support.'[7]

In an interview with *Ramparts*, Fred Hafner, a Reagan aide, parroted the campaign's new message: 'Ronnie is a pretty flexible guy – he has conservative leanings; but he's not black and white on issues. We don't expect the lunatics to stay with him, and we don't care.'[8] The only prominent Republican who refused to join the bandwagon was Kuchel, who had backed Christopher and now endorsed Brown. He lost more because of that decision than Reagan ever did. Even Christopher eventually came around, formally endorsing Reagan in July, though he couldn't resist the occasional snide remark.

Party harmony made mincemeat of the pollsters' predictions. Before the primary, the California Poll had suggested that Christopher was the stronger candidate and that Reagan would not be able to woo sufficient Democratic support to beat Brown. Immediately afterwards, the same poll revealed exactly the opposite: Reagan led Brown by 52 to 37 per cent. Mervin Field blithely turned error into logic: 'Reagan's impressive showing ... is the result of his appeal to voters of both parties: four out of five Republicans and one-third of Democrats say today that they would vote for Reagan over Brown.'[9]

Brown, meanwhile, struggled to find significance and direction for his campaign. Berkeley, Watts and Rumford had worn him down. Politics had lost its lustre; it was difficult to get anything important done. The historian Ethan Rarick has perfectly encapsulated a Shakespearean tragedy:

> For Brown, there was a special misery. All that he had fought for was coming down around him. He had built universities; now the campuses were hotbeds of rebellion. He had signed civil rights laws; now black Californians were rising up in rage. He had counseled justice and inclusion; now whites were buying pistols and threatening vigilantism. Brown's second term, launched with an affirming victory, was ending with a horrifying thud.[10]

As Brown confessed to Vice President Hubert Humphrey, the Republican resurgence made campaigning like a bar fight. The party was using social issues 'more viciously than at any time in my career, and there are a whole slew of them who slug at me every hour on the hour'.[11] Even more unsettling, however, was the heat from within. The California Democratic Council had been causing trouble because of its outspoken opposition to the Vietnam War. Campaigning on Reagan's behalf, Nixon slammed the Council for 'harbor[ing] draft card burners, troop train blockers, and beatniks', an intentional link to the turmoil at Berkeley. He further alleged that the Council 'advocates appeasement of Hanoi, Havana, and Peking'.[12] When Simon Casady, the CDC president, seemed to confirm Nixon's allegations by attacking Johnson's policy in Vietnam, Brown responded by trying to force his long-time friend from office. That alienated those on the left. At the convention in February, Casady lost a bitter no-confidence vote by 1,001 to 859. Brown had won, but his narrow victory proved that his influence was evaporating.

Much more formidable were the attacks from the right, in particular from Los Angeles Mayor Sam Yorty. Brown had fought Yorty ever since the latter's election as mayor in 1961. '[He] was sly,' Brown reflected. '[He] ... was a contemptible, under-the-table fighter with a capacity of meanness second to none.'[13] In 1964, an argument over delegate selection in the Democratic presidential primary turned ugly when Yorty accused Brown of harbouring vice-presidential ambitions. Brown won that argument, leaving Yorty seeking revenge. Further trouble arose the following year when Brown refused to endorse Yorty's re-election campaign, backing Jimmy Roosevelt instead. Yorty's easy victory made Brown look vindictive.

Yorty chose not to challenge Brown for the gubernatorial nomination in 1962 because he was unassailable. Four years later, however, he seemed vulnerable to an assault from the right. Yorty threw out vague allegations that Brown was a communist; though ridiculous, these resonated in the paranoid southern part of the state. Despite being a Democrat, Yorty was closer in political sympathies to Reagan than to Brown. He made law and order a big issue in the primary, in particular by focusing attention on Watts. Polls had revealed that racial violence had replaced the Vietnam War as the number one concern of the American people. Though the riots had occurred in Yorty's city, he cleverly shifted blame to Brown. The crisis, he argued, had arisen because the civil rights movement, the Great Society and Brown's overt empathy toward blacks had encouraged a sense that they were 'abused and mistreated'.[14] That was like throwing petrol on a smouldering fire. Brown, he claimed, had compounded the problem by initially refusing to cut short his holiday in Greece after the riots broke out. (The fact that Yorty was also absent when the riots erupted was apparently immaterial.)

Yorty argued that Watts, like Berkeley, revealed the dangers of bleeding-heart liberalism. Brown, he claimed, spent too much effort trying to understand problems, instead of stamping them out. There was enough truth to this allegation to render it effective: after first stressing the law-and-order line in response to the riots, Brown had argued that racism, poor living conditions and poverty were contributory factors. That annoyed white voters who did not want to share culpability for the riots, preferring instead to see them as symptomatic of the black character. Brown's opponents benefited immensely from the fact that the governor confessed surprise that riots had broken out at all. 'I don't think any of us had any idea this would happen,' he admitted. 'No one advised me that Los Angeles was in a turbulent situation.'[15] When riots again erupted in Watts in March 1966, the issue received renewed attention at the worst possible time. Reagan weighed in, alleging that Brown had prior warning of the trouble but had failed to act. In an unfortunate coincidence, Brown was again out of the state, allowing Reagan to accuse him of a 'flagrant dereliction of duty'.[16] That delighted Yorty.

In stark contrast to the previous eight years, it was now the Democratic Party that looked hopelessly divided. 'Yorty was a very clever ... fighter,' Brown recalled. '[He] attacked me in the primaries viciously, to such an extent that even if he had gotten the nomination my people would have walked away from him in the general election. They would have been so damn mad at him.' In the end, Brown got 1,355,000 votes and Yorty 981,000 – under the circumstances, an embarrassingly small margin. 'That was a close fight,' Brown reflected. 'If I couldn't beat Yorty who I always felt was a yokel and a bad guy, then I knew I was in trouble. Then Reagan winning by such a big vote over ... Christopher indicated that I was really in trouble.'[17] The statistics certainly did not bode well. Brown's vote total was less than Reagan's, despite the fact that registered Democrats significantly outnumbered Republicans. Champion decided that the general election was already lost:

> Yorty has never been a big vote-getter. He has always been an accumulator of resentments of people who want to vote no, and he gives them lots of reasons to vote no on a whole lot of things.
>
> The heavy vote he got in the Democratic primary against Pat really showed how much trouble we were in with Pat's basic

constituency. It wasn't just the conservative Democrats. We were in great trouble with everybody.[18]

Years later, the bitterness of that primary still prevented Brown from understanding what had happened. Because he was able to dismiss his opponent as sly, mendacious, vindictive and paranoid, he failed to appreciate why he was popular. The primary was a mandate on Brown's social policy, and he had not fared well. Brown dismissed both Yorty and Reagan as extremists, failing to grasp just how much the electorate, tired of 'responsible liberalism', had moved rightward. Rather than accept these truths, Brown instead blamed foul play. 'To this day I always felt that [Yorty] was financed by the Republicans in this campaign against me and he undermined me in the primary so that I became an easy target for Reagan in the final.'[19] The irony of that assessment did not trouble Brown.

Yorty continued to do damage after the primary. 'The discredited Brown machine has become an albatross around the neck of the Democratic Party,' he announced on 8 June. 'Brown and his supporters appear determined to hang on until they drag the Democratic Party down to defeat.' Continuing that rant, he added that 'moderates in both parties will not like the choice with which they are now confronted. Many will sit this one out. I will make no decision ... relative to what position, if any, I will take in the coming general election.'[20] That was simply a selfish attempt to make sure that journalists continued to pay attention to him. He kept them waiting until early October, when he announced that he would not support Brown, whom he now accused of corruption. Reagan exploited Democrat discomfiture by appearing with Yorty at a birthday celebration for the City of Los Angeles and by boasting that he had defended the mayor against attacks by the eastern Democratic establishment.

Yorty supporters who were obsessed with law and order drifted toward Reagan. The California Poll at the beginning of the general election campaign ranked crime the top issue amongst voters, followed closely by 'racial problems' – another way of saying the same thing.[21] Responsible liberalism had not, it seemed, made the streets safer. Fed up with attempts to understand the causes of crime, the voters were inclined to see criminality as a problem for the police, not social workers. Reagan understood that every occurrence of disorder caused a shift in support toward him:

> a helpful thing happened in Oakland when I went to ... one of the government job-training centers there ... Some local unions had organized a big demonstration. Literally the police had to clear a way through them from the bus to the school for me to get through. They were violent. I mean, they were trying to swing sticks and everything ... it was all over television, I think that was worth a few thousand votes.[22]

Reagan used Watts as an example of lawlessness, just as he used Berkeley to highlight moral decay. His campaign cleverly turned quite localized problems into issues supposedly affecting every voter. For instance, a pamphlet argued that crime cost the average family of four $1,000 per year, even if they were not direct victims. Lawlessness was blamed on 'judicial rulings that took much of the law-enforcement authority away from the local police and left them handicapped in their efforts to protect the law-abiding citizen from the increasingly insolent criminal element'.[23] The pamphlet also pointed out that Brown had vetoed a crime-prevention bill as governor, a vague allegation but one no less powerful for being so. Reagan's solution was to put law enforcement back into the hands of local officials, a strategy designed to empower individual communities.

While Reagan's rise and Brown's decline had caused a 5.3 per cent increase in Republican registrants and a 0.4 per cent decrease in Democrat ones since November 1964, Democrats still had an advantage of 1.3 million registered voters.[24]

Reagan's goal was to get 90 per cent fealty from Republicans while making serious inroads into Democratic support. This meant that an appeal had to be made to white workers. Reagan did so by playing on their fears, emphasizing crime and student unrest. References to Rumford were coded warnings about blacks moving in next door. He courted organized labour by stressing that the interests of employers and employed were essentially the same – both required a healthy economy. California, he argued, was teetering on the brink of recession because Brown's policies were anti-business. 'The business climate was bad,' he later explained.

> We had dropped drastically in the desirability of California as a place for new businesses and industries ... I was able to state that major industries, several of them, had passed the word down from their headquarters ... that no expansion of any branch in California was to take place because of the poor business climate here ... I think that ... [Brown's] chickens came home to roost.[25]

Reagan drew attention to the fact that California's unemployment rate was above the national average, blithely ignoring that this was due in part to recently arrived jobless migrants who still considered the state a promised land.

'Which candidate is the friend of the working man?' a Reagan pamphlet asked. There followed allegations of how Brown had betrayed the workers, buttressed by evidence suggesting that Reagan was worthier of trust. He played upon his long membership of the Screen Actors' Guild, which apparently made him a comrade of every trade unionist. Boasts about his role in stopping a communist takeover of the guild were designed to appeal to the stridently anti-communist sympathies of unionized workers. 'With a background of 22 years as a member of a working union, 20 years on the executive board and 6 terms as president,' the pamphlet maintained, 'Ronald

Reagan will bring to Sacramento more extensive experience in labor-management relations than any previous governor.'[26] It was certainly a novel approach for a Republican candidate to brag of his strike experience and success in winning pay settlements. 'I happen to be part of that rank and file of labor,' Reagan told the Republican State Convention in August, with a straight face.[27] Even Spencer thought the 'union man' line ridiculous. 'I laughed about it. He always considered himself a labor union guy and I used to say, "There is no similarity between the Screen Actors' Guild and the teamsters."'[28]

Reagan tried to drive a wedge between union workers and their leaders, especially after the latter officially endorsed Brown. His proposal to set up tribunals to settle labour disputes was presented as being in the workers' best interests, when in fact it was designed to weaken union power. The same was true of his promise to impose secret ballots on industrial action, a union-busting initiative sold as a sacred democratic principle designed to give workers self-determination. Union bosses were presented as selfish, power-hungry demagogues who operated without the consent of the workers and did not keep their best interests in mind – rather like those folks in Washington.

Reflecting on the overtures made to the working class, Weinberger commented that Reagan 'appealed to a very broad segment who don't care about politics or politicians or parties or issues, but vote on the individual personality'.[29] This was possible because the new prosperity of the working class had inspired a change in political sympathies – the strife was gone, and with it the anger. In the *Christian Science Monitor*, Kimmis Hendrick recognized that: 'Mr. Reagan ... is approaching his campaign on the premise that "working people" in California's highly technical industry represent suburban attitudes.'[30] Those who had migrated to the state in search of work were now enjoying the fruits of prosperity and were disinclined to be charitable toward the next generation of downtrodden. Reagan, fully in tune with this change, presented welfare as an insult to decent working people who 'should not be asked to carry the additional burden of a segment of society capable of caring for itself but which prefers making welfare a way of life, freeloading at the expense of more conscientious citizens'.[31] Alarmed by this shift in sympathy, Jimmy Hoffa, the Teamsters leader, complained that 'labor isn't hungry anymore. My men each have a cottage at the lake, and they want to spend their holiday there, not at a rally where there are no parking places. Most of them don't remember the old days.' Echoing that theme, Drew Pearson remarked that: 'In California, the election of governor will partly depend on whether labor remembers those who helped them in the old days, when they were hungry, or whether they are carried away by present-day television glamour.'[32] Memories were short.

Bill Boyarsky, covering the campaign for the Associated Press, witnessed the new zeitgeist in Norwalk, a Southern California suburb where aerospace workers lived. Pollsters saw it as a bellwether neighbourhood – 'the reaction of the crowds almost as sound a test of public opinion in the area as a scientific poll'. A clue to local sympathies could be derived from a huge billboard which overlooked the freeway: 'IMPEACH EARL WARREN'. When Reagan spoke at the Lakewood Shopping Center, a massive crowd gathered. That in itself astonished Boyarsky, given that it was noon on a weekday. Cheers erupted when Reagan lambasted the high cost of welfare and blasted the kooks at Berkeley. When Brown visited the same site a few weeks later, he was heckled. Norwalk, it should be noted, was three-quarters registered Democrats.[33]

Norwalk was concrete proof of what the polls had long been suggesting: Brown was having trouble holding onto his core support. Field noted 'the relatively faint-hearted support he gets from rank-and-file Democratic voters' and predicted that 'a sizeable number of Democrats [will] defect.' This apparently had more to do with Brown than with his party, as a private Democratic poll demonstrated. In one district of Los Angeles, it found 72 per cent support for the Democratic State Assemblyman, but 68 per cent support for Reagan. In other words, the voters had not switched parties; they were simply more fickle in their sympathies. The California Poll showed that while 78 per cent of union members were likely to support Brown in 1958, only 57 per cent were inclined to do so eight years later. A similar decline was discovered among those with less than a high-school education, from 71 to 53 per cent. Field put this down to the 'white backlash'.[34] Clearly, Yorty supporters were switching to Reagan in droves. The unions, in particular the AFL-CIO, tried to counteract this drift by emphasizing classic union issues, but workers were much more concerned about Rumford, urban riots, crime and student unrest.[35] Impressive in its ability to state the obvious, the *Los Angeles Times* observed: 'It is doubtful ... to what extent union members nowadays follow their leaders' advice in voting.'[36]

Reagan combined a fiercely anti-union attitude with a remarkable ability to attract union members. Keen to alert workers to the danger he posed, union bosses in August promised to spend $1,400,000 to defeat him.[37] That, however, was money wasted. Weinberger observed that:

> our polls afterward showed that he got something in excess of forty percent of the union labor vote and he did that because he was talking about things they were very interested in. Union labor was very much more affluent at that time, and when he talked about low taxes and keeping government small and less intrusive ... he was striking a very strong chord with the individual union member ... he just talked about things they were interested in, all from a very conservative viewpoint.

Reagan had even more success with the wives of the union members. 'He ... got something around forty-nine percent of union wives' votes,' Weinberger recalled. 'That's because he's extremely attractive to women and they liked what he was saying too. He said things that appealed to them as people who had family responsibilities.'[38]

Reagan had similar success in the agricultural sector. The big landowners were natural Republican supporters, but Reagan also went after farm labourers. They tended to be conservative in their political sympathies and deeply self-reliant, which meant that they were susceptible to Reagan diatribes. His appeal to them nevertheless required considerable subtlety since they habitually clashed with landowners. The Reagan team addressed this problem by arguing that Brown's agricultural policies had been detrimental to both owners and labourers. Government tinkering in the agricultural sector, he claimed, had increased the costs of food processing, causing canning and packing companies to move to Mexico, with the consequent loss of jobs in California. This line of argument appealed not only to the farm owners and labourers in the fields, but also to workers in the processing factories and to the business sector in general.

While Spencer-Roberts sold Reagan like a shiny new car, Brown's team tried desperately to cultivate enthusiasm for a used governor with a dodgy transmission and more than 100,000 miles on the clock. 'I think there was a kind of malaise in that campaign that probably reflected a real malaise of how things might have been functioning in the later days of the administration,' his close aide Meredith Burch admitted. A big problem, she felt, was 'a lack of leanness and commitment':

> At that campaign headquarters you walked in and you knew there was something wrong. There were hundreds of people on the payroll. It was an enormously expensive campaign. I don't think there were four volunteers around. It just wasn't the lean hard days that you remember when you started out, when it was a kind of guerrilla warfare and you had a small staff and everyone was really hucklety bucklety. This one was overstaffed. Every place you looked there was some portentous, fat, young advance man. We used to call them 'the young old

farts' ... there were lots of those. Everyone was paid. There was lots of money.[39]

After the primary debacle, Brown brought in Fred Dutton, his campaign manager in 1958, and Champion, a close adviser over the previous eight years. This might have helped, if not for Brown's simultaneous refusal to dismiss Bradley. 'You can imagine how well that worked,' Burch recalled. 'It didn't work at all.'[40] It later emerged that Bradley was stealing from the campaign's war chest – to the tune of around $85,000. At the time, however, it was his mismanagement, not his larceny, that caused the real problems. Since the specific roles of Bradley, Dutton and Champion were never defined, chaos reigned, punctuated always by poisonous bickering. One aide called it 'the perfect bastard troika'.[41] Dutton, Burch explained, thought he had been recruited to run the campaign. 'It then became apparent that ... there were three people who thought they were running the campaign ... It was just an untenable situation; three people don't run a campaign; somebody's in charge ... It was unfortunately typical that [Brown] would allow that kind of a mushy situation to develop.'[42] Champion agreed that Brown's great weakness was that he hated to see once-enthusiastic supporters leave the campaign team. 'So he tended to want to bring them all back in, even though they didn't get along together and sometimes made almost hysterical accusations about each other.'[43] Policies agreed one day would be rescinded the next, simply because a different member of the troika was in the office. The chaos gave rise to some ridiculous mistakes. On one occasion, Brown's office announced a series of rallies around the state. One was scheduled for Santa Barbara, where a large crowd duly gathered. As Brown's plane approached the airport, the pilot discovered that the runway was too short to accommodate his DC-7. The plane circled for ten minutes, then took off for Fresno, leaving the crowd below lacking a candidate to cheer. These little disasters exacerbated the simmering rivalries. 'There were big fights,' Brown admitted.[44] 'I had my people going in every direction and it showed ... I didn't handle it well at all.' This was partly because he seldom visited headquarters. 'I didn't know what was going on,' he confessed. 'But people have told me later ... that it was just terrible down there. Dutton ... was tossing people around and everything else; Bradley and Dutton hated each other and it was a very badly run campaign.'[45] Champion felt that morale was low because of a prevalent sense of impending defeat. 'I spent a large part of that ... campaign trying to keep the peace ... trying to keep people's spirits up because everybody felt that the chances were not good.'[46] 'It was a nightmare,' Dutton agreed. 'It was like ... sitting on a plane going through a thunderstorm, and you knew it was going to crash ... and there's not a damn thing you can do about it.'[47]

A week after arriving from Washington, Dutton concluded that the election was unwinnable. 'A Brown victory probably was never doable in '66,' he reflected, 'including long before Yorty damaged him in the primary.'[48] Dutton felt that Brown failed to address the natural deterioration in support that comes after two terms in office. 'He had gotten governmental instead of political. He had let his administration bureaucratize. His creativeness at the start had gotten stuck in the concrete of rectitude.' The Irish street fighter from south of Market in San Francisco had turned into a career politician who derived too much enjoyment from the privileges of office. By 1966, 'you'd have thought that Pat Brown had been born to the purple. He had too many ... state troopers wherever he went, too many big black limousines, too many people deferring and calling him governor for too long.'[49] No wonder, then, that Reagan the non-politician struck a chord with the people. The fact that Brown still delivered good government was no longer enough. 'The point of elective officers', Dutton argued, 'is not to be just administrators and policy-makers but also to rally the public, maintain strong support to expand where needed substantively and, in essence, to be political figures. That latter role had very seriously deteriorated.'[50]

Mills concurred with that analysis. 'We all thought he was going to lose.' He formed that opinion by observing Reagan: 'watching his primary campaign, watching how smooth he was, watching how much he understood ... the media, how to use television, how he understood the temper of the people ... People believed in him.'[51] 'Reagan made ... good speeches,' Brown admitted. 'He had good quips. He had good writers ... and he was personable in appearance.' In contrast, 'my speeches ... were really a recounting of what I had accomplished rather than ... a vision [for] the future, I didn't speak extemporaneously because I think I was afraid I'd say something wrong ... My campaign lacked spontaneity.'

Because he had to spend so much of his time defending his past record, he had little opportunity to speak positively about the future. 'I had the Watts riot to defend, I had the fair housing bill to defend, I had the Free Speech Movement,' he recalled, 'and then above all, wherever I'd go to the universities, even where they were for me because I was a liberal ... they'd say, "Do you think we should get out of Vietnam?"'[52] As *Ramparts* noticed, Brown had nothing to say: 'Reagan speaks ... about Watts, Berkeley and Vietnam. He does not say what liberals want to hear, and his analyses are simplistic if not Mesozoic, but he is saying *something*. Pat Brown, on the other hand, is saying nothing, except what a terrible right winger and inexperienced neo-fascist Ronald Reagan is.'[53] Brown was handicapped by his own honesty. For instance, he admitted throughout the campaign that, if re-elected, he would have to raise taxes. This, of course, seemed to confirm allegations that he was a tax-and-spend liberal who could not be trusted with the public purse. As Mills recalled, 'Ronald Reagan said that if people wanted to vote for someone who was going to raise taxes, they should vote for Pat Brown, but he wasn't going to do it. Of course, after he was elected, he was responsible for the biggest tax increase in the history of California.'⁵⁴ Reagan also continued to promise an across-the-board cut of 10 per cent in every department budget. That idea had no substance or feasibility, but sounded wonderful. 'Pat was being driven from pillar to post,' Dutton reflected.⁵⁵ He had no answer to Reagan's simple solutions that resonated so well with voters who abhorred big government and craved easy answers. On one occasion, when questioned about how he would implement his fiscal prudence, Reagan actually replied, 'Let's not get bogged down in specifics.'⁵⁶

Reagan, not Brown, now dominated the middle ground. Lewis described the constituency Reagan had found, or rather that had found Reagan:

> He appeals to the 'forgotten man': California's anonymous millions, neither rich nor poor, who live nine to five lives, fight freeways and crabgrass, sweat out thirty-year mortgages and escape to their television sets at night. They are essentially apolitical, and their ranks include well-paid blue-collar workers as well as technicians and Ph.D.s. They are united in a desire to escape the demands of a complicated and interdependent society. Reaganism appeals to them like the soft, blurry edges of a well-remembered old movie; it is a call to the nostalgia and a return to the verities of a generation that believed in itself and the sound dollar.⁵⁷

On social issues – welfare, civil rights, student unrest, taxation, crime, etc. – Reagan was in tune with this constituency. Brown, on the other hand, was weighed down by his own past. 'It isn't that people are tired of Brown,' an aide remarked, rather perceptively. 'They just wish all these problems he keeps talking about would go away.'⁵⁸ Having won two elections on a platform of 'responsible liberalism', he could not abandon his liberal image simply because the voters had grown tired of what it implied. Winslow Christian, Brown's executive secretary, tried nevertheless to encourage a shift of focus: 'There are several substantively valid proposals that can re-identify you as a wise and progressive law enforcement officer rather than as a coddler of hoodlums and distributor of welfare checks.' Christian nevertheless understood that such a makeover would be difficult to carry off convincingly. 'People think that welfare is supporting hordes of illegitimate Negro children produced by women who probably welcome a new pregnancy as a chance to augment the welfare check. Rational argument will not put this idea down.' He nevertheless urged Brown to adopt new policies that would 'be both highly conspicuous and ... gratifying to the prejudices I have mentioned'.[59] Brown, however, understood that playing to the crowd in this way would expose him to charges of hypocrisy. A liberal could not transform himself into a conservative populist this late in the campaign.

Brown not only found it difficult to promote himself, he also struggled to find an effective way to attack Reagan. In desperation, he stressed the actor issue. 'We did go heavily on the theme ... of Reagan being an actor to try to show that he was unqualified,' Champion admitted. 'I think ... [that] played into their hands.'[60] When asked why the team had opted for this tactic, Dutton gave the lame excuse that 'it goes over big with the farmers in the San Joaquin Valley, the guys who think an actor isn't a man's man.'[61] The jibes merely emphasized Reagan's message that he was a fresh face in politics, uncorrupted by government. This worked particularly well against Brown, the career politician. Christopher, at least, could claim to have been a businessman once. Brown was nothing but a politician. In addition, the tactic demonstrated just how empty the Democrat campaign actually was. 'This was intellectual snobbery at its worst,' Weinberger felt. 'If anybody had criticized a Democrat as being a mere college professor or something, why, they would have been all over the lot with how bigoted the remark was. But it was perfectly all right for them to say that somebody was a mere actor and so shouldn't run for office.'[62] In retrospect,

Champion felt that the mistake lay in the delivery, not the message itself. 'It came through not that we were trying to show Pat as being the more experienced, steady old hand, but that we were attacking Reagan for being an actor. Well, that's just a bad piece of execution.'[63] No, it was a lot more than that. It was a tired tactic that had never yielded much and which grew ever more tiresome each time it was used.

Though the actor line was a non-starter, a California Poll in early September did suggest that Brown was highlighting precisely what voters considered Reagan's weaknesses, namely inexperience (71 per cent), his failure to disown the Birchers (43 per cent) and his links to Goldwater (30 per cent). Polls of this sort were, however, probably misleading since they asked respondents to list weaknesses without measuring whether these weaknesses were actually important to voting intention. In truth, they were probably not very important. More significant was a poll in June that listed the issues most significant to the voters (crime, racial problems, taxes, welfare) and revealed that 55 per cent felt Reagan more likely to do a better job handling these issues, compared to 31 per cent for Brown.[64] 'While there appeared to be general public agreement that the state was facing complex and difficult social and economic issues,' wrote the political analysts Totten Anderson and Eugene Lee, 'there was equal agreement that a new administration – regardless of its lack of experience – should be entrusted with their solution.'[65] Since Brown was blamed for these problems, his greater experience was irrelevant.

The Reagan team responded to the acting jibes by trotting out a few well-loved actors. A television ad featured the widely respected John Wayne presenting a montage of three actors who had served their country with distinction: Jimmy Stewart, a World War II bomber pilot; George Murphy, the current senator from California, and Irene Dunne, an alternate delegate to the United Nations. 'So what's this empty nonsense about Ronald Reagan being just an actor?' Wayne asked in his trademark gravelly voice. 'I watched Ronald work his entire adult life preparing for public service. His will be a new, informed, dedicated leadership.' The ad was significant not only because it addressed doubts about Reagan's fitness for office but also because it underlined the fact that he was a fresh alternative to the career politicians.[66] The Brown strategy also alienated a large number of high-profile Democrat supporters, since most of Hollywood was Democrat. Jack Palance walked out of a Democratic telethon exclaiming: 'Attack him if you wish for his lack of experience, but don't go after him just because he is an actor.'[67] A joke circulated the state: 'Why not an actor? We've had a clown for eight years.'[68]

The actor complaint implied that Reagan was a mere mouthpiece for other people's lines. Reagan destroyed that allegation by performing so well in front of journalists. He may have been inexperienced, but he was not ill-informed. 'We had people out there asking ... tough questions,' Champion recalled. 'Only once or twice did we catch him completely unprepared.' A media event at Oroville Reservoir designed to highlight water policy was a case in point. Brown thought he had a huge advantage since he had been deeply involved in water law over the past two decades. Reagan, however, held his own. 'Reagan really did his homework,' Champion recalled. 'It was not deep homework, but ... enough to appear knowledgeable, which is all he has ever done ... You don't find him making big, detailed speeches ... He just makes knowledgeable-like remarks ... and that's the technique.'[69]

The advantages of being a 'non-politician' were driven home when Reagan began to hit Brown hard with allegations of nepotism. When asked whether he could think of anything good to say about the governor, Reagan, with perfect timing, quipped: 'Well, he is good to his family ... he puts a lot of relatives on the payroll.'[70] The criticism was effective because the charges were true. 'I was guilty of nepotism,' Brown admitted. 'They were all able people, but people resent a whole family being on the state payroll.[71] Though Brown understood that he was vulnerable on this point, he failed to anticipate how cleverly Reagan would exploit it. Nepotism, Reagan argued, was a morality problem. 'There has been a conspicuous lack of morality and a consequent decline in the quality of leadership emanating from Sacramento,' a briefing document argued. 'The basis of effective and honest leadership is morality, and morality in turn is promoted by and should be synonymous with honest leadership.' By this means, a rather small issue was turned into a 'major problem facing Californians'.[72]

When the actor line wore thin, critics began instead to concentrate on Reagan's policies – or lack of them. 'When on script, Reagan has been glib and unnourishing,' the *Bee* commented. 'He has sounded often as if he were running for the presidency instead of the governorship. Evasive, photogenic, given to generalities and angelic sounding platitudes, Reagan has left his public almost completely in the dark as to how he will accomplish the things he says he will.'[73] In the *Examiner*, Stanley Kossen still complained about Reagan's 'appalling ignorance of California problems', but that accusation was contradicted by the Q&A performances.[74] At times, however, the candidate seemed *too* good. 'Reagan is a "quick study" on politics and state government,' wrote Richard Wilson in the *Los Angeles Times*. 'He left behind the impression that if he does not know what he is talking about, he has at least got his script down letter perfect.'[75] The syndicated columnist Stewart Alsop, no left-winger, complained that Reagan 'resembles a carefully designed, elaborately "customerized" supermarket package, complete with the glossiest wrapping and the slickest sort of eye appeal'.[76] That was true, but the electorate hardly cared.

The criticism was symptomatic of the way politics was changing, much to the chagrin of seasoned journalists. Reagan seemed a product of the television age, his soundbites written in advance and assembled for the effect they would produce. In a rather lovely metaphor, the *Bee* complained that his canned remarks sounded like 'a broom sweeping up broken glass'.[77] The *New Republic* likewise poked fun at the steady stream of glib one-liners:

> Reagan ... [has] an air of modest decency, a fine crop of hair and a homogenized mind. 'One of the great problems of economics', he explained, 'is unemployment'. The crowd cheered. 'For every ounce of federal help we get we surrender an ounce of personal freedom.' 'There's no such thing as left or right any more, it's up or down.' Steady cheers right along ... We knew that pretty soon he was going to say 'I am not a politician' (he did), and add, 'Ordinary citizens created this country of ours' (Flourish, Cheers) ... 'I'm against the idea that the criminal must be protected from society, rather than the other way around!' Applause.[78]

Addicted to wishful thinking, the *Bee* repeatedly insisted that the voters would not be fooled:

> The more Reagan reveals himself the more ridiculous he appears as a gubernatorial candidate, and the more amazing it becomes [that] he could ever have been taken seriously ... by either party. He is revealing not only ignorance about the facts of California life, he is exhibiting that inclination of all political dilettantes – the penchant for the easy, glib answer when the solution calls for hard, searching reason.[79]

These journalists simply did not realize (or chose to ignore) that political communication had changed. They looked nostalgically to the candidate who could speak from the stump for hours, displaying a vast and deep knowledge of the issues. They seemed to think that complaining about the dumbing down of politics would encourage the voters to demand greater intellectual substance. Like poor Canute, they tried to hold back the irresistible waves of anti-intellectualism. Reagan did not create the climate of vacuity that now typified campaigning, but he did know how to thrive in it. A few journalists eventually came to appreciate that he was re-writing the playbook. 'Ronald Reagan is shaking up the GOP as the old elephant has not been shook up since it fell from power in 1960,' wrote William White in the *Washington Post*. 'And should he beat the hard-pressed Gov. Brown in November the thing would amount to nothing less than an earthquake of change.'[80]

Bradley eventually discovered that, rather than being a liability, Reagan's acting experience gave him an advantage that Brown could not counter.

> We got into all kinds of arguments about policy, and his method was to pick some small aspect of something, and with his dramatic ability, build it up into one of the most fiendish crimes that had ever been committed on the people, and he did it very effectively. They weren't very interesting, really, but he made them fairly interesting. He was very effective with that. He'd come up with all these statistics about '88,000 unwed mothers', and things like that, and he did it quite well.[81]

This talent was all the more important because of the role television played in the campaign. Television is the perfect medium for conveying the reductive arguments that are the populist's ammunition. Analysing the ads produced by the two candidates, Rose and Fuchs found that 'while Reagan might have been able effectively to project himself in a 20 second time slot, Brown lacked both the visual appeal and the "star" aura to do this well.'[82] Seldom was Reagan required to elaborate on a point. Soundbites became an acceptable substitute for policy.

Rhetorical skill allowed Reagan to maintain the image of moderation so important to his success. Tone superseded policy. He did not hide his conservative values, but avoided speaking too specifically about their implications. 'My definition of a Republican conservative', he proclaimed, 'is an American of integrity, progressive in his creative thinking, who strives to make this a better place in which to live and to raise children, and accomplishes that result by the application of hard work and sound common sense. A conservative Republican is a good American citizen with both feet on the ground.'[83] Substitute 'Democrat' and 'liberal' for 'Republican' and 'conservative' in the two sentences and they make equal sense. It sounded beautiful, but meant nothing. In a similar way, Reagan made extensive use of a rhetorical device known at the time as the 'Nixon segue'. The speaker starts with a statement designed to encourage agreement: 'Now, none of us would care to abridge in any way the principle of academic freedom...' Having established an entirely reasonable point of consensus, the speaker then exploits that harmony by proposing what is presented as a sensible limitation on the established principle, pivoting on an all important 'but', as in '...but academic freedom must stop short of indoctrinating students with an alien philosophy'. The listener is swept along on what seems a tide of reasonableness, despite the end point being quite extreme. 'All of us agree that California must take responsibility for the welfare of its genuinely needy citizens, but...'; 'Teachers, like everyone else, have the inalienable right to strike, but...'[84] By this means, a radical proposal is made palatable by a coating of sugary logic.

Nofziger thought Reagan 'the best television candidate in the history of television'.[85] Playing to this strength, the campaign team organized a special collection to pay for television time. Wary of slick ads that implied clever marketing, Spencer and Roberts spent most of the money on telethons. These live programmes were designed to bring Reagan into direct contact with the voters, who could phone in questions. In effect, this was an extension of the Q&A format that had already served Reagan well and also reiterated that he was a man of the people. Edited versions of these sessions were then incorporated into ads and short 'key issue' films broadcast on local television in target areas. A similar innovation was the 'Reagan Team Barbecue', held on 16 October, a pioneering version of the campaign house party. A large gathering at Reagan's Malibu ranch took place simultaneously with barbecues organized by volunteers across the state, enhancing the folksy, inclusive image of the campaign. Through television, the various parties were amalgamated into one big event. This allowed Reagan to communicate with his supporters in a relaxed situation. They responded by volunteering and donating money.

The key, Spencer and Roberts insisted, was to keep the campaign simple. This meant not overwhelming the voters with complex issues or torrents of detail and statistics. 'Normally you can't get through more than two or three issues,' the campaign managers confessed. They settled on 'three main ones ... morality; then taxes, spending, that whole ball of wax; and then eight years of incumbency'. 'Morality' included student unrest, obscenity, crime, nepotism, etc. 'Spending' included welfare, property taxes, the cost of big government. The incumbency issue was self-explanatory and the flip-side of Reagan's claim to be a non-politician. These three broad issues were the labelling that defined Reagan and which established a clear and sharp contrast with Brown.[86]

Spencer felt that Reagan's enormous appeal and Brown's tendency to self-destruct rendered this an easy campaign. The hardest task, he felt, was 'to keep from screwing up':

> We had a good thing going. We had the ideal candidate. We had the money. We had the troops. It was, *don't do something stupid ...* just deal with what you've got and do it right. It's almost like a football team. Whatever your system is, keep running the ball until you have to pass it. Just don't start throwing the ball all over the field. I think that was our biggest challenge, to not screw it up.[87]

The remark about not screwing up was an oblique reference to BASICO. Spencer remarked that Reagan 'was green, and he had some supporters who wanted to go out and do some things that Goldwater did. Overstate the case for example.'[88] Plog and Holden misinterpreted the Reagan phenomenon as a massive swing toward the hard right. They felt that Spencer and Roberts were inhibiting Reagan's effect by camouflaging his radicalism. Roberts admitted to a 'general personality disagreement' with BASICO, who had an annoying tendency to 'offer, gratuitously, an opinion ... that we did not ask for. As a matter of fact, my unhappiness with their approach grew during the campaign.' Through careful management, the problem was kept under control. 'During the general election they had very little to do with his issue work ... I was not satisfied with the way it was going and the way it was being presented.'

Roberts would not allow Plog and Holden to jeopardize the packaging of Reagan. 'It could have been around issues. It could have been around their general conduct, but I do know that I was not happy with them toward the end of the campaign.' As a result, 'they did not have as much access ... in the general election as they did in the primary.'[89] This was especially true when Battaglia, who could never see the point of Plog and Holden, took over as campaign chairman, after the primary. 'Placing Battaglia in the campaign was a clear attempt to guide the candidate toward a more moderate position in the party,' Holden complained. 'It was a mistake that almost ruined Reagan's political career.'[90] When Salvatori tried to force a new contract on Plog and Holden that required them to report to Roberts and Battaglia, they refused, complaining that: 'those two guys were salmonella.'[91] Salvatori relented, but found a different way to keep Plog and Holden sidelined. For the final months of the campaign, they were paid to be ciphers.

The BASICO problem was minor in comparison to the chaos in the Brown camp. Having spent the first half of the year targeting Christopher, Brown was ill-prepared to take on Reagan, whom he still underestimated. 'We were always trying to do something [big],' Champion reflected. 'You know a campaign's in trouble when it is trying to get the one big thing that's going to turn everything around, instead of doing the daily hard work that always accumulates.'[92] (One is reminded of Spencer's football metaphor.) In desperation, they played the extremist card. A pamphlet entitled 'The Target is Your Family' posed a stark question: 'Governor Pat Brown or Actor Ronald Reagan?' The latter was described as dangerous, unhinged and unpredictable, rather like Goldwater had once been. 'THE CHOICE IS YOURS ... GOVERNOR PAT BROWN, who works with moderates of both political parties to assure a better life for you and your family ... or RONALD REAGAN, who condones the John Birch Society, and proposes costly disruptions to California's way of life.'[93] Another leaflet, entitled 'Here's the *REAL* REAGAN!', provided quotes and allegations highlighting his extremism, including that he was a 'paid propagandist for Barry Goldwater'. Brown supporters in Los Angeles distributed a political cartoon of 'fat cat rightwing millionaires' pulling on the strings of an evil-looking Reagan puppet. The message read: 'STOP and THINK, DON'T LEAP!'[94]

'We tried to establish his positions from things he said in the primary campaign and other speeches that he made which indicated both stupidity and right-wing tendencies,' Brown reflected. 'I thought we did it very well, but we apparently didn't.' His aide Bob Coate produced a 30-page dossier of evidence purporting to prove once and for all Reagan's extremism. The material was then distilled into a highly inflammatory summary:

> RONALD REAGAN is the extremists' candidate for governor of California. He is the extremists' collaborator in California. He endorses their products, promotes their policies, takes their money. He is their 'front man'. Meanwhile, he pretends to be a moderate, middle-of-the-roader. The record belies him. It shows – that he has collaborated directly with a score of top leaders of the super-secret John Birch Society. That he supports the

programs, policies and projects of numerous extremist fronts. That extremist money from California and Eastern states is an important source of his campaign financing. That he uses his acting skill and TV charm to soft-sell the doctrines of radical rightists who condemn Social Security and other social advances as Communist-inspired.[95]

Coate reiterated the message at a series of press conferences, with the widely respected State Controller Alan Cranston lending support. The approach backfired because many of the quotes used were not, by that stage, considered extreme. For instance, Reagan was quoted as saying, in reference to juvenile delinquents, 'I'd like to harness their youthful energy with a strap.'[96] To many voters, that seemed entirely sensible. Brown inadvertently fed the public more reasons to like Reagan.

Brown also tried to link Reagan to notorious extremists like Gerald Smith of the National Christian Crusade, an avowed anti-Semite and former supporter of Nazi Germany. Smith had indeed used a Reagan speech in one of his publications, but no direct connection between the two individuals could be proven. The Reagan camp lambasted the tactic as 'McCarthyism of the left'.[97] 'It looks like a case of guilt by association,' Reagan remarked, 'but in this instance, there isn't even an association.'[98] For the most part, however, Reagan responded to the extremist jibes by not responding. Bradley confirmed that: 'We made a considerable effort to establish the right-wing connections Reagan had and Reagan was making every effort to keep as far away from it as he could.'[99] Within that recollection lies a good explanation of what happened. Brown wanted a mudfight, but Reagan refused to join in. As a result, the only one who looked dirty was Brown.

Lending support to Reagan, Robert Sutton, vice president of CBS Radio, attacked Cranston for using 'every technique of smear, of distortion, and of guilt-by-association'. He also maintained that, when challenged, Coate was forced to admit that: 'he has no evidence – I repeat, no evidence – that any John Birch member is an adviser of Mr. Reagan.'[100] Roberts identified a clear flaw in the Democratic strategy:

> In 1966 the Birchers weren't throwing Molotov cocktails and hitting policemen; the Negroes were. You might disagree with the Birch Society, even disagree violently, but they weren't practicing violence to get their viewpoint across. Besides, we learned in the 1964 election that it's tough to put over the right-wing issue. Most people don't know how to define an extremist; the average Bircher looks, acts and talks pretty much like everyone else. If you meet him, say at a cocktail party, you're not going to start looking for a bomb shelter. The Bircher isn't identifiable, but the Negro is. When California was talking about Negro rioters, Pat Brown was talking about Birchers.[101]

The strategy was clearly bankrupt, but the Democrats stuck with it, in the vain hope that the voters would eventually see the light. 'At this stage of the game you are so deeply committed to what you are doing that you can't worm out of it,' a Brown aide candidly admitted.[102] The political commentators Rowland Evans and Robert Novak pinpointed a common error:

> What is happening here is the old problem of campaign strategists saying what their supporters want to hear rather than what might win votes. For among Brown's backers and particularly among his prominent Jewish supporters there is a genuine fear of Reagan in Sacramento as a dangerously sharp turn to the right ... But the Jewish and Negro votes, who might most be affected by the extremist issue are in Brown's pocket anyway.
> 
> The votes that Brown must win are the lower income and lower middle income white and Mexican Democrats in the Los Angeles area who gave Mayor Sam Yorty his anti-Negro backlash vote against Brown in last June's primary ...

Conceivably, these key voters might turn against Reagan if they are convinced he is an inexperienced incompetent. But, for them, the extremism issue doesn't exist.[103]

Dutton admitted that there was an inherent contradiction in the Democratic campaign. On the one hand, the Brown team was 'trying to paint Reagan as the big black reactionary who would suppress democratic institutions or poor people'. On the other hand, 'it was trying to say he was the B movie actor who was totally ineffective and couldn't do anything. We were aware at the time that the approaches were inconsistent.'[104] In other words, if Reagan was a lightweight, how was he also dangerous?

The Bircher issue was important to voters. A California Poll in February 1966 found that 55 per cent disapproved of the Society, while only 6 per cent approved. The poll further revealed that 53 per cent would be less likely to vote for a candidate if he welcomed support of the Birchers. These findings seem to contradict the reaction to Reagan, who steadfastly insisted that he welcomed support from any quarter. Clearly, the voters accepted Reagan's denials of affiliation and excused his refusal to condemn because he seemed an honest man. He responded as he had over the previous year, reiterating that he was not a Bircher but could not control the fact that Birchers liked him. 'It [has] never occurred to me to give saliva tests to my supporters,' he quipped.[105] That was apparently enough to satisfy the voters, yet Brown stubbornly refused to drop the issue. On 9 October, he claimed that Reagan would have no qualms about appointing a Bircher to his staff. 'The threat of the John Birch Society is the greatest threat we have in California.' He accused Reagan of ducking this issue: 'If he doesn't believe that Birchers are dangerous,' Brown spat, 'why does he deny – against the flat, published evidence – that they are all around him in his campaign? ... Is it because he believes as they do, but knows he can't be elected if the voters find out?'[106] The histrionics were impressive for their intensity, but not for their effect. To the electorate, the allegations at first seemed insubstantial, then boring, then annoying. 'If Brown loses,' George Todt wrote in the *Los Angeles Herald-Examiner*, 'it will be largely because the odiferous "extremist" warfare has offended the good taste of the electorate. The latter is weary of hatemongering.'[107]

Reagan, in contrast to Goldwater, did not make a credible extremist. 'All of this just completely backfired,' Smith argued, 'because when Reagan goes on television ... he does not create [look like] an extremist ... So that campaign just fell absolutely flat. And by the time they realized that, it was ... too late, and they couldn't do anything right.'[108] This was ironic given that, in private, Reagan was happy to acknowledge his ties to Goldwater. In a letter to the Arizona senator just after his primary victory, he wrote:

> No need to tell you, of course, what's in my mind about the coming campaign. You set the pattern and perhaps it was your fate to just be a little too soon, or maybe it required someone with the courage to do what you did with regard to campaigning on principles. I have tried to do the same and have found the people more receptive because they've had a chance to realize there is such a thing as truth.[109]

The Brown camp hoped that the voters would automatically assume that a candidate from the far right was a monster. 'It didn't work,' Bradley admitted.[110] Reagan seemed unworthy of hate or fear. He was the favourite uncle: the man who made one feel good. In the charm contest, Reagan annihilated Brown. 'Reagan was a very electric, dynamic, charismatic figure and a magnificent speaker, and Brown was nothing like that at all,' Weinberger reflected. 'I think the contrast was just too great.'[111] Feeling cheated, Brown concluded, perhaps correctly, that Reagan had won because his handlers had successfully camouflaged his extremism. 'The speeches and things like that were really very deceiving and very deceptive.' The voters' refusal to see what seemed so readily apparent was frustrating. 'By the end of the first week of October we all admitted failure on the extremism issue. We couldn't make him an extremist even though he was.'[112]

Given Reagan's adroit handling of the press and coolness under cross-examination, Spencer and Roberts were eager to organize a debate with Brown. This would play to Reagan's strengths, not only that he was telegenic, but also his ability to craft clever one-liners. The Brown team hedged whenever the issue was raised. 'We tried frantically ... to arrange a debate,' Weinberger maintained. 'We soon learned ... that one thing the Brown representatives did not want was a debate with Reagan and they would go to any ends to avoid it by putting up new conditions and constantly changing.'[113] Reagan demanded a 'traditional face-to-face, no-holds-barred format'.[114] Brown wanted to avoid that at all costs, but did not want to seem cowardly. His team proposed instead a straightforward news conference with both candidates present but not able to ask questions of, or rebut, one another. Negotiations remained deadlocked through most of September and October. 'Probably the biggest shock of the entire story was that Brown ever accepted Reagan's challenge,' a leader in the *Pasadena Star News* commented. 'It seems clear that he never intended to follow through ... The governor's only reason for accepting ... was to create the illusion that he did not fear the possibility that Reagan would dominate philosophically as well as forensically.'[115] While the *Star News* was an unashamedly right-wing paper, that was probably true.

Brown somehow managed to convince himself that a debate did take place. 'We had a debate and I thought I did well ... I know that I did.'[116] He perhaps had in mind two appearances on television with Reagan, the first on NBC's *Meet the Press* on 11 September and the second on ABC's *Issues and Answers* on 2 October. Since the debate negotiations continued while these broadcasts were aired, they are clearly not what Reagan had in mind. On both occasions, the candidates were questioned separately, ruling out genuine rebuttal. The programmes were highly scripted affairs with the candidates repeating arguments now boringly familiar. Reagan won the encounter because he did not lose – Brown came up with nothing new to damage him.

Meanwhile, Reagan was hammering Brown at grassroots level. Spencer-Roberts repeated the techniques used during the primary to ensure that potential supporters were identified, contacted and then mobilized on election day. There were three phases to this operation. The first involved establishing an efficient organization in each precinct, headed by a chairman who then recruited precinct captains who identified potential supporters. Contacts were mainly made in person by door-to-door canvassing. This phase was completed by 31 May, in other words before the primary was actually won. The second phase reinforced this link through telephone calls and extended the network of support in areas where shifts of allegiance were discerned through PIPS. Localized polls were used to craft messages appropriate to each area and to discover trends. The final phase took place on election day, when 'Victory Squads' of volunteers made certain that every person who had pledged support actually made it to the polls.

Frustrated at his inability to make serious inroads into Reagan's lead, Brown turned to smear in the last few weeks of the campaign. That proved difficult, however, because Reagan, unlike Christopher, had no obvious skeletons in his closet. Pro-Brown reporters dug up his divorce from actress Jane Wyman, but that tactic collided head-on with evidence of his stable and loving marriage to Nancy. Supporters also took to sabotaging Reagan's radio phone-ins with bogus calls. On 24 October 1966, for instance, a caller identifying himself as 'Colonel Moore' claimed on KNX Radio's *Firing Line* that he had served in the same Air Force unit as Reagan and had witnessed his involvement in the illegal trading of mess supplies. Reagan handled the situation well, eventually accusing the caller of being a phony and a Brown plant. Further investigation revealed that the real Colonel Moore had not called the programme, but it was impossible to prove a direct connection to Brown. Reagan nevertheless used the incident to accuse Brown of 'riding out the last days of his campaign on a sea of smear'.[117] Given the hard evidence of Brown's earlier dirty tricks, that allegation sounded plausible.

The Brown campaign was not only poorly conceived, it was also badly stage-managed. An example of this fault came when Robert Kennedy arrived to lend Brown a hand. No one bothered to make sure that Kennedy stayed on script. As Brown recalled:

> Senator Kennedy came into the state to campaign for me, but he was really campaigning for himself. He attracted so much attention that when we'd get on the platform all the young people would watch Bobby Kennedy. They loved him and it was obvious they ignored me. It was kind of a mistake because the governor has to be number one; he can never be number two.[118]

'There were a lot of big spectaculars with visitors from out of the state,' Champion recalled. 'They didn't do very much good ... They got lots of publicity and so on but it didn't seem to change the character of the campaign.'[119] Shiny celebrities made Brown look grey. The Reagan team, realizing they could not possibly mobilize personalities of similar political stature, made a virtue of this deficiency. They decided to stress that, in their view, the campaign 'was between the candidates and the people of California, and it was the other side bringing in the carpetbaggers'.[120] The strategy had the additional benefit of keeping Goldwater at bay, without causing offence to those who still had a soft spot for the Arizona senator. By refraining from drafting in celebrities, Spencer and Roberts also ensured that Reagan was always the star.

Brown had a large budget for television, but the money was mainly spent attacking Reagan. After the primary, the filmmaker Charles Guggenheim was brought in to make a series of ads and short films. David Wolper, used during the primary, was pushed aside in the quest for something flashier and more aggressive. Guggenheim's ads were much more cinematically impressive than Reagan's, but the content was unimaginative, as he admitted:

> the whole idea was to just sort of make ludicrous Reagan's candidacy, that an actor should try to run the biggest state in the union. They got caught up in that strategy and they devoted all of their time to that thing. When I got there it was already in motion and instead of separating myself ... from it I got caught ... going after Reagan rather than trying to build up Brown. In retrospect ... it was a mistake.[121]

One particular script demonstrates this lack of imagination:

> Thomas Jefferson once said, 'That which would best warrant the public trust will secure to itself men of uncommon worth and integrity.' Integrity – still a good word. Ronald Reagan has made it the foundation of his campaign. Is it integrity for Mr. Reagan to deny all connection with the John Birch Society, when his state labor chairman and four members of his finance committee are known members of this secret society? Is it integrity for Mr. Reagan to spend ten years fighting Medicare, Social Security, the union shop and now pretend to support them? Integrity is a good word, but in Mr. Reagan's case, is it the right word? Vote for a real governor, not an acting one ... Pat Brown.[122]

Another ad strung together brief clips of Reagan in his various Hollywood roles, from cowboy, to gunslinger, to jilted lover, to frontman for Boraxo. Toward the end of the sequence, the narrator, in a grave tone, asks: 'Ronald Reagan has played many roles.

This year he wants to play governor. Can you afford the price of admission?'[123] Burch felt that the ads betrayed a lack of ideas:

> the negative campaign was turned off a number of times. I can't remember if it was the governor or Fred [Dutton] I heard say, 'God, we turn it off every Friday and every Monday I come in and there are those big manila envelopes going out to the press.' But it was an aspect of the campaign that seemed to have a life of its own. It seemed that no matter how often decisions were made in so-called strategy meetings, that we weren't going to pursue that effort anymore, the operation continued to flourish.[124]

Leaving aside the actual content, the Reagan team was delighted that the shoe was on the other foot – Brown could now be criticized for spending vast sums on a slick, Hollywood-influenced campaign. 'Mr. Guggenheim's big problem with his new star is to teach him to smile,' a mischievous press release quipped. 'Informed sources say the Governor tends to … talk too much on camera … As a result a drama coach has been called in to teach Pat to smile and relax and to talk less.'[125] In the end, well-produced ads simply drew attention to the negativity and emptiness of the campaign.

One of Guggenheim's tasks was to produce a 30-minute campaign film that was all about Brown, without the negative stuff. He followed the governor on the campaign trail, taking candid shots designed to show him at his best – relaxed, warm, happy, joking. On the whole, the project went well and Guggenheim was proud of the footage. 'He was … very open and made you feel good to be around him.'[126] One small scene, however, backfired. In it, Brown is seen chatting informally to a few black children. He asks them: 'Do you know who killed Lincoln?' 'No,' they reply. Brown then says: 'It was an actor.'[127] The remark was typical of Brown: he had an endearing tendency to talk without thinking. 'I could never keep my mouth shut,' he admitted.[128] 'When you tell the story it sounds absolutely horrible,' Guggenheim explained. He insisted that it was completely unscripted and totally innocent. 'If you see the film then you have to make your own judgment. It was an endearing moment because of the fact that the teachers were laughing, the black kids were laughing, everybody was laughing.'[129]

'I thought it was the funniest thing in the world,' Brown reflected. He saw no problem with including the scene in the documentary. 'But the Republicans picked it up right away and attacked me for attacking the acting profession, and a lot of the actors that liked me very much ... turned against me ... it was just a misjudgment.'[130] Spencer felt that the documentary itself was superb, but 'The whole essence of it went out the window because of this one lousy sixty seconds ... I never could figure that one out.'[131]

Dutton was flabbergasted. 'He did say it, and ... decided to use it. It couldn't have been more wrong ... It was politically harmful from the time it was first shown.'[132] Reagan's team took full advantage of the gaffe. 'Whoever authorized that ad should get some kind of an award,' Smith felt. 'We couldn't believe it, but we loved every minute of it. They finally took it off, and we were very sorry about that.'[133] Given his background, Reagan was genuinely offended and astonished at its insensitivity. The ad nevertheless had an unanticipated effect:

> Hollywood was pretty predominantly Democrat. So even people that I had worked with and who were friendly to me just wouldn't desert their party. A number of them, after he did that, just walked away from him ... I couldn't understand the stupidity of it. Because he not only did it once, he kept on running that ad on television. I just never responded to it.[134]

Spencer confirmed that effect:

> That got under Hollywood's skin. Frank Sinatra was on our phone the next day. Frank was a big Democrat for whom I had

done work before. 'What can I do?' he asked in that voice. 'What can I do?' Man, they were coming out of the woodwork. A lot of them were hidden Reaganauts, but they were Democrats and they didn't want to get out front.[135]

In retrospect, Guggenheim admitted his error. 'It was a mistake not to take it out. It read terribly. Word of mouth was horrible. It just didn't sound right.'[136]

On the ballot in California, candidates are given the opportunity to list their occupation below their name. Brown listed 'governor'; Reagan left the space blank, choosing not to identify himself as an actor. The uncertainty over definition did not seem to bother the voters. On 8 November, Reagan won by a margin of 56.7 per cent to 41.6 per cent, or nearly a million votes. He won 55 of 58 counties, thus demonstrating that, in contrast to Goldwater and Nixon, his brand of conservatism had broad appeal. 'This is indeed a great victory,' Reagan proclaimed. 'It is a clear mandate from the people of California that they want and demand a change in the direction of their government.' It is difficult to argue with that assessment. The landslide was, Reagan claimed, 'clear evidence that this was not a narrow, factional victory ... We could not have won without the votes of hundreds of thousands of concerned Democrats from every county and city and town in the state.' The changing nature of politics in the United States was written in the faces of those who voted for Reagan. These people had, he felt, supported him 'not because we are Republicans, but because we offered an alternative to Big Brother government'. He stressed once again that government works best when it 'leads, but does not rule'.[137] What that meant in practice was still unclear, but it sure sounded good.

Brown subsequently insisted that he had drawn level by the final weeks of the campaign. This was not exactly true, since the California Poll gave Reagan a three-point lead in September, seven points in October and five just a week before the election.[138] That moment in September when the candidates drew closest together nevertheless explains a great deal about this election. Brown told friends that 'Ronnie ... is beginning to wear a little bit thin.'[139] He convinced himself that he would be able to engineer another miraculous victory by campaigning hard in the autumn. But then, on 27 September, a white policeman fatally shot a black teenager in Hunters Point, a predominantly black neighbourhood of San Francisco. Riots immediately erupted. Reagan weighed in with his usual soundbites about law and order and the irresponsibility of black leaders. An angry Brown replied that Reagan was more to be 'pitied than condemned' because he was pretending to be an authority on matters 'he never has had to deal with ... in his entire life'.[140] Given the state of white opinion in California, Reagan was always destined to win that argument. Game over.

Brown blamed the discrepancy between the final polls and the actual result on the fact that 'we had another riot in San Francisco. All the undecideds switched and I lost practically 90 percent of the undecided vote.'[141] There was some truth to that claim. The California Poll was accurate as far as Brown's share was concerned, which suggests that the 10 per cent listed as undecided did indeed overwhelmingly go for Reagan, despite two-thirds of them being Democrat. The Hunters Point riot might have had a lot to do with that shift, but the statistics also demonstrate in stark terms the success Spencer and Roberts had in targeting swing voters. The revolution was revealed most clearly in the 12 most working-class towns in California, most of them Los Angeles commuter suburbs that housed aerospace workers. Four years earlier, Brown had won all 12. Against Reagan, he managed to win only one.

'The voters failed to appreciate my greatness,' Brown later quipped.[142] Rather than take the blame for a badly managed campaign, Brown convinced himself that he had been defeated by events beyond his control, including the riot in San Francisco. Bradley, to his credit, had a firmer grasp on reality.

He blamed Reagan's ability to attract white working-class support. 'We lost the campaign by the same margin we were behind when we started,' he remarked. 'So we never really made any dent in it.' In just a few sentences, Bradley summarized a revolutionary change in American politics: 'We ... lost votes with the conservative Democrats. I'd say the backbone of the party, the blue-collar majority worker. That's who we lost.'[143] The working class had grown sceptical of liberalism.

# 10

# 'Hey, This Guy Could Be President Someday'

After Reagan's victory in the primary, political commentators struggled to make sense of what had happened. Liberal journalists on the East Coast, with typical snobbery, were inclined to dismiss California as simply weird. 'The California Republicans, against all counsels of common sense and political prudence, insisted upon nominating actor Ronald Reagan for Governor,' an editorial in the *New York Times* remarked. 'Mr Reagan ... is innocent of experience in government, and his speeches suggest he is equally innocent of knowledge.'[1] 'California has always been one of those states whose politics makes no sense at all to the outside,' wrote Pete Hamill in the *New York Post*.[2] In *Newsweek*, Emmet Hughes declared that the Reagan victory 'dramatizes the virtual bankruptcy, politically and intellectually, of a national party'.[3]

Another set of commentators took a completely opposite view. Nofziger, after his first campaign tour with Reagan, remarked: 'Hey, this guy could be president some day!'[4] Before long, that notion was rumbling across the country like the aftershocks of an earthquake. A Gallup poll just after the primary showed the first hints of support for Reagan as the Republican presidential nominee in 1968.[5] The *New York Times* correspondent David Broder, reporting on Reagan's visit to

Washington in August, remarked on what seemed, 'in the eyes of many of those present, the Washington debut of a potential presidential candidate'.[6] After Reagan's landslide victory on 8 November, papers across America began reporting on, and spreading, rumours of a presidential bid. Reagan himself feigned innocence: 'gosh, it's taken me all my life to get up the nerve to do what I'm doing. That's as far as my dreams go.'[7]

Both responses to the Reagan phenomenon confirm that this was no ordinary candidate and no ordinary election. It was clearly meaningful, but what precisely did it mean? In short, why did Reagan win?

Some critics jumped to the conclusion that Reagan won because big money bought him the election. That notion was reinforced by the actions of Republican State Assemblyman Howard Thelin, who, just before polling day, slammed the Reagan campaign as 'a conspiracy of powerful, well financed forces dominated by extreme views'. He insisted that Reagan's defeat was 'vital to the future of the Republican Party', and therefore pledged his support to Brown.[8] (That action qualifies as one of the rare instances of a rat boarding a sinking ship.) Granted, Reagan spent more than any previous candidate in California history, but that says more about trends in American politics than about his profligacy. The decline of party organizations and voter loyalty meant that campaigns became much more expensive, a trend exacerbated by television. Vast networks of research and communication needed to be set up in order to enable a candidate to identify potential supporters and court their support. By the next election, the amount Reagan had spent would seem unremarkable. By the one after that, it would appear minuscule.

Reagan did not buy this election. He spent $544,199 to win the primary, less than the $561,876 spent by Brown to defeat Yorty. In the general election campaign, Reagan spent $2.6 million, Brown $2.0 million.[9] While this is a significant difference, it is not astronomical, especially since Brown was the incumbent and did not therefore need to start from scratch. Reagan also spent a great deal because he had a great deal to spend – grassroots fundraising was so superbly managed that he ended up with a surplus. His approach to fundraising foreshadowed that of Barack Obama in 2008, in that thousands of ordinary people were persuaded to donate small amounts. 'The only thing I know', he reflected, '[is that] I broke all records in California for the number of contributors so that ... the average contribution was something under $20 ... In other words, we were not basically funded by fat cats.'[10] In any case, much more important than the amount of money collected was the way it was spent. Brown wasted $2 million on a poorly managed campaign. Reagan paid $2.6 million for a good one. Reagan paid 69 cents for each vote gained, Brown 72 cents.

Dutton felt that Reagan won not because his campaign was particularly brilliant, but because his opponent was so weak. 'The main problem was the Brown administration. Democrats lost in droves in '66 across the country.'[11] Bagley felt the same. 'You don't "win" an election against an incumbent. The incumbent loses ... Pat was at the end of his trail and he lost.'[12] Champion likewise concluded that 'There were a series of things and all of them hurt us during that campaign because all of them were sort of regarded as a signal of Pat's being too permissive, of people feeling threatened.' It seemed, therefore, that any liberal running in California in 1966 was doomed. 'There wasn't anything Pat could do about it. Pat never really had very much of a chance.'[13]

Reagan undoubtedly benefited from a significant backlash against the Democrats. Republicans captured five out of six partisan, statewide positions, five new Senate seats and seven new Assembly seats. On the surface, then, his victory does not seem to be any more remarkable than that of his party. Bagley, in fact, felt that Christopher would have won by a greater margin. That in turn suggests that Brown's strategy of targeting Christopher during the primary might have been sound. As evidence, Bagley noted that Robert Finch, the Republican nominee for lieutenant governor, achieved an even bigger landslide than did Reagan, beating the Democrat Glenn Anderson by 1.3 million votes.[14] 'I'm not even sure that if it had been the other way around', Champion admitted, 'we would have done any better; I think we might have had a lot of trouble with Christopher, too.'[15]

While it is pointless to speculate about counterfactuals, it is nevertheless undeniable that Reagan benefited from a massive shift rightward between 1964 and 1966. This was noticeable across the nation, but especially in California. Thus, almost any credible Republican candidate would have defeated Brown in 1966, the only variable being the margin of victory. 'If I had known how far behind I was,' Brown reflected, 'I might have gone fishing.'[16] Reagan won because the Democratic core collapsed. Reflecting on that collapse during a reception overlooking the San Fernando Valley, Bradley gave Guggenheim a candid observation:

> You see all those people down there? ... You know where they're from, Guggenheim? They're from Peoria. They're from Kankakee. They're from Pittsburgh ... You know why they're here? Well, they're back in Peoria and their kids are on drugs and their wife is unhappy because there's all kinds of crap in the streets and there's all kind of problems and the schools are not good and the blacks are coming in.
>
> So they move. They move west ... Their kids are still on drugs. There's still violence in the schools. There's still problems with blacks ... They can't go any further. The ocean is there. And they're still unhappy. And you know something? That's why we're going to get our ass beat.[17]

The promised land no longer seemed promising. Democrats failed to react effectively to this groundswell of white discontent. It was perfectly expressed in a letter to the *San Diego Union*:

We are tired of picket lines and sit-ins by dirty unwashed never-do-wells who rush to man the barricades against law-and-order. We are tired of seeing mobs of scabby-faced, long-haired youths and short-haired girls who claim to represent the 'new wave' of America and who sneer at the virtues of honesty, integrity, and morality on which this country achieved its greatness.

We are tired of the lazy do-nothings who wouldn't take a job if they were driven back and forth to work in a Rolls Royce.

We are tired of the people who try to peddle the belief in schools and colleges that capitalism is a dirty word and that free enterprise and private enterprise are synonyms of greed. They say they hate capitalism, but are always at the head of the line demanding their share of American life.

Last but not least, most of us are fed up with the colleges which are tax supported ... having disgraceful demonstrations by youths who are trying to dictate the policies of an institution of education.[18]

White voters in California never managed to conform to the noble illusions Brown held about them. He kept insisting that ordinary people were big-hearted, generous, tolerant, unselfish and liberal, but their behaviour suggested they were mean-spirited, selfish and bigoted. The gap between his illusions and their reality explains why so many white working-class voters walked away. Since he would not compromise on his liberal principles, he found it increasingly difficult to accommodate their prejudices. His difficulty arose in part because of the racial undertones of white discontent. As the journalist Marianne Means remarked with perfect precision, 'There is not much the governor can do to counteract this, except to make the idea of Reagan in the statehouse a more frightening prospect than the possibility of a Negro living next door.'[19] A frustrated Brown complained on 28 October that Reagan was 'riding the [white] backlash ... and perhaps even subtly contributing to it'.[20] Reagan vehemently denied that allegation, but it was true.

While it is credible to suggest that Christopher would also have won, perhaps even by a wider margin, that should not detract from the dramatic nature of Reagan's victory. He was, after all, a far-right conservative, notorious for his support of Goldwater in 1964 and his refusal to repudiate the Birchers. The reason he had to fight so hard to counter the extremist label was because there was so much truth to it. Recall what Goldwater said about extremism in 1964. Recall how enthusiastically Reagan campaigned for Goldwater. Recall that, on some issues, like social security and the TVA, Reagan was to the right of Goldwater.

In measuring the magnitude of Reagan's achievement, it is helpful to bear in mind the two previous elections in California. Brown beat Nixon by nearly 300,000 votes in 1962. In 1964, Lyndon Johnson, a man of similar political temperament to Brown, defeated Goldwater by nearly 1.3 million votes in California. While it is undoubtedly true that white workers deserted the Democrats in droves between 1964 and 1966, it is astonishing that they would move so willingly from a liberal Democrat to a conservative Republican. Thus, what is remarkable about Reagan's success is not his margin of victory, but rather that he achieved that margin with policies not distinctly different from Goldwater's. Despite the attempts of Spencer-Roberts to make his conservatism palatable, the fact remains that he was unashamedly right wing. As Goldwater remarked after Reagan's primary victory, 'All I know is, he was billed as a conservative, and he won.'[21] An editorial in the *San Diego Union* astutely concluded that 'Reagan proved in the primary election that the people have not rejected conservatism, when it is constructive and there is the opportunity to properly present it and make it understandable. That, Mr. Reagan succeeded in doing.'[22]

Reagan's appeal to the core values of blue-collar workers presaged the 'southern strategy' that would be used to such good effect by Richard Nixon in 1968 and 1972. Nixon learned a great deal from Reagan about how to play to the prejudices of the white working class. This constituency was particularly susceptible to campaigns based on emotion rather than reason – fear and hopes more than policies or ideology – and to the techniques associated with the television age, in particular cleverly crafted soundbites, nostalgic images, romantic promises and apocalyptic warnings. By these means, working-class loyalty to the Democratic Party was comprehensively undermined in the 1960s. The workers would support the Democrats in the future, but never again instinctively as they had once done. Democrats, in order to win back the workers, would have to imitate Reagan's style and approach. This meant communicating in a language that the workers could understand and find inspiring. As Means recognized, 'This is the land of Hollywood and the hard sell, and political pitches, like modern TV commercials, must somehow be louder than life.'[23] In time, the California style of campaigning would spread outwards, across the United States.

Reagan's victory was, above all, a reaction against the liberalism that had dominated American politics since Franklin Roosevelt's election in 1932. 'Liberal' was fast becoming a dirty word, as it is today. As Reagan explained to a correspondent, he did not like the word because it meant different things to different people. He associated it with 'those people who are willing to sacrifice our traditional way of individual freedom for some kind of government-controlled, semi-socialist society'. He accepted that 'to other people this word is used only to describe those who are moved by compassion and want to help the less fortunate', an inclination which he claimed to share.[24] In his attack upon liberalism, Reagan conducted a modern campaign, but one with its themes drawn from the past. He appealed to those who worshipped a romantic notion of frontier self-reliance. To these people, the New Deal was warm-hearted but wrong-headed. Robert Alcorn, a Denver doctor, captured this sentiment perfectly, when he wrote a letter of complaint to the *Denver Post*:

> In an editorial on Jan. 6th, you bushwhacked Ronald Reagan for taking us back to the Death Valley Days. I agree, things were different then. The Constitution, not the Supreme Court, was the law of the land. The currency was sound, backed by gold and silver and not by 'promises to pay'. The government was on a pay-as-you-go basis, not borrowing from children and unborn grandchildren to finance harebrained extravaganzas. The dollar was worth 100 cents, not 45, bread was 8 cents a loaf, not 28, bacon was 30 cents a pound, not a dollar ten and for five cents you could get all the coffee you could drink with a couple of doughnuts on the side.

To voters like Alcorn, the present was objectionable, the future frightening. By evoking traditional values while intentionally avoiding complex issues, Reagan appealed to those who believed that politics could be distilled down to the price of bacon. 'We're going to hitch up those mules, all twenty of them, give the reins to Ronald Reagan and take off cross-country for Washington,' Alcorn concluded. 'There we're going to put the driver in the White House and use the Borax to clean out the Capitol.'[25] Reagan could not have said it better.

At the heart of liberalism lies a belief in change and progress. The liberal seeks perpetual improvement of the human condition and thinks that government is the best mechanism for achieving this. Each stage of improvement, however, produces a group satisfied with the scope of progress and unwilling to make the sacrifices necessary to extend it further – nor indeed to see the point of doing so. More and more people begin to question the continued relevance of the ideology to their lives. Liberalism becomes, in effect, a victim of its own success. The left-wing journal *Ramparts* reflected on this effect and its consequences in California:

> The failure of Pat Brown's liberalism is its unwillingness to grow out of the New Deal, in the assumption that with welfare laws, labor legislation, and social security the job has been finished. It was the promise of liberalism in America to expand men's horizons, to create new potentialities in society by education and leadership. This is the promise that Pat Brown has failed to keep, and in the affluent uneasiness of California lies the 'grass roots' of Ronald Reagan.[26]

Liberalism, for all its benefits, is expensive, or at least seems so to those who have to bear the largest burden of funding. For each individual voter, a moment arrives when the expense overwhelms the justification. Liberalism is also complex. It is an ideology difficult to reduce to basic notions of cause and effect – black and white – and therefore difficult to defend in a simplistic age of soundbite politics.

In the 1960s, those bewildered by what passed for progress looked for some way to apply the brakes. Workers whose fathers had been rescued by the alphabet programmes now agitated noisily for small government, while worshipping self-reliance. Many wondered whether, if the end result of all that good intention of the 1930s was the hedonism and turmoil of the 1960s, perhaps liberalism itself was misconceived. John Steinbeck, once the arch-enemy of anti-communists because of his unfettered exposure of capitalist injustice, eventually grew appalled at the incessant complaints of baby boomers. He condemned the 'fallout, drop-out, cop-out insurgency of our children and young people, the rush to stimulant as well as hypnotic drugs ... the mistrust and revolt against all authority – this in a time of plenty such as has never been known.'[27] In other words, liberalism had overtaken one of its greatest champions. As Reagan argued:

> I am wholeheartedly in support of the humanitarian goals of practically all of the social legislation we have ever had. I am

violently opposed to some of the methods we have chosen because they have not brought the good they were supposed to bring. I don't think there is any real good to humanity or compassion in adopting some kind of welfare that perpetuates poverty and puts people for three and four generations ... onto the public dole instead of getting them off the public dole and out as self-sustaining citizens.[28]

It seemed to many that all that money and good intention were actually detrimental to social harmony. 'Is America's star rising toward a great new Utopia, or sinking into a morass of overpopulation, poverty and crime?' one study asked. 'Are we making enormous strides toward a golden era of peace and prosperity, or rapidly digging our own collective grave?'[29] This new zeitgeist allowed conservatives to express what was once taboo, sweeping aside the verities of the 1930s. Ideals once labelled extreme now seemed moderate. Shell-shocked liberals had no answer to the erosion of their faith.

No wonder, then, that a silver-tongued conservative should prosper during an era when liberalism was everywhere in decline. As Joseph Lewis remarked,

Reaganism, a refinement of Goldwaterism, appeals ... because it neither threatens nor challenges; it demands neither sacrifice nor money, and it seeks no new insights. Instead, it reassures the majority of Americans that they possess virtue and truth almost by divine right of numerical superiority. It is a counter-revolution of the well-fed, well-housed and well-educated against the great social movement of the last three decades. It is capable of mobilizing millions who never cared before about politics.[30]

Thus, the first reason why Reagan won was because he ran for election at precisely the right moment and was perfectly in tune with the new mood. 'I think the main reason that Reagan won', Nofziger argued, 'was because ... he was a candidate who not only had a unique appeal to the people, but [also] that ... [the] people were looking for something, and he happened to fit what they were looking for.'[31]

The political climate does not, however, provide the full explanation for his victory. Substantive issues like fair housing, race riots and student unrest tend to distract attention from equally important, but less dramatic, factors like strategy, tactics and management– the nuts and bolts of a campaign. There was something very impressive about the way this election was conducted. The control, creativity and direction provided by Spencer-Roberts were transformative. The firm's approach would eventually become the playbook for any serious candidate. Yet because the changes were not particularly dramatic and some were indeed prosaic, a great deal of what went on escaped attention. Stories about 'behaviour engineering' make more dramatic copy than mundane accounts of volunteers knocking on doors, even if the latter was far more important to the final result.

The campaign's uniqueness has customarily been attributed to the unusual nature of the candidate, not to his management. Observers assumed that he had opted for a slick, media-driven campaign because that accorded with his Hollywood background. Others surmised that he needed Spencer-Roberts precisely because he was an inexperienced lightweight. A veteran candidate, it was thought, would still be able to campaign in the old way. When asked why Brown did not hire a team of handlers like Spencer and Roberts, Champion ridiculed the idea. 'That's not necessary,' he insisted. 'Spencer-Roberts were essential to a guy like Reagan, who'd never run for office before, who didn't have any background or experience, who didn't have a campaign structure.' In contrast, 'Brown had won ... at least five straight elections.' Champion insisted that his past successes were proof that the traditional campaign was still relevant.[32] In fact, contrary to what Champion claimed, Brown did hire a professional management team – Baus and

Ross – who had previously handled Goldwater. The issue, however, was not whether a firm was hired, but what it was allowed to do. Because Brown's inner circle was so confident of their ability to win elections, they used Baus and Ross in an advisory, as opposed to management, capacity. The firm did not do anything to shape Brown's image, yet the candidate's image was his weakest point. 'I have no style and I know it,' he admitted. 'I'd give anything to have it, but it's just not there.'[33] Given the chaos caused by the 'bastard troika', it is clear that more dispassionate, professional management was needed. In observing the Reagan campaign, Champion and others saw only a polished PR effort and assumed that was the essence. They failed to notice that Spencer-Roberts were not just spin doctors, but full service managers who coordinated every aspect of the campaign, including, in particular, the grassroots effort and precinct profiling that attracted so little attention from the Brown camp and, subsequently, from historians. The success of those efforts can be demonstrated from the fact that 84 per cent of registered Republicans actually voted in the election, compared to 77 per cent of registered Democrats.[34] (And, of the latter, an extraordinary proportion actually voted for Reagan.)

Thus, the second reason why Reagan won was because he had behind him the best campaign managers that money could buy. While Reagan was a superb candidate, he nevertheless benefited enormously from those who surrounded him – Spencer-Roberts and the Friends. It was a team effort that included the candidate, his backers, his managers and an army of volunteers. 'Bill or myself ... built a massive organization of people,' Spencer explained. 'We put a good organization together ... one of the best they ever had in the state ... it was a volunteer campaign, it was a melding of all the resources better than any other campaign.'[35]

The implications of modern campaign management caused considerable concern – at the time and since. Because an avowed non-politician had succeeded so brilliantly in a politician's world, many began to fear that politics had been hijacked by Madison Avenue. 'This idea that you can merchandise candidates for high office like breakfast cereal', Adlai Stevenson complained, 'is, I think, the ultimate indignity to the democratic process.'[36] The future looked frightening. The Ripon Society, a moderate group of Republicans, warned that campaign managers were usurping the power of the party:

> In radically changing the image of a candidate, they are beginning to assume responsibility for the candidate's program. Approaching the point where they will be able to 'sell' a prospect a 'campaign package' for Congress or the Assembly or whatever, they will be dictating candidate selection, with the party only able to protest weakly and attempt to pick up the pieces afterwards.[37]

Inadvertently lending credence to the group's concerns, Baus and Ross asserted that: 'Political campaigns are too important to be left to the politicians, too rich the prize, too complex and costly the process to entrust the struggle for political power entirely to party chieftains, political bosses, committee chairmen, hopeful candidates, ambitious insiders and political "volunteers".'[38] The manipulative potential of campaign managers was compounded by the power of television, another serious concern for those worried about the future. Would the tyranny of television and image shapers give way to a raft of actor-candidates and rule out dull geniuses like Thomas Jefferson or physically unattractive men like Abraham Lincoln?

Another concern raised was that Reagan's campaign had played upon the fears of the electorate, fears created by the candidate himself. This was, after all, the notion central to PIPS. In 1968, Barabba explained the potential of PIPS to a conference in Chicago sponsored by the Republican Congressional Campaign Committee. Tom Littlewood, reporting for the *Sun Times*, summarized Barraba's presentation:

Using computers, Datamatics devised a way of simulating a campaign in much the same way that Pentagon consultants practice waging wars in the gaming room and economists project Gross National Product ... For about $250,000, a party or candidate could 'program' a computer to respond like the voting public. The machine would be fed sociodemographic information, past voting and other statistics, and a polling sample of current attitudes of various segments of the population. Then, options could be 'bounced' at groups of voters.[39]

The word 'program' caused hackles to rise. What was being programmed? The election? The electorate? The candidate? 'Do we really want to fully program an election?' David Hardin, a corporate market researcher, asked. 'Opinion polling puts some real pressure on the candidate to adjust. We're getting real close to the programmed candidate.'[40] These protests provided as much protection as a tent in a hurricane. What candidate would not want to make use of these tools in order to find out what made the voters tick? Since the future promised better computers and more accurate data, the advent of the programmed candidate was inevitable. Reagan was a symptom of what happened when computer technology was applied to elections. He demonstrated what could be achieved if the tools were used effectively. He was not, however, the cause of that transformation.

These concerns seemed all the more credible because an actor had been turned into a governor. Serious questions were therefore raised about the difference between electability and fitness for office. What would happen if the perfect candidate proved to be a disaster as governor – or president? Critics reacted as if that was a new possibility, yet American history is littered with individuals who were brilliant campaigners but hopeless leaders. In any case, these fears were inappropriate to the Reagan story. Reagan highlighted the problems discussed but did not epitomize them. He benefited from excellent management, but his managers did not make a governor from a lump of Hollywood clay. Furthermore, those who decry the role of Spencer and Roberts in this election miss an essential point: in modern politics *every* candidate is shaped by his managers. Lewis felt that Reagan had an enormous advantage because he appealed to the public's hunger for glamorous figures: 'He did not create that demand for political sex appeal, which has been fed by television and public relations, but he is a logical consequence of it.' Lewis noted rather wryly that 'The opposition, which complains about the slick marketing techniques in selling Reagan, uses the same tools but not as skilfully.'[41]

As Spencer, Roberts, Nofziger and others concluded, Reagan won because he was a consummate and talented politician long before they met him. 'His strength', Lewis remarked in 1968,

> is his shining image as the earnest, pleasantly naïve 'citizen politician', a role of dewy-eyed ingenuousness which he plays exquisitely, having prepared for it in fifty films ... he is a master politician who senses where the power lies and acts accordingly ... He flourishes precisely because he appears to be what he is not: an amateur ... Reagan differs from the herd because he is so skillful at playing the game while pretending not to.[42]

Reagan was successful because he was perfectly in tune with the political sympathies of Californians at a moment of profound political change within the state. These qualities were not the creation of his managers, though they did help to bring them to the fore and promote them among the people. To judge the importance of Reagan against that of his handlers, we should imagine the counterfactual: while Brown conducted an atrocious campaign, it is inconceivable that a firm like Spencer and Roberts could have turned him into a winner in 1966. In other words, while some of the best campaign managers in the business were on Reagan's side, none of those talented men made him or won him the election.

Thus, the third reason why Reagan won was because he was Ronald Reagan – the Great Communicator. Though Republicans did well across the country, the 1966 gubernatorial victory was in truth the triumph of an individual. 'It was an easier campaign than people think,' Spencer remarked. He always believed that, 'once we've got him over the hump and headed in the right direction, he's going to win it with us or without us. The only thing we were able to do was … to keep him from making mistakes.'[43] As has been stressed throughout this book, the election confirmed that the voters in California cared more about character and personality than about specific policies. American elections are often the triumph of an individual who happens to capture the imagination of the electorate at a specific moment – as Kennedy, Carter, Clinton, Reagan and Obama have demonstrated. At elections of this sort, policy is less important than personality. 'It is the character of the man, rather than the position he takes on public issues, which so often wins an election,' the syndicated columnist David Lawrence argued. 'In fact, there are many cases where the candidate who says less than his opponent on specific issues and sticks to general principles turns out to be the victor – very largely because of a winning personality.'[44] That perfectly summed up Reagan.

This also explains why Reagan could win with so little experience of campaigning. We return to a question posed earlier: why did an obvious non-politician succeed so brilliantly and with such apparent ease in a politician's world? The answer lies in the question. The essence of Reagan's 1966 revolution was that he gave expression to the voters' profound estrangement from traditional politics. The fact that Reagan was an actor made his job of convincing voters easier, but it does not explain his success. That success may seem annoyingly simple, but its simplicity lies in Reagan's paper-thin manifesto and in his intentionally unsophisticated nature. The campaign itself was refined and complex, requiring skills for which Reagan is seldom credited, namely shrewdness, sensitivity, perfect timing and an extraordinary memory for detail. Beyond those substantial personal attributes and talents, he was also willing to heed advice.

The crucial period came at the very beginning when the extremist issue was buried. Spencer felt that: 'how he handled the extremism question, was probably the biggest contribution we made.'[45] For all the praise heaped upon Reagan for his honesty and lack of guile, the fact is that he was a one-time extremist who was marketed as a moderate. Journalists frequently disparaged the makeover that had been done on him. 'He is a product, as carefully processed and packaged as Lucky Filters,' argued the editors at *Ramparts*.[46] Spencer was always sensitive to these charges. 'I hate the word packaging ... I come from the school of thought that you just can't fool all the people; that they can see through what you're doing.' He nevertheless accepted that Reagan's beliefs needed careful presentation. 'How it is produced and what is said is very important, but it is very difficult to change a candidate's philosophy and beliefs. And I don't think you can and I don't think you should try.' Instead,

> We try to work with the framework of what they believe. We may emphasize one thing and de-emphasize something else, get them to do that sort of thing. But that's where the press comes in. They're the big referee of this whole ball game. And they have to ... make all these value judgements as to whether the person is being packaged and tinselled and saying things that they really don't believe or that the record doesn't show. And this is true of all candidates, not just Ronald Reagan.[47]

So, according to Spencer, Reagan was carefully presented, but not packaged. Campaign professionals often insist that they are image-conveyors, not image-makers.[48] Yet that seems a contrived distinction and one all the more suspect because it comes from a profession whose product is spin. If there is a subtle difference between presentation and packaging, it is perhaps a distinction only discernible to someone like Spencer. One striking feature to emerge from a close examination of this election is that Reagan was sold by a very talented sales team.

We mine the past for insights into our world, lessons that might make the confusing events of today more understandable or manageable. To do so, however, is dangerous, misleading and often facile. The effort to extract lessons relevant today usually means imposing the present upon the past. Factors that render a bygone event unique to its own context are ignored so that it can be shoehorned into preconceived notions of how we wish to see our world today. Drawing profound conclusions from contrived comparisons might suit the fairground fortune teller, but not the serious historian.

The passage of time can quickly make a fool of the historian who tries to find parallels in the past. For this reason, I am reluctant to go down that road and impose on the reader lessons that should be derived from Reagan's 1966 campaign. If parallels seem apparent, that is fine. That said, there are trends noticeable back then which remain relevant to this day. The most important one is anti-intellectualism or what can more crudely be described as the dumbing down of politics. Christopher complained bitterly of that problem in 1966, yet he would be appalled at what passes for political dialogue today. We now live in a world where political discourse is often reduced to what can be said in 140 characters. The populist thrives amongst an electorate disinclined to explore or understand the complexity of problems.

Another notable trend is the diminishing importance of the party and the consequent prominence of the individual. That development, too, is even more pronounced than it was in the 1960s and is exacerbated by what the talented and attractive politician can do with the ever-developing media. (Imagine what Reagan could have achieved with the tweet.) A weak party system allows fringe groups and rogue demagogues to thrive. On the other hand, as Reagan demonstrated, this situation also offers opportunities for a talented politician to take hold of the party and impose unity upon it.

Plog and Holden always insisted that they made the Great Communicator. Every other aide who worked closely with Reagan scorned that contention as a forlorn attempt to siphon the greatness of a massive individual. Aside from Plog and Holden, almost everyone argues that success was mainly due to Reagan himself. Neil Reagan had no doubt why his brother won so handsomely in 1966 and in every subsequent election: 'there isn't a better communicator in the business ... There wasn't anything you had to teach him about communication.'[49] McDowell agreed: 'He is one of the best campaigners, or probably the best campaigner, that I've ever had anything to do with.'[50] He was, as Nofziger felt, the perfect candidate, but his perfection was not limited to aspects of delivery usually associated with the 'Great Communicator' image. He was not simply a handsome and articulate spokesman for a pre-arranged package of policies. He had an instinctive understanding of modern politics which allowed him to sense how to tailor his message to his audience. He was not, in other words, an ideologue who abhorred nuance or compromise. Nor was he weighed down by how campaigns had been conducted in the past. The avowed non-politician was in fact one of the most skilled politicians in American history. 'Politics has always been his first love,' wrote Lewis, 'acting is what Reagan did for a living.'[51]

The constituency that supported Reagan in 1966 would remain loyal to him for the rest of his political career. To them, he would always be the citizen-politician, the man who knew the pain of those who despised politics. The tactics that had allowed that constituency to be mobilized would become gospel for every aspiring politician who subsequently sought office in the United States. The Republicans used those tactics to great effect in the period from 1966 to 2008. Reagan's success had demonstrated that conservative Republican policies, if properly packaged and delivered with charisma, could be sold to white workers who might otherwise have identified Republicanism with the banker, the boss and the factory owner. The success of the Reagan formula spelled disaster for the Democrats, who were forced to re-think their strategy for winning elections. Workers could no longer be won over simply by dangling liberal reforms in front of them, nor by repeating the rhetoric of class, nor by promising to protect their union rights.

In 2008, Barack Obama managed to win the presidency with the most liberal platform since Lyndon Johnson. Liberals optimistically celebrated the apparent revival of their creed. The 2012 election seemed to confirm that interpretation. Yet given the deep divisiveness of so many of Obama's policies, it is difficult to believe that he has managed to revive the old loyalties of the working class to the Democratic Party or to liberalism. His victories are more a measure of Republican weakness than of Democratic strength. The same could be said of the victories of Brown in 1958 and 1962. The Republican Party of today resembles that of the early 1960s – a party in which moderates and extremists engage in bitter internecine warfare and campaign as if purity is more important than success. After Goldwater's debacle of 1964, many judged the party to be doomed. There did not seem to be a way out of the hole it had dug for itself. Similar comments are made about the party today. Yet it is well to remember that, just two years after the Goldwater disaster, Reagan won a victory that heralded a long period of Republican dominance in Washington. This achievement was possible because of his ability to rise above the ideological battle and impose his charismatic will upon the party. As Weinberger reflected, Reagan's great achievement was his ability to unite the party at a moment when it seemed hopelessly fractured: 'He was very strongly conservative; he was consciously so. He never hid it for a minute, but he also strongly believed in party unity … He was very, very good at building party unity.'[52]

In other words, Democrats today who carelessly dismiss the Republicans as too divided and ideologically stubborn to compete effectively on a national stage should beware of what Reagan achieved in 1966. His victory was not a miracle that can never be repeated. Reagan was special, but not unique. His victory simply demonstrates that modern politics is about people – that it is always a mistake to underestimate the power of personality.

# Notes

The author would like to express his gratitude to Jennifer Mandel of the Reagan Presidential Library, Pruda Lood of the Hoover Institution Library, and the entire staff of the Bancroft Library, University of California, Berkeley.

**Introduction**
1. Lewis, p. 19.
2. Lewis, p. viii.
3. *Newsweek*, 22 June 1966.

**1 The Speech**
1. Dunckel transcript, pp. 10–11.
2. Ibid.
3. Lewis, p. 28.
4. Pemberton, p. 42.
5. Cannon (2003), p. 108.
6. Reagan (1965), p. 311.
7. Dunckel transcript, p. 4.
8. Reagan (1965), p. 292.
9. Ibid., p. 108.
10. Ibid., p. 295.
11. Dunckel transcript, p. 12.
12. Edwards, p. 456.
13. Dunckel transcript, p. 20.
14. Weinberger transcript (2002), p. 4.
15. Ibid.
16. Neil Reagan transcript, n.p.
17. Dunckel transcript, p. 14.
18. Edwards, p. 460.

19 Dunckel transcript, p. 10.
20 Ibid., p. 28.
21 Weinberger transcript (2002), p. 3.
22 Reagan (1990), p. 129.
23 Hofstadter, pp. 4–5.
24 'infotrage', 'Reagan's Populist Conservatism', *Daily Kos*, 16 February 2007. Available at www.dailykos.com/story/2007/02/16/302603/-Reagan-s-Populist-Conservatism# (accessed 25 February 2015).
25 *Sacramento Bee*, 9 August 1966.
26 *Sarasota Herald-Tribune*, 24 August 1980.
27 R. Dallek, p. 13.
28 Perlstein (2014), p. 31.
29 Ronald Reagan, 'A Time for Choosing', 27 October 1964. Available at www.reagan.utexas.edu/archives/reference/timechoosing.html (accessed 25 February 2015).
30 Reagan (1965), p. 7.
31 Wills, p. 343.
32 Cannon (2003), p. 121.
33 Neil Reagan transcript, n.p.
34 Ronald Reagan, testimony before the House Committee on Un-American Activities, 23 October 1947. Available at www.cla.calpoly.edu/cla/legacies/rsimon/rsimonsite/Hum410/ReaganHUAC.htm (accessed 25 February 2015).
35 R. Dallek, p. 24.
36 Reagan (1990), pp. 128–9.
37 Dunckel transcript, p. 30.
38 Ibid., p. 44.
39 Edwards, p. 480.
40 R. Dallek, p. 26.
41 Dunckel transcript, p. 40.
42 Ibid., p. 38.
43 Boyarsky (1968), p. 11.
44 Wills, p. 337.
45 Edwards, p. 457.
46 Cannon (2003), p. 109.
47 Edwards, p. 457.
48 Reagan (1990), p. 137.
49 Reagan (1965), p. 310.
50 Reagan (1990), p. 134.
51 Perlstein (2014), p. 406.
52 Ronald Reagan transcript, p. 1.
53 Edwards, p. 475.

54 'Losing Freedom by Instalments', RRGP, Box C35, pre-1966 speeches.
55 Perlstein (2014), pp. 400–1.
56 Reagan (1990), p. 135.
57 Gentry, p. 35.
58 Edwards, p. 461.
59 Reagan (1965), p. 297. The emphasis is Reagan's.

## 2 Hardening of the Categories

1 Kahn, loc. 3262.
2 Ibid., loc. 3269.
3 Ibid., loc. 3271.
4 See Phyllis Schlafly, *A Choice, Not an Echo*.
5 Lewis, pp. 75–6.
6 Weinberger transcript (1978–9), p. 54.
7 M. Dallek, p. 38.
8 Bagley transcript, p. 32.
9 Weinberger transcript (1978–9), p. 57.
10 M. Dallek, p. 38.
11 Edwards, p. 480.
12 M. Dallek, pp. 22–3, 25.
13 Parkinson transcript, p. 93.
14 Champion transcript, p. 60.
15 1960, 1970 censuses. Available at www.census.gov (accessed 25 February 2015).
16 Nofziger transcript (1978), p. 38.
17 Spencer transcript (1978), p. 20.
18 Reagan to John Collier, 24 February 1966, RRGP, Box C5.
19 M. Dallek, p. 26.
20 Telegram, Dick Biggy to Reagan, 9 September 1966, RRGP, Box C2.
21 Weinberger transcript (1978–9), p. 54.
22 Lewis, pp. ix–x.
23 M. Dallek, p. 45.
24 Ibid., p. 54.
25 Parkinson transcript, p. 112.
26 Champion transcript, p. 58.
27 M. Dallek, p. 55.
28 Rarick, p. 290.
29 Reagan to Dale Baldwin, 31 May 1966, RRGP, Box C1.
30 Gentry, p. 184.
31 'Reagan's Stand on the Rumford Act', RRGP, Box C32, Folder '66 Campaign, 3/4'.

32 Bradley transcript, p. 175.
33 Brown transcript, p. 525.
34 Ibid., p. 526.
35 Kline transcript, pp. 18–19.
36 Haas transcript, p. 72.
37 Ronald Reagan transcript, p. 1.
38 Kahn, loc. 3696.
39 www.salon.com/2015/03/18/noam_chomsky_intentional_ignorance_fuels_american_racism (accessed 30 April 2015).
40 Ibid., loc. 3703.
41 Spencer transcript (1978), p. 24.
42 Bagley transcript, p. 39.
43 Perlstein (2001), p. 335.
44 Ibid., p. 166.
45 Weinberger transcript (1978–9), p. 78.
46 Lewis, p. 70.
47 Reagan (1990), pp. 138–9.
48 Ronald Reagan transcript, p. 2.
49 Cristina transcript, p. 44.
50 Spencer transcript (2001), p. 6.
51 Ibid.
52 M. Dallek, p. 65.
53 Holden, p. 72.
54 Spencer transcript (2001), p. 6.
55 Roberts transcript, p. 157.
56 Ibid., pp. 154–5.
57 Spencer transcript (1978), p. 6.
58 Roberts transcript, p. 158.
59 Goldwater, p. 15.
60 Cristina transcript, p. 33.
61 Barry Goldwater, acceptance speech to the Republican National Convention, San Francisco, 16 July 1964. Available at www.washingtonpost.com/wp-srv/politics/daily/may98/goldwaterspeech.htm (accessed 25 February 2015).
62 Walker transcript, p. 3.
63 Weinberger transcript (2002), p. 60.
64 Kahn, loc. 3740.
65 Walker transcript, p. 3.
66 Weinberger transcript (1978–9), p. 82.
67 Ronald Reagan, 'A Time for Choosing', 27 October 1964. Available at www.reagan.utexas.edu/archives/reference/timechoosing.html (accessed 25 February 2015).
68 Reagan (1990), p. 143.

69   Broder and Hess, pp. 253–4.
70   Reagan (1990), p. 143.
71   Spencer transcript (2001), p. 8.
72   M. Dallek, p. 69.
73   Wills, p. 345.
74   Parkinson transcript, p. 93.
75   *National Review*, 1 December 1964.
76   Cristina transcript, p. 48.
77   Ibid.

## 3 'You Guys Are Absolutely Crazy'
1   Kahn, loc. 3767.
2   Ibid., loc. 3776.
3   Edwards, p. 488.
4   Ronald Reagan transcript, p. 4.
5   Cristina transcript, p. 48.
6   Ibid.
7   Ronald Reagan transcript, p. 3.
8   Spencer transcript (2001), p. 17.
9   Nofziger transcript (2003), p. 35.
10  Lewis, p. 9.
11  Parkinson transcript, p. 119.
12  Nofziger, p. 44.
13  Smith transcript, pp. 8–9.
14  Nofziger transcript (1978), p. 35.
15  Spencer transcript (2001), p. 18.
16  Ronald Reagan transcript, p. 6.
17  Ibid., p. 4.
18  Parkinson transcript, p. 56.
19  Weinberger transcript (1978–9), p. 49.
20  Ibid., p. 53.
21  Parkinson transcript, p. 114.
22  Ibid., p. 118.
23  Spencer transcript (2001), p. 9.
24  Ibid., p. 3.
25  Ibid., p. 4.
26  Roberts transcript, p. 153.
27  Ibid., p. 151.
28  Spencer transcript (1978), p. 6.
29  Spencer transcript (2001), p. 4.
30  Roberts transcript, p. 157.
31  Spencer transcript (1978), p. 6.
32  Roberts transcript, p. 152.

33 Gentry, p. 78.
34 Agranoff, p. 94.
35 Lewis, p. 64.
36 Gentry, p. 294.
37 Lewis, pp. 54–5.
38 Agranoff, p. 65.
39 Lewis, p. 55.
40 Ibid., p. 56.
41 Roberts transcript, p. 161.
42 Spencer transcript (2001), p. 9.
43 Spencer transcript (1978), p. 25.
44 Roberts transcript, p. 164.
45 Ibid., p. 165.
46 Ibid.
47 Ibid., p. 162.
48 Spencer transcript (1978), p. 27.
49 Ibid., p. 8.
50 Spencer transcript (2001), p. 5.
51 Ibid., p. 14.
52 Roberts transcript, p. 12.
53 Lewis, pp. 108–9.
54 Gentry, p. 289.
55 Neil Reagan transcript, n.p.
56 Spencer transcript (2001), p. 12.
57 Ibid., p. 16.
58 Spencer transcript (2001), p. 10.
59 Nofziger transcript (1978), p. 44.
60 Spencer transcript (2001), p. 10.
61 Nofziger transcript (1978), p. 44.
62 Spencer transcript (1978), p. 28.
63 Bagley transcript, p. 40.
64 Spencer transcript (2001), p. 11.
65 Cristina transcript, p. 53.
66 Spencer transcript (2001), p. 9.
67 Cyril Stevenson to Reagan Campaign, 14 July 1965, RRGP, Box C20.
68 O. L. Bane to Fred Hafner, RRGP, Box C1.
69 Stevenson to Reagan, 27 July 1965, RRGP, Box C20.
70 Roberts transcript, p. 25.
71 Spencer transcript (1978), p. 7.
72 Transcript of 'George Putnam News', KTTV, Los Angeles, 1 June 1965, RRGP, Box C32, Folder '66 Campaign 1/4'.
73 Spencer transcript (1978), p. 29.

74 Edmund G. Brown, speech to California Federation of Young Democrats, 1 May 1965, RRGP, Box C32, Folder '66 Campaign 1/4'.
75 Roberts transcript, p. 164.
76 Ibid., p. 172.
77 Spencer transcript (1978), p. 32.
78 Spencer transcript (2001), p. 25.
79 Walker transcript, p. 5.
80 Weinberger transcript (2002), p. 2.
81 Smith transcript, p. 14.
82 Sturgeon transcript, p. 12.
83 Reagan to Goldwater, 11 November 1965, RRGP, Box C29, Folder 'Goldwater (2)'.
84 Ronald Reagan transcript, p. 9.
85 John Harmer to Bill Roberts, 12 July 1965, RRGP, Box C32, Folder '66 Campaign 1/4'.
86 Ronald Reagan transcript, p. 9.
87 Spencer transcript (2001), p. 27.
88 Roberts transcript, p. 165.
89 Spencer transcript (1978), p. 30.
90 California Poll, 9 August 1965, RRGP, Box C32, Folder 'Campaign Polls'.
91 'The Voice of 300 Californians in Yellow Zones', 7 May 1965, RRGP, Box C32, Folder 'Campaign Polls'.
92 Transcript of *KNXT News*, 9 August 1965, RRGP Box C32, Folder '66 Campaign 2/4'.
93 *Beverly Hills Courier*, 24 September 1965.
94 Resolution of the Los Angeles County Young Republicans, 7 September 1965, RRGP, Box C32, Folder 'Kuchel'.
95 Roberts transcript, p. 174.
96 Nofziger transcript (1978), p. 63.
97 Parkinson transcript, p. 46.
98 Smith transcript, p. 13.
99 Mr and Mrs F. L. Alberts to Reagan, 16 August 1966, RRGP, Box C1.
100 Daniel Arthur to Reagan, n.d., RRGP, Box C1.
101 Rita Brown to Reagan, n.d., RRGP, Box C1.
102 Reagan news release, 13 June 1966, RRGP, Box C32, Folder '66 Campaign 1/4'.
103 Roberts transcript, p. 164.
104 Ibid., p. 174.
105 Baus and Ross, pp. 342–3.
106 Spencer transcript (2001), p. 11.

107 Nofziger transcript (1978), p. 64.
108 Spencer transcript (2001), p. 27.
109 Smith transcript, p. 15.
110 Spencer transcript (1978), p. 30.
111 Spencer transcript (2001), p. 25.
112 Friends of Ronald Reagan Letter, 10 August 1965, RRGP, Box C33, Folder 'RR-Friends 1/2'.
113 Ronald Reagan transcript, p. 5.
114 Reagan to Hurst Amyx, 16 September 1965, RRGP, Box C32, Folder '66 Campaign 1/4'.
115 Ronald Reagan transcript, p. 5.
116 Reagan to Anita Rutsky, 21 December 1965, RRGP, Series IV, Box C32, Folder '66 Campaign 1/4'.
117 Ronald Reagan transcript, p. 5.

## 4 Old Tactics, New Faces

1 Weinberger transcript (1978–9), p. 88.
2 Nofziger transcript (1978), p. 66.
3 Roberts transcript, p. 174.
4 Nofziger transcript (1978), p. 8.
5 Lewis, pp. 133–4.
6 James Alleman to Reagan, RRGP, Box C1.
7 *Los Angeles Times*, 15 June 1966.
8 Spencer transcript (1978), p. 16.
9 *Sacramento Bee*, 11 February 1966.
10 Weinberger transcript (1978–9), p. 48.
11 Lewis, p. 59.
12 Parkinson transcript, p. 105.
13 Ibid.
14 'Youth for Reagan', RRGP, Box C33, Folder 'RR Committee 2/4'.
15 McKenna, pp. 42–3.
16 Reagan Girls Information Sheet, RRGP, Box C33, Folder 'RR Committee 1/4'.
17 Memo, Jack Wheeler to All Youth for Reagan, 12 May 1966, RRGP, Box C33, Folder 'RR Committee 2/4'.
18 Reagan Girls Information Sheet, RRGP, Box 25, Folder 'RR Committee 1/4'.
19 Reagan Girls Manual, RRGP, Box C33, Folder 'RR Committee 1/4'.
20 Clipping from unknown newspaper found at https://picasaweb.google.com/SherryLynnK/ReaganGirls#5186861297652201874 (accessed 25 February 2015).

21  Open letter to Senior Citizens from Francis Bushman and Charles Skoien, n.d., RRGP, Box C32, Folder '66 Campaign Files 3/4'.
22  Phil Saenz to Reagan, 28 April 1965, RRGP, Box C21.
23  Francisco Bravo, 'The Hour of Decision', 1 August 1966, RRGP, Box C32, Folder '66 Campaign 3/4'.
24  Lewis, p. 152.
25  Roberts transcript, p. 171.
26  Barabba transcript, p. 2.
27  Agranoff, p. 193.
28  Ibid., p. 200.
29  Barabba transcript, p. 3.
30  Issenberg, pp. 42–3.
31  Spencer transcript (2001), p. 22.
32  Nofziger transcript (1978), p. 59.
33  Spencer transcript (2001), p. 24.
34  Ibid.
35  Rose and Fuchs, p. 250.
36  Ibid., p. 252.
37  Dutton transcript, p. 163.
38  Nofziger transcript (1978), p. 58.
39  Ibid., p. 46.
40  Nofziger, p. 18.
41  Nofziger transcript (1978), p. 69.
42  Ibid.
43  Ibid., p. 60.
44  Ibid., p. 67.
45  Ibid., p. 58.
46  Ibid., p. 60.
47  Spencer transcript (2001), p. 19.
48  Spencer transcript (1978), p. 35.
49  Nofziger transcript (1978), p. 51.
50  Ibid.
51  See, for instance, *Sacramento Bee*, 16, 18 and 24 August 1966.
52  Nofziger transcript (1978), p. 52.
53  Weinberger transcript (2002), p. 3.
54  Ibid.
55  Cristina transcript, p. 48.
56  Plog transcript, p. 9.
57  *Riverside Press*, 11 January 1966.
58  *New York Times*, 5 January 1966.
59  *San Francisco Chronicle*, 9 January 1966.
60  *Sacramento Bee*, 9 January 1966.
61  Ibid., 12 June 1966.

62. *San Francisco Chronicle*, 19 September 1966.
63. Ronald Reagan, 'A Plan for Action', 4 January 1966, RRGP, Box C30, 'RR Speeches and Statements (1)'.
64. Ronald Reagan transcript, p. 18.
65. Nofziger transcript (1978), p. 49.
66. McKenna, pp. 56–7.
67. Gentry, p. 122.
68. *CBS Reports:What About Ronald Reagan*, 12 December 1967.

## 5 Those Boys from BASICO

1. *San Francisco Chronicle*, 20 April 1966.
2. *Esquire*, February 1966.
3. *Daytona Beach Morning Journal*, 25 February 1965.
4. *Boston Herald*, 11 June 1966.
5. Plog transcript, p. 21.
6. Cannon (2003), pp. 138, 139, 141.
7. Baus and Ross, p. 260.
8. Reagan (1990). Ronald Reagan transcript, pp. 9–10.
9. Wills, pp. 350–4.
10. Ibid., p. 350.
11. *Anchorage Daily News*, 14 November 1985.
12. Gentry, pp. 285–6. Plog and Holden in fact had a very small staff of three professionals and assorted clerical workers.
13. Ronald Reagan, 'A Plan for Action', 4 January 1966, RRGP, Box C30, 'RR Speeches and Statements (1)'.
14. Plog transcript, p. 5.
15. Plog transcript, cf. Wills's inflated assessment of BASICO's importance comes from taking Plog at his word.
16. Holden's book, published in 2013, is titled *The Making of the Great Communicator*. The blurb boasts that 'Holden and Plog ... shaped an actor into a governor, but they were also turning a governor into a president.'
17. Plog transcript, p. 6.
18. Spencer transcript (2001), p. 19.
19. Ibid., p. 14.
20. Spencer transcript (2001), p. 19.
21. Roberts transcript, p. 167.
22. Ibid.
23. Ibid.
24. Spencer transcript (2001), p. 19.
25. Roberts transcript, p. 167.
26. Spencer transcript (2001), p. 20.
27. *San Francisco Chronicle*, 26 January 1966.

28  Baus and Ross, p. 37.
29  Roberts manuscript, p. 19.
30  Reagan, 'A Plan for Action'.
31  *Sacramento Bee*, 6 January 1966.
32  Reagan, 'A Plan for Action'. The welfare figures might have been a mistake, but could also have been an indicator of Reagan's ideology. He was probably including those on state pensions, Medicare and social security, since he considered these a form of welfare.
33  *Sacramento Bee*, 6 January 1966.
34  *Riverside Press*, 11 January 1966.
35  *Washington Post-Intelligencer*, 11 January 1966.
36  *San Francisco Chronicle*, 9 January 1966.
37  Ibid., 7 January 1966.
38  Plog transcript, p. 3.
39  Roberts transcript, p. 168.
40  Ibid.
41  'Operations Manual: Southern California Reagan for Governor Committee', p. 8, RRGP, Box C33, Folder '1966 Campaign Roster'.
42  Roberts transcript, p. 167.
43  Cannon (2003), p. 138.
44  Spencer transcript (2001), p. 21.
45  Ibid.
46  Reagan transcript, p. 21.
47  Holden, p. 133.
48  Ibid., p. 132.
49  Boyarsky (1968), p. 143.
50  Ronald Reagan transcript, p. 10.
51  Nofziger transcript (1978), p. 68.
52  Perlstein (2014), p. 48.
53  Weinberger transcript (2002), p. 4.
54  Spencer transcript (2001), p. 12.
55  Plog transcript, p. 3.
56  Ibid., p. 4.
57  *Sacramento Bee*, 11 February 1966.
58  Plog transcript, p. 14.
59  Ibid., p. 21.
60  Boyarsky (1968), p. 143.
61  Plog transcript, p. 5.
62  Nofziger, p. 42.
63  Holden, p. 144.
64  Ibid., p. 169.

65 Ibid.
66 McDowell transcript, p. 12.
67 *National Observer*, 10 January 1966.
68 Spencer transcript (2001), p. 11.
69 Ronald Reagan transcript, p. 21.
70 Weinberger transcript (2002), p. 4.
71 Spencer transcript (1978), p. 31.
72 Roberts transcript, p. 168.
73 McDowell transcript, p. 95.
74 Ibid., p. 82.
75 *Newsweek*, 22 July 1966.
76 *Los Angeles Times*, 11 January 1966.
77 *The Times-Voice*, 31 May 1966.
78 Reagan press release, 18 March 1966, RRGP, Box C32, Folder '66 campaign, 2/4'.
79 Holden, p. 233.
80 Ibid., p. xi.
81 Spencer transcript (2001), p. 23.
82 Nofziger transcript (1978), p. 47.
83 Holden, p. 239.
84 Reagan to Stanley Plog, 1 December 1966, copy in Plog transcript, pp. 22–3. Note how Reagan thanked Plog and Holden for the research they provided, not the coaching in communication skills.
85 Neil Reagan transcript, n.p.
86 Ronald Reagan transcript, p. 10.
87 Holden, p. 209.
88 *Sacramento Bee*, 25 October 1966.
89 Transcript of 'George Putnam News', KTTV, Los Angeles, 1 June 1965, RRGP, Box C32, Folder '66 Campaign 1/4'. In 2001, Spencer claimed he had been involved in more than 500 campaigns since his firm was founded in 1960.
90 Spencer transcript (2001), p. 21.
91 Plog transcript, pp. 23–4.
92 Holden, p. 135.
93 Wills, pp. 344–54.

## 6 The Great Pretender

1 Ronald Reagan, 'A Plan for Action', 4 January 1966, RRGP, Box C30, 'RR Speeches and Statements (1)'.
2 Hall transcript, p. 2.
3 Transcript of 'George Christopher Aired', KPOL Radio, 28 September 1965, RRGP, Box C31, Folder 'George Christopher'.
4 *Oakland Tribune*, 27 October 1965.

5  Parkinson transcript, p. 94.
6  Ibid., p. 104.
7  Ibid., p. 108.
8  Roberts transcript, p. 169.
9  Walker transcript, p. 37.
10 Parkinson transcript, p. 107.
11 Roberts transcript, p. 170.
12 Nofziger transcript (1978), p. 42.
13 Roberts transcript, p. 170.
14 'Reagan Answers the Press', transcript of press conference, 30 March 1966, RRGP, Box C30, Folder 'Speeches and Statements'.
15 Parkinson transcript, p. 109.
16 Walker transcript, p. 29.
17 *Oakland Tribune*, 27 October 1965.
18 Parkinson transcript, p. 108.
19 Christopher transcript, p. 45.
20 Parkinson transcript, p. 101.
21 Nofziger transcript (1978), p. 42.
22 Walker transcript, p. 37.
23 Cristina transcript, p. 49.
24 Brown transcript, p. 170.
25 Parkinson transcript, p. 118.
26 *National Observer*, 10 January 1966.
27 Nofziger transcript (1978), p. 48.
28 Agranoff, p. 65.
29 Christopher transcript, p. 47.
30 Cristina transcript, p. 54.
31 Perlstein (2008), p. 91.
32 Parkinson transcript, p. 46.
33 Ibid., p. 109.
34 Ibid.
35 Monagan transcript, p. 251.
36 Smith transcript, p. 10.
37 Spencer transcript (2001), pp. 23–4. v
38 Ibid., p. 23.
39 Nofziger transcript (1978), p. 66.
40 Lewis, pp. 46–7.
41 Speech at USC, 19 April 1966, RRGP, Box C30, 'RR Speeches and Statements (1)'.
42 Weinberger transcript (1978–9), p. 87.
43 Kline transcript, p. 228.
44 Bimes, p. 4.
45 Brown transcript, p. 85.

46 Ronald Reagan transcript, p. 26.
47 California Poll, 6 September 1966, private collection.
48 Smith transcript, p. 14.
49 Spencer transcript (2001), p. 24.
50 Plog transcript, p. 12.
51 W. S. McBirnie to Ronald Reagan, 30 November 1965, RRGP, Box C31, Folder 'Creative Society'. When asked who came up with the Creative Society idea, Reagan replied: 'Dr McBirnie as a matter of fact, I have to give him credit.' Ronald Reagan transcript, p. 23.
52 McBirnie to Reagan, 30 November 1965.
53 Ronald Reagan, 'The Creative Society', n.d., RRGP, Box C31, Folder 'Creative Society'.
54 Speech to fundraising dinner, Delano, n.d., RRGP, Box C30, Folder 'Speeches and Statements'.
55 'The Creative Society', RRGP, Box C31, Folder 'Creative Society'.
56 Reagan to Hank Bartholomew, 14 March 1966, RRGP, Box C2.
57 Steve Murdock, 'In Reagan's Deck the Right is Wild', *People's World*, 22 October 1966.
58 Ronald Reagan transcript, p. 23.
59 Spencer transcript (2001), p. 24.
60 Spencer transcript (1978), p. 8.
61 Ronald Reagan transcript, p. 16.
62 Ibid., p. 15.
63 Broyles, pp. 66–7.
64 Spencer transcript (2001), p. 28.
65 *Beverly Hills Courier*, 17 September 1965.
66 Reagan to Rousselot, 16 September 1965, RRGP, Box C21, Folder 'Campaign Correspondence'.
67 Spencer transcript (2001), p. 29.
68 'Statement of Ronald Reagan Regarding the John Birch Society', 24 September 1965, RRGP, Box C31 Folder 'Birch Society (1/2)'.
69 Spencer transcript (2001), p. 29.
70 Brown transcript, p. 447.
71 Spencer transcript (1978), p. 32.
72 H. Albright to Reagan, 8 October 1965, RRGP, Box C1.
73 Josephine Powell Beaty to Reagan, n.d. [1965], RRGP, Box C2.
74 M. Dallek, p. 126.
75 Perlstein (2008), p. 73.
76 *San Francisco Chronicle*, 27 March 1966.
77 Parkinson transcript, p. 114.
78 Spencer transcript (1978), p. 27.

79  Bagley transcript, p. 32.
80  Ibid., p. 41.
81  Transcript of 'George Putnam News', KTTV, Los Angeles, 1 June 1965, RRGP, Box C32, Folder '66 Campaign 1/4'.
82  Everett Andrews to Reagan, n.d., RRGP, Box C1.
83  Lewis, p. 100.
84  Champion transcript, p. 60.
85  Ibid., p. 62.
86  Ronald Reagan transcript, p. 19.
87  Author unknown, 'An Alternative to the Rumford Act', n.d., RRGP, Box C32, Folder '66 Campaign, 3/4'.
88  Ronald Reagan transcript, p. 19.
89  Spencer transcript (1978), p. 32.
90  Ibid., p. 19.
91  Ibid., p. 15.
92  Brown transcript, p. 526.
93  Lewis, p. 103.
94  Evelyn Anderson to Reagan, 12 October 1966, RRGP, Box C1.
95  Louis Berger to Reagan, 9 November 1965, 15 August 1966, RRGP, Box C2.
96  Jack Barron to Ronald Reagan, n.d., RRGP, Box C2.
97  Coffey transcript, p. 9.
98  Brown transcript, p. 84.
99  *San Francisco Examiner*, 16 October 1966.
100  Champion transcript, p. 59.
101  Perlstein (2008), pp. 70–1.
102  Champion transcript, p. 59.
103  *New York Post* article reprinted in *Sacramento Bee*, 11 September 1966.
104  Perlstein (2008), p. 115.
105  *New York Post* article reprinted in *Sacramento Bee*, 11 September 1966.
106  Champion transcript, p. 70.
107  Reagan, 'A Plan for Action'.
108  Champion transcript, p. 70.
109  Parkinson transcript, p. 113.
110  *Sacramento Bee*, 6 February 1966.

## 7 Drowning in Milk

1  Christopher transcript, p. 43.
2  Ibid.
3  Ibid., p. 47.
4  Ibid., p. 42.

5 Transcript of 'The California Gubernatorial Race', KPOL Radio, Los Angeles, 23 September 1965, RRGP, Box C32, Folder '66 Campaign 1/4'.
6 Christopher transcript, p. 42.
7 Ibid., p. 45.
8 M. Dallek, p. 200.
9 Lewis, p. 115.
10 *Sacramento Bee*, 20 June 1966.
11 Ronald Reagan transcript, p. 27.
12 Spencer transcript (2001), p. 26.
13 Ronald Reagan transcript, p. 27.
14 *Sacramento Bee*, 18 March 1966.
15 Nofziger transcript (1978), p. 50.
16 Spencer transcript (2001), p. 26.
17 Ibid.
18 Holden, p. 177.
19 Ibid.
20 This is how Plog and Holden described the incident to the author.
21 Gentry, p. 133.
22 Reagan press release, 6 March 1966, RRGP, Box C32, Folder '66 campaign, 2/4'.
23 *San Francisco Chronicle*, 13 March 1966.
24 *Sacramento Bee*, 26 April 1966.
25 Nofziger, p. 39.
26 Ibid., pp. 39–40.
27 *Oakland Tribune*, 18 March 1966.
28 Ronald Reagan transcript, p. 28.
29 *Oakland Tribune*, 18 March 1966.
30 Spencer transcript (2001), p. 26.
31 Boyarsky (1968), p. 112.
32 Lewis, p. 153.
33 Brown transcript, p. 566.
34 *San Francisco Chronicle*, 3 June 1966.
35 Mills transcript, p. 171.
36 M. Dallek, p. 204.
37 Champion transcript, p. 58.
38 Kline transcript, p. 29.
39 Press release 507, Field Research Corporation, personal collection.
40 Press releases 523 and 525, Field Research Corporation, personal collection.
41 Bagley, Milias and Pattee to Reagan, 15 April 1966, RRGP, Box C32, Folder '66 Campaign 2/4'.

42  Nofziger transcript (1978), p. 39.
43  Ibid.
44  Ibid., p. 40.
45  Drew Pearson, 'Washington Merry-Go-Round', syndicated copy, printed as handout, n.d., RRGP, Box C32, Folder '66 Campaign 2/4'.
46  Gentry, p. 131.
47  *Los Angeles Times*, 12 June 1966.
48  Bagley transcript, p. 15.
49  Brown transcript, p. 566.
50  Christopher transcript, p. 44.
51  Champion transcript, p. 72.
52  *San Francisco Chronicle*, 3 June 1966.
53  Bradley transcript, p. 181.
54  Ibid., p. 182.
55  Champion transcript, p. 73.
56  Christopher speech, 1 June 1966, RRGP Box C31, Folder 'George Christopher'.
57  *San Francisco Chronicle*, 28 May 1966.
58  Christopher transcript, p. 42.

## 8 'What Are You Going to Do About Berkeley?'

1  Goines, pp. 485–6.
2  Brown, commencement speech at the University of Santa Clara, 3 June 1961, quoted in Draper, p. 120.
3  *San Diego Union*, 11 December 1964.
4  *Ramparts*, October 1966, p. 26.
5  Goines, pp. 490–1.
6  Ibid., pp. 489–90.
7  Ibid., p. 491.
8  Ibid., p. 490.
9  Ibid., p. 505.
10  Ibid., p. 506.
11  Spencer transcript (1978), p. 33.
12  Ronald Reagan, 'Denouncing the Morality Gap at Berkeley', speech at the Cow Palace, San Francisco, 12 May 1966, RRGP, Box C30, Folder 'Speeches and Statements'.
13  Roberts transcript, p. 33.
14  Rubin, p. 38.
15  Transcript of *Meet the Press*, NBC News, 11 September 1966, RRGP, Box C30, Folder 'Speeches and Statements'.
16  Ronald Reagan transcript, p. 21.
17  Dutton transcript, p. 145.

18  Ronald Reagan transcript, p. 21.
19  Spencer transcript (1978), p. 31.
20  Ronald Reagan, 'A Plan for Action', 4 January 1966, RRGP, Box C30, 'RR Speeches and Statements (1)'.
21  Dutton transcript, p. 167.
22  Reagan press release, 28 March 1966, RRGP, Box C32, Folder '66 campaign, 2/4'.
23  Ibid.
24  Transcript of *Issues and Answers*, ABC Television, n.d., RRGP, Box C30, Folder 'Speeches and Statements'.
25  Reagan, 'Denouncing the Morality Gap at Berkeley'.
26  Perlstein (2008), p. 91.
27  California Legislature, pp. 133–4.
28  Ibid., p. 65.
29  *Los Angeles Times*, 15 May 1966.
30  Reagan, 'Denouncing the Morality Gap at Berkeley'.
31  Reagan, speech at San Jose City Auditorium, 2 April 1966 RRGP, Box C30, Folder 'Speeches and Statements'.
32  Reagan, 'Denouncing the Morality Gap at Berkeley'.
33  Reagan, 'A Plan for Action'.
34  Reagan press release, 9 September 1966, RRGP, Box C32, Folder '66 campaign, 2/4'.
35  Ibid.
36  Reagan telecast, 9 September 1966, RRGP, Box C30, Folder 'Speeches and Statements'.
37  John and Lola Bergman to Reagan, 8 June 1966, RRGP, Box C2.
38  Dutton transcript, p. 146.
39  Ibid.
40  Reagan press release, 9 September 1966, RRGP, Box C34, Folder 'University of California'.
41  Champion transcript, p. 70.
42  Boas transcript, p. 13.
43  Champion transcript, p. 70.
44  *Los Angeles Times*, 15 May 1966.
45  *Sacramento Bee*, 12 July 1966.
46  Ibid.
47  Ibid.
48  *San Diego Union*, 9 October 1966.
49  Press release, University Community for Brown, n.d., RRGP, Box C34, Folder 'University of California'.
50  *San Diego Evening Tribune*, 7 May 1966.
51  Kenneth Holden, 'Academic Freedom', RRGP, Box C33, Folder 'RR Committee (1)'; 'Ronald Reagan Speaks Out on the Issues:

Academic Freedom', RRGP, Box C30, Folder 'Handouts and Issue Statements'.
52 Spencer transcript (1978), p. 31.
53 Kline transcript, p. 26.
54 BASICO to Reagan, 12 October 1966, RRGP, Box C33, Folder 'Campus Unrest'.
55 Reagan campaign news release, 18 October 1966, RRGP, Box C33, Folder 'Campus Unrest'.
56 *San Francisco Chronicle*, 11 October 1966.
57 Krassner, p. 26.
58 *San Francisco Chronicle*, 2 November 1966.
59 Transcript of *Meet the Press*, NBC News, 11 September 1966.
60 Dutton transcript, p. 146.
61 Perlstein (2014), p. 88.
62 *Los Angeles Times*, 7 January 1973.
63 Perlstein (2014), p. 87.
64 Transcript of *Issues and Answers*, ABC Television, 2 October 1966.
65 Reagan campaign memo, n.d., RRGP, Box C34, Folder 'University of California'.
66 Ronald Reagan transcript, p. 22.
67 Reagan, Boalt Hall speech, n.d., RRGP, Box C34, Folder 'University of California'.
68 Dutton transcript, p. 167.
69 Ibid.
70 Galbraith transcript, p. 150.
71 Spencer transcript (2001), p. 25.
72 *Ramparts*, October 1966, p. 27.

## 9 'Who Shot Lincoln?'
1 Parkinson transcript, p. 101.
2 *New York Times*, 16 June 1966.
3 Bagley transcript, p. 41.
4 Spencer transcript (1978), p. 29.
5 Nofziger transcript (1978), p. 41.
6 Reagan to George Murphy, 19 August 1966, RRGP, Box C29.
7 Cannon (1969), p. 18.
8 *Ramparts*, October 1966, p. 28.
9 Press release 527, Field Research Corporation, personal collection.
10 Rarick, p. 340.
11 M. Dallek, p. 150.
12 *Chicago Tribune*, 24 June 1966.

13  Brown transcript, p. 331.
14  M. Dallek, p. 145.
15  Rarick, p. 333.
16  Reagan press release, 16 March 1966, RRGP, Box C34, Folder 'Watts'.
17  Brown transcript, p. 567.
18  Champion transcript, p. 66.
19  Brown transcript, p. 331.
20  Yorty press release, 8 June 1966, RRGP, Box C31, Folder 'EGB'.
21  Press release 528, Field Research Corporation, personal collection.
22  Ronald Reagan transcript, p. 25.
23  'Ronald Reagan Speaks Out on the Issues: Crime', RRGP, Box C32, Folder 'Crime'.
24  Anderson and Lee, p. 541.
25  Ronald Reagan transcript, p. 26.
26  'Which Candidate is the Friend of the Working Man?', RRGP, Box C32 Folder '66 Campaign 3/4'.
27  Reagan, speech to Republican State Convention, Sacramento, 6 August 1966, RRGP, Box C30, Folder 'Speeches and Statements'.
28  Spencer transcript (2001), p. 14.
29  Weinberger transcript (1978–9), p. 87.
30  *Christian Science Monitor* article reprinted in *Sacramento Bee*, 13 August 1966.
31  Ronald Reagan, 'A Plan for Action', 4 January 1966, RRGP, Box C30, 'RR Speeches and Statements (1)'.
32  *San Francisco Chronicle*, 20 September 1966.
33  Boyarsky (1968), pp. 132–4.
34  Press release 544, Field Research Corporation, personal collection.
35  *Park City Daily News*, 12 October 1966.
36  *Los Angeles Times*, 5 September 1966.
37  *Christian Science Monitor* article reprinted in *Sacramento Bee*, 13 August 1966.
38  Weinberger transcript (1978–9), p. 88.
39  Burch transcript, p. 24.
40  Ibid., p. 23.
41  Kent transcript, p. 268.
42  Burch transcript, p. 23.
43  Champion transcript, p. 75.
44  Brown transcript, p. 569.
45  Ibid., p. 570.
46  Champion transcript, p. 75.

47 Dutton transcript, p. 165.
48 Ibid., p. 157.
49 Ibid., p. 137.
50 Ibid., p. 138.
51 Mills transcript, p. 171.
52 Brown transcript, p. 566.
53 *Ramparts*, October 1966, p. 27.
54 Mills transcript, p. 172.
55 Dutton transcript, p. 146.
56 Gentry, p. 183.
57 Lewis, p. x.
58 Gentry, p. 279.
59 M. Dallek, pp. 224–5.
60 Champion transcript, p. 83.
61 Lewis, p. 136.
62 Weinberger transcript (1978–9), p. 85.
63 Champion transcript, p. 83.
64 Anderson and Lee, p. 550.
65 Ibid.
66 John Wayne advert, available at www.hulu.com/watch/40611.
67 Lewis, p. 136.
68 Personal recollection.
69 Champion transcript, p. 83.
70 Lewis, p. 139.
71 Brown transcript, p. 569.
72 'Leadership and Morality', BASICO briefing paper, n.d., RRGP Box C30, Folder 'Handouts and Issue Statements'.
73 *Sacramento Bee*, 22 July 1966.
74 *San Francisco Examiner*, 7 August 1966.
75 *Los Angeles Times*, 21 June 1966.
76 *Sacramento Bee*, 6 November 1966.
77 *Sacramento Bee*, 23 August 1966.
78 *New Republic* article reprinted in *Sacramento Bee*, 9 August 1966.
79 *Sacramento Bee*, 4 October 1966.
80 *Washington Post*, 21 June 1966.
81 Bradley transcript, p. 203.
82 Rose and Fuchs, p. 253.
83 Reagan to Kats Kunitsugu, 1 November 1966, RRGP, Box C13.
84 Gentry, p. 120.
85 Nofziger transcript (1978), p. 59.
86 Anderson and Lee, p. 543.
87 Spencer transcript (2001), p. 28.
88 Spencer transcript (1978), p. 31.

89  Roberts transcript, p. 169.
90  Holden, p. 199.
91  Ibid., p. 224.
92  Champion transcript, p. 75.
93  'The Target is Your Family', RRGP, Box C32, Folder 'RR Material (2)'.
94  'STOP and THINK, DON'T LEAP!', RRGP, Box C32, Folder 'RR Material (2)'.
95  'The Target is Your Family'.
96  'Ronald Reagan, Extremist Collaborator – An Exposé', RRGP, Box C32, Folder 'RR Material (4)'.
97  *New York Times*, 12 August 1966.
98  *Los Angeles Times*, 14 August 1966.
99  Bradley transcript, p. 193.
100 Transcript of 'Extremists on the Left', KNX News, 15 August 1966, RRGP, Box C31, Folder 'Birch Society (1/2)'.
101 Lewis, pp. 134–5.
102 *Middlesboro Daily News*, 1 November 1966.
103 *Pittsburgh Post-Gazette*, 24 September 1966.
104 Dutton transcript, p. 158.
105 Gentry, p. 182.
106 *San Diego Union*, 9 October 1966.
107 *Los Angeles Herald-Examiner*, 21 October 1966.
108 Smith transcript, p. 15.
109 Reagan to Goldwater, 11 June 1966, RRGP, Box C29, Folder 'Correspondence Personal: Goldwater (1)'.
110 Bradley transcript, p. 197.
111 Weinberger transcript (1978–9), p. 86.
112 Brown transcript, p. 573.
113 Weinberger transcript (1978–9), p. 88.
114 Philip Battaglia to Seth Hufstedler, 22 September 1966, RRGP, Box C31, Folder 'Debate'.
115 *Star News*, 10 October 1966.
116 Brown transcript, p. 569.
117 Reagan press release, 25 October 1966, RRGP, Box C32, Folder 'Campaign RR 4/4'.
118 Brown transcript, p. 572.
119 Champion transcript, p. 76.
120 Reagan to Frederick Ayer, 7 July 1966, RRGP, Box C1.
121 Guggenheim transcript, p. 6.
122 Rose and Fuchs, p. 254.
123 Burch transcript, p. 20.
124 Ibid., p. 22.

125 Reagan press release, 8 September 1966, RRGP, Box C32, Folder '66 Campaign, 2/4'.
126 Guggenheim transcript, p. 9.
127 Champion transcript, p. 82.
128 *Los Angeles Times*, 19 October 1996.
129 Guggenheim transcript, p. 10.
130 Brown transcript, p. 571.
131 Spencer transcript (2001), p. 29.
132 Dutton transcript, p. 164.
133 Smith transcript, p. 15.
134 Reagan transcript, p. 24.
135 Spencer transcript (2001), p. 29.
136 Guggenheim transcript, p. 11.
137 Reagan victory statement, RRGP, Box C32, Folder 'Election Night'.
138 Press releases 534, 543 and 547, Field Research Corporation, personal collection.
139 Rarick, p. 358.
140 Ibid., p. 359.
141 Brown transcript, p. 570.
142 *Los Angeles Times*, 19 February 1966.
143 Bradley transcript, pp. 191–2.

## 10 'Hey, This Guy Could Be President Someday'

1 Quoted in *South Bay Daily Breeze*, 29 June 1966.
2 *New York Post* article reprinted in *Sacramento Bee*, 11 September 1966.
3 *Newsweek* article reprinted in *Sacramento Bee*, 26 June 1966.
4 Nofziger transcript (1978), p. 47.
5 *Sacramento Bee*, 16 June 1966.
6 Ibid., 9 August 1966.
7 Perlstein (2008), p. 93.
8 *Washington Post*, 28 October 1966.
9 Anderson and Lee, p. 553.
10 Ronald Reagan transcript, p. 16.
11 Dutton transcript, p. 143.
12 Bagley transcript, p. 41.
13 Champion transcript, p. 65.
14 Bagley transcript, p. 68.
15 Champion transcript, p. 65.
16 Lewis, p. 123.
17 Rarick, p. 364.
18 *San Diego Union*, 2 August 1966.

19  Gentry, p. 280.
20  Rarick, p. 356.
21  *San Diego Union*, 10 June 1966.
22  Ibid., 17 June 1966.
23  *San Francisco Examiner*, 16 October 1966.
24  Reagan to H. C. Armstrong, 16 September 1965, RRGP, Box C1.
25  Robert Alcorn to *Denver Post*, 9 January 1966, RRGP, Box C1.
26  *Ramparts*, October 1966, p. 28.
27  Perlstein (2008), p. 94.
28  Lewis, p. 201.
29  Perlstein (2008), p. 183.
30  Lewis, p. xi.
31  Nofziger transcript (1978), p. 65.
32  Champion transcript, p. 82.
33  Edwards, p. 490.
34  Anderson and Lee, p. 542.
35  Spencer transcript (1978), p. 38.
36  Agranoff, p. 42.
37  Gentry, p. 291.
38  Ibid., p. 292.
39  Ibid., p. 290.
40  Ibid., p. 291.
41  Lewis, p. 203.
42  Ibid., pp. 14–15, 18.
43  Spencer transcript (1978), p. 38.
44  *Los Angeles Times*, 13 June 1966.
45  Spencer transcript (1978), p. 31.
46  *Ramparts*, October 1966, p. 27.
47  Spencer transcript (1978), p. 37.
48  Agranoff, p. 40.
49  Neil Reagan transcript, n.p.
50  McDowell transcript, p. 114.
51  Lewis, p. 19.
52  Weinberger transcript (1978–9), p. 90.

# Bibliography

### Document Collections
Ronald Reagan Gubernatorial Papers (RRGP), Reagan Presidential Library, Simi Valley, California.
Social Protest Project, Bancroft Library, University of California, Berkeley, California.

### Oral Interviews
*Government History Documentation Project, Ronald Reagan Gubernatorial Era, Regional Oral History Office, Bancroft Library, University of California, Berkeley, California:*

> Bagley, William, 'Some Complexities of Social Progress and Fiscal Reform', interview conducted by Gabrielle Morris, 1981.
> Boas, John Roger, 'Democratic State Central Committee Chairman, 1968–1970', interview conducted by Sarah Sharp, 1982.
> Christopher, George, 'Mayor of San Francisco and Republican Party Candidate', interview conducted by Sarah Sharp and Miriam Stein, 1977–8.
> Cristina, Vernon J., 'A Northern Californian Views Conservative Politics and Policies, 1963–1970', interview conducted by Sarah Sharp, 1983.
> Dunckel, Earl B., 'Ronald Reagan and the General Electric Theater, 1954–1955', interview conducted by Gabrielle Morris, 1982.
> Hall, James, 'Supporting Reagan: From Banks to Prisons', interviews conducted by Nicole Biggart and Gabrielle Morris, 1978, 1984–5.
> McDowell, Jack S., 'Press Work and Political Campaigns, 1966–1970', interview conducted by Gabrielle Morris, 1985.
> Mills, James R., 'A Philosophical Approach to Legislative and Election Realities, 1959–1981', interview conducted by Gabrielle Morris, 1980–1.

Monagan, Robert T., 'Increasing Republican Influence in the State Assembly', interview conducted by Gabrielle Morris, 1981.

Nofziger, Franklyn C., 'Press Secretary for Ronald Reagan, 1966', interview conducted by Sarah Sharp, 1978.

Parkinson, Gaylord B., 'California Republican Party Official, 1962–1967', interview conducted by Sarah Sharp, 1978.

Reagan, Ronald, 'On Becoming Governor', interview conducted by Gabrielle Morris, 1979.

Roberts, William E., 'Professional Campaign Management and the Candidate, 1960–1966', interview conducted by Sarah Sharp, 1979.

Rodda, Albert, 'Sacramento Senator: State Leadership in Education and Finance', interview conducted by Gabrielle Morris and Sarah Sharp, 1979–81.

Smith, William French, 'Evolution of the Kitchen Cabinet, 1965–1973', interview conducted by Gabrielle Morris, 1988.

Spencer, Stuart, 'Developing a Campaign Management Organization', interview conducted by Gabrielle Morris, 1978.

Sturgeon, Vernon, 'State Senator, Reagan Adviser, and PUC Commissioner', interview conducted by Sarah Sharp, 1982.

Watts, Norman (Skip), 'Observations of a Youthful Political Pro', interview conducted by Gabrielle Morris, 1983.

Weinberger, Caspar W., 'California Assembly, Republican State Central Committee, and Elections, 1953–1966', interview conducted by Gabrielle Morris, 1978–9.

*Government History Documentation Project, Oral History Interviews of the Goodwin Knight – Edmund G. Brown, Sr, Gubernatorial Eras, 1953–1966, Regional Oral History Office, Bancroft Library, University of California, Berkeley, California:*

Bradley, Don, 'Managing Democratic Campaigns, 1954–1966', interview conducted by Amelia Fry, 1977–9.

Brown, Edmund G., Sr, 'Years of Growth, 1939–1966; Law Enforcement, Politics, and the Governor's Office', interviews conducted by Malca Chall, Amelia Fry, Gabrielle Morris and James Rowland, 1977–81.

Burch, Meredith, 'Political Notes', interview conducted by Eleanor Glaser, 1977.

Champion, Hale, 'Communication and Problem Solving: A Journalist in State Government', interview conducted by Amelia Fry and Gabrielle Morris, 1977–9.

Coffey, Bertram, 'Reflections on George Miller, Jr, Governors Pat and Jerry Brown, and the Democratic Party', interview conducted by Gabrielle Morris, 1978.
Dutton, Frederick G., 'Democratic Campaigns and Controversies, 1954–1966', interview conducted by Amelia Fry, 1977–8.
Guggenheim, Charles, 'The Use of Film in Political Campaigning', interview conducted by Eleanor Glaser, 1977.
Kent, Roger, 'Building the Democratic Party in California', interview conducted by Anne Brower and Amelia Fry, 1976–7.
Kline, Richard, 'Governor Brown's Faithful Advisor', interview conducted by Eleanor Glaser, 1977.
Mosk, Stanley, 'Attorney General's Office and Political Campaigns, 1958–1966', interview conducted by Amelia Fry, 1979.
Yorty, Samuel, 'Samuel Yorty: A Challenge to the Democrats', interview conducted by Julie Shearer, 1979.

*Government History Documentation Project, Ronald Reagan Gubernatorial Era, Regional Oral History Office, Powell Library, University of California, Los Angeles, California:*

Galbraith, John S., 'Academic Life and Governance in the University of California', interview conducted by Harry Tuchmayer, 1981.
Plog, Stanley, 'More than Just an Actor: The Early Campaigns of Ronald Reagan', interview conducted by Stephen Stern, 1981.
Reagan, Neil, 'Private Dimensions and Public Images: The Early Political Campaigns of Ronald Reagan', interview conducted by Stephen Stern, 1981.

*California State Archives, State Government Oral History Program, Sacramento, California:*

Haas, Lucien, 'Interview with Lucien Haas', interview conducted by Carlos Vásquez, 1989.

*Ronald Reagan Oral History, Miller Center, University of Virginia, Charlottesville, Virginia:*

Nofziger, Lyn, 'Interview with Lyn Nofziger', interview conducted by Stephen Knott and Russell Riley, 2003.
Spencer, Stuart, 'Interview with Stuart Spencer', interview conducted by Jim Young, Russell Riley, Gar Culbert, Paul Freedman and Stephen Knott, 2001.

Weinberger, Caspar, 'Interview with Caspar Weinberger', interview conducted by Stephen Knott and Russell Riley, 2002.

*United States Office of Census:*

Barabba, Vincent, 'Oral History', interview conducted by Barbara Milton and David Pemberton, 7 August 1989. Available at www.census.gov/prod/2003pubs/oh-Barabba.pdf (accessed 25 February 2015).

*Personal Collection:*

Field Research Corporation, California Polls, 1964–6.

## Books and Articles

Agranoff, Robert, *The New Style in Election Campaigns*, Boston: Holbrook Press, 1972.

Anderson, Totton J. and Eugene C. Lee, 'The 1966 Election in California', *Western Political Quarterly*, 20 (July 1967).

Baus, Herbert and William Ross, *Politics Battle Plan*, New York: Macmillan, 1968.

Bimes, Terri, 'Ronald Reagan and the New Conservative Populism', working paper, Institute of Governmental Studies, UC Berkeley. Available at http://escholarship.org/uc/item/08s0f26b (accessed 25 February 2015).

Blum, John M., *Years of Discord*, New York: W. W. Norton, 1991.

Bollens, John C. and Grant B. Geyer, *Yorty: Politics of a Constant Candidate*, Pacific Palisades, CA: Palisades Publishers, 1973.

Boyarsky, Bill, *The Rise of Ronald Reagan*, New York: Random House, 1968.

—— *Ronald Reagan: His Life and Rise to the Presidency*, New York: Random House, 1981.

Brennan, Mary C., *Turning Right in the Sixties: The Conservative Capture of the GOP*, Chapel Hill, NC: University of North Carolina Press, 1995.

Brinkley, Alan, *Liberalism and its Discontents*, Cambridge, MA: Harvard University Press, 1998.

Broder, David and Stephen Hess, *The Republican Establishment*, New York: Harper and Row, 1967.

Brown, Edmund G., *Reagan: The Political Chameleon*, New York: Praeger Publishers, 1976.

Broyles, J. Allen, *The John Birch Society: Anatomy of a Protest*, New York: Beacon, 1964.

California Legislature, *13th Report of the Senate Factfinding Committee on Un-American Activities*, Sacramento, 1965
Cannon, Lou, *Ronnie and Jesse: A Political Odyssey*, New York: Doubleday, 1969.
—— *Governor Reagan: His Rise to Power*, New York: Public Affairs, 2003.
D'Souza, Dinesh, *Ronald Reagan: How an Ordinary Man Became an Extraordinary Leader*, New York: Free Press, 1997.
Dallek, Matthew, *The Right Moment: Ronald Reagan's First Victory and the Decisive Turning Point in American Politics*, New York: Free Press, 2000.
Dallek, Robert, *Ronald Reagan: The Politics of Symbolism*, Cambridge, MA: Harvard University Press, 1984.
DeGroot, Gerard J., 'The Limits of Moral Protest and Participatory Democracy: Vietnam Day Committee', *Pacific Historical Review*, 64 (1995).
—— 'Ronald Reagan and Student Unrest', *Pacific Historical Review*, 65 (1996).
—— '"A Goddamned Electable Person": The 1966 Gubernatorial Campaign of Ronald Reagan', *History: The Journal of the Historical Association*, 82 (1997).
—— *Student Protest: The Sixties and After*, London: Routledge, 1998.
—— *The Sixties Unplugged*, Cambridge, MA: Harvard University Press, 2008.
Draper, Hal, *New Student Revolt*, New York: Grove Press, 1965.
Dunn, Charles W. and J. David Woodard, *The Conservative Tradition in America*, Lanham, MD: Rowman and Littlefield Publishers, 1996.
Edwards, Anne, *Early Reagan*, New York: William Morrow and Co., 1987.
Farber, David and Jeff Roche (eds), *The Conservative Sixties*, New York: Peter Lang Publishing, 2003.
Gentry, Curt, *The Last Days of the Late Great State of California*, Ithaca, NY: Comstock Publishing Associates, 1977.
Goines, David, *The Free Speech Movement: Coming of Age in the 1960s*, Berkeley, CA: Ten Speed Press, 1993.
Goldwater, Barry, *The Conscience of a Conservative*, Shepherdsville, KY: Vicor Publishing, 1960.
Hayward, Steven F., *The Age of Reagan: The Fall of the Old Liberal Order, 1964–1980*, Roseville, CA: Prima Publishing, 2001.
Hofstadter, Richard, *Anti-Intellectualism in American Life*, London: Jonathan Cape, 1964.
Holden, Ken, *The Making of the Great Communicator*, New York: Lyons Press, 2013.

Horne, Gerald, *Fire This Time: The Watts Uprising and the 1960s*, Charlottesville, VA: University Press of Virginia, 1995.
Issenberg, Sasha, *The Victory Lab: The Secret Science of Winning Campaigns*, New York: Broadway Books, 2012.
Isserman, Maurice, and Michael Kazin, *America Divided: The Civil War of the 1960s*, New York: Oxford University Press, 2004.
Jacoby, Susan, *The Age of American Unreason*, London: Old Street Publishing, 2008.
Kahn, Roger, *Into My Own*, New York: Diversion Books, 2012 (Kindle Edition).
Kazin, Michael, *The Populist Persuasion: An American History*, New York: Basic Books, 1995.
Kopel, David, 'Ronald Reagan's Extremism and the 1966 California Gubernatorial Election'. Available at www.britannica.com/blogs/2011/02/ronald-reagan's-"extremism"-and-the-1966-california-gubernatorial-election (accessed 1 September 2014).
Krassner, Paul, et al., *We Accuse*, Berkeley, CA: Diablo Press, 1965.
Lee, Eugene C. and Bruce E. Keith, *California Votes 1960–1972*, Berkeley, CA: University of California Press, 1974.
Levy, Peter (ed.), *America in the Sixties: Left, Right and Center*, London: Praeger, 1998.
Lewis, Joseph, *What Makes Reagan Run? A Political Profile*, New York: McGraw-Hill Book Company, 1968.
McGirr, Lisa, *Suburban Warriors: The Origins of the New American Right*, Princeton, NJ: Princeton University Press, 2001.
McKenna, Kevin, 'The "Total Campaign": How Ronald Reagan Won the California Gubernatorial Election of 1966', senior thesis, Columbia University, 2010.
McWilliams, Carey (ed.), *The California Revolution*, New York: Grossman Publishers, 1968.
Mitchell, Greg, *The Campaign of the Century: Upton Sinclair's Race for Governor of California and the Birth of Media Politics*, New York: Random House, 1992.
Morris, Edmund, *Dutch: A Memoir of Ronald Reagan*, New York: Harper Collins, 1999.
Nofziger, Lyn, *Nofziger*, Washington, DC: Regnery Gateway, 1992.
Owens, John R., et al., *California Politics and Parties*, London: Macmillan Company, 1970.
Patterson, James T., *Grand Expectations*, New York: Oxford University Press, 1996.
Pemberton, William, *Exit with Honor: The Life and Presidency of Ronald Reagan*, New York: M. E. Sharpe, 1998.

Perlstein, Rick, *Before the Storm: Barry Goldwater and the Unmaking of the American Consensus*, New York: Hill and Wang, 2001.
—— *Nixonland: The Rise of a President and the Fracturing of America*, New York: Scribner, 2008.
—— *The Invisible Bridge: The Fall of Nixon and the Rise of Reagan*, New York: Simon and Schuster, 2014.
Phillips-Fein, Kim, *Invisible Hands: The Making of the Conservative Movement from the New Deal to Reagan*, New York: W. W. Norton and Company, 2009.
Rarick, Ethan, *California Rising: The Life and Times of Pat Brown*, Berkeley, CA: University of California Press, 2005.
Reagan, Ronald, *Where's the Rest of Me?*, New York: Duell, Sloan and Pierce, 1965.
—— *An American Life*, New York: Simon and Schuster, 1990.
Reinhard, David W., *The Republican Right Since 1945*, Lexington, KY: University Press of Kentucky, 1983.
Rogin, Michael Paul and John L. Shover, *Political Change in California: Critical Elections and Social Movements, 1890–1966*, Westport, CT: Greenwood Publishing Corporation, 1970.
Rorabaugh, William J., *Berkeley at War: The 1960s*, New York: Oxford University Press, 1989.
—— *The Real Making of the President: Kennedy, Nixon, and the 1960 Election*, Lawrence, KS: University of Kansas Press, 2009.
Rose, Ernest and Douglas Fuchs, 'Reagan vs. Brown: A TV Image Playback', *Journal of Broadcasting*, 12 (summer 1968).
Rubin, Jerry, *Do It!: Scenarios of the Revolution*, New York: Simon and Schuster, 1970.
Scheitle, Christopher and Roger Finke, *Places of Faith: A Road Trip Across America's Religious Landscape*, New York: Oxford University Press, 2012.
Schlafly, Phyllis, *A Choice, Not an Echo*, Alton, IL: Pere Marquette Press, 1964.
Schrag, Peter, *California: America's High-Stakes Experiment*, Berkeley, CA: University of California Press, 2006.
Schuparra, Kurt, *Triumph of the Right: The Rise of the California Conservative Movement, 1945–1966*, New York: M. E. Sharpe, 1998.
Shea, Daniel M. and Michael Burton, *Campaign Craft: The Strategies, Tactics, and Art of Political Campaign Management, Revised and Expanded Edition*, Westport, CT: Praeger Publishers, 2001.
Starr, Kevin, *California: A History*, New York: Modern Library, 2005.
Steigerwald, David, *The Sixties and the End of Modern America*, New York: St Martin's Press, 1995.

White, Thomas, 'Why Anti-Intellectualism is Dumb', *Huffington Post*, 23 February 2014. Available at www.huffingtonpost.com/thomas-white/why-anti-intellectualism-is-dumb_b_4842808.html (accessed 25 February 2015).
Wilentz, Sean, *The Age of Reagan: A History, 1974–2008*, New York: HarperCollins, 2008.
Wills, Garry, *Reagan's America*, New York: Penguin, 1988.

## Newspapers and Magazines
*Anchorage Daily News*
*Beverly Hills Courier*
*Boston Herald*
*Chicago Tribune*
*Christian Science Monitor*
*Daytona Beach Morning Journal*
*Denver Post*
*Esquire*
*Los Angeles Herald-Examiner*
*Los Angeles Times*
*Middlesboro Daily News*
*National Observer*
*National Review*
*New Republic*
*New York Times*
*Newsweek*
*Oakland Tribune*
*Park City Daily News*
*People's World*
*Pittsburgh Post-Gazette*
*Ramparts*
*Riverside Press*
*Sacramento Bee*
*San Diego Evening Tribune*
*San Diego Union*
*San Francisco Chronicle*
*San Francisco Examiner*
*Sarasota Herald Tribune*
*Saturday Evening Post*
*South Bay Daily Breeze*
*Star News*
*Time*
*The Times-Voice*
*Washington Post*
*Washington Post-Intelligencer*

# Index

'A Time for Choosing' 47–51
ABC 178, 190, 239
academic freedom 183, 186, 192, 203
Adams, Cherie 91
advertising 97
AFL-CIO 21, 219
agricultural sector 220, 225
Alameda County 182
Alarcón, Arthur 35
Alcorn, Robert 254–5
Alexander, Jane 151–2
Alleman, James 87
Alsop, Stewart 228
American Council of Education 197
American Dream 31, 147
American Medical Association 61
American Nazi Party 35, 156
American Revolution 13, 49, 157, 205
Amerine, Mervin 87
Anderson, Evelyn 159
Anderson, Glenn 251
Anderson, Totten 226
anti-communism 28, 32, 48, 79, 154, 256
anti-intellectualism 182–3, 194, 203–5, 229, 265
Arizona 37, 41, 51, 238, 241

Associated Press 218
atomic weapons 39, 42

baby boomers 256
Bagley, William 27, 39, 70, 155, 174, 209, 250–1
Bagshaw, Al 175
Bagshaw, Fred 175
Bane, O. L. 71
Barabba, Vince 95–6, 118, 260
Barnett, Ross 29
Baroody, William 47
Barron, Jack 159
BASICO 109–10, 116–18, 125, 127–8, 134–6, 149, 199–201, 232
Bastiat, Frédéric 123
Battaglia, Philip 82, 85–6, 233
Baus, Herbert 109, 114, 258–60
Baxter, Leone 61
Bay Area 25, 30–1, 179
Beats 33
Beaty, Josephine Powell 153
*Bedtime for Bonzo* 172
behaviour engineering 3, 109, 118, 134–6, 258
Bell, Bernard 13
Berkeley 33, 74, 104, 179–206, 210–12, 215, 218, 223
*Beverley Hills Courier* 152

'Big Business' 80
bigotry 35–6, 39, 155–61, 167–70, 225, 252, 254
Birchers *see* 'John Birch Society'
black Muslims 153
blacks 24, 34, 38, 55, 92, 158–61, 167–70, 206, 211–13, 216, 225, 236, 246, 251–2
Boas, Roger 197
*Bonanza* 20
*Boston Herald* 108
Boyarsky, Bill 19, 218
Braceros 93
Bradley, Don 36, 177, 221–2, 230, 235, 238, 247, 251
Bravo, Francisco 93
Broder, David 51, 248
Brown, 'Colonel' 240–1
Brown, Edmund G. (Pat) 2, 25, 27, 29, 31, 34–5, 58, 69, 92–3, 97, 130–1, 139–40, 151, 156–7, 166, 173–7, 193, 198, 202, 208, 210–47, 249, 251, 253
  advisers 131, 173, 189, 197, 220–2, 237–9, 241, 243, 258–9
  campaign budget 242–3, 249–50
  fair housing 35
  on Reagan 73, 134, 143, 148, 153, 171–2, 223
  racism issue 35–7, 155–62
  'responsible liberalism' 26–7, 34, 155, 214–15, 224
  student unrest issue 180–3, 195, 198, 211
  vulnerability 70, 102, 147, 173, 180–2, 185, 195–6, 199–200, 206, 211, 220, 223–5, 259
  weaknesses 94, 146, 148, 162, 203–4, 210, 214, 216, 221, 223, 230, 232, 238, 243–4, 250, 252, 256, 259
Brown, Harold 175
Bryan, William Jennings 51
Buckley, William F. 67
Burch, Meredith 220–1, 243
Burghardt, Franklin 158
Bush, Prescott 42

Cagney, James 58
California 2, 4, 5, 25, 29–30, 32–3, 37, 40–3, 46, 56, 59, 61, 63–5, 69, 75–6, 82, 111, 113–14, 120, 134, 149, 151, 156, 159–61, 165, 179, 182, 189, 194, 203, 217–18, 220, 236–7, 251–2, 256, 262–3
  Northern California 37, 86
  Southern California 32, 34, 86, 105, 164–5, 177, 218
  uniqueness 2, 75, 103, 248, 254
California Aqueduct 26, 32
California Assembly 35, 250
California Democratic Committee 159
California Democratic Council 31, 211
California Negro Republican Assembly 167–70
California Poll 78, 210, 214–15, 219, 226, 237, 245–6
California Real Estate Association 156
California Republican Assembly 39, 71
California Senate 35, 250
California Senate Sub-Committee on Un-American Activities 191–2
California Supreme Court 36
campaign management 3–4, 44, 61–2, 64, 83, 85–6, 117,

119, 128–9, 143, 155, 240,
    246, 258–60, 262–5
campaigns
    1958 gubernatorial 267
    1962 gubernatorial 27, 119,
        212, 253, 267
    1964 presidential 51–3, 86,
        119, 253, 267
    1964 Republican primary
        40–5, 119, 139, 208
    1966 California Democratic
        gubernatorial primary 83,
        208, 211–15, 223, 236
    1966 California Republican
        gubernatorial primary
        164–78, 234, 248, 253
    1968 presidential 73, 253
    1970 gubernatorial 135
    1972 presidential 253
    2008 presidential 250, 267
    2012 presidential 267
    financial contributions 3–4, 44,
        51
Cannon, Lou 109
capitalism 15–16, 252
Carmichael, Stokely 201–2
Carson, Johnny 178
Carter, Jimmy 263
Casady, Simon 211
CBS 235
Champion, Hale 29, 35, 157,
    160–2, 176–7, 196–7, 200,
    213, 221–2, 225–7, 233,
    241, 250–1, 258–9
Chandler, Buffie 170–1
China 159
Chomsky, Noam 38
Christian Anti-Communist
    Crusade 28, 149
*Christian Science Monitor* 217
Christian, Winslow 224–5
Christopher, George 69–70, 78,
    138–42, 144, 147, 164–78,
209–10, 213, 225, 233, 240,
    250, 253, 265
CIA 198
civil liberties 183
civil rights 55, 156, 159, 188,
    211, 224
Civil Rights Act 167
Cleveland, Grover 50
Clinton, Bill 263
Coate, Bob 131–2, 234–5
Coffey, Bertram 159
Cold War 104
Columbia University 57
communism 18, 21–2, 28–9,
    49–50, 55, 111, 151, 153,
    169, 192–4, 197–9, 212,
    216, 235
*Congressional Quarterly* 63
Conrad, Charles 88, 112–13
Conrad, Paul 170–1
*Conscience of a Conservative, The*
    40, 44
conservatives and conservatism
    13–14, 18, 26, 35, 46–7,
    52–3, 55, 64, 206, 225, 245,
    253, 257
Constitution, U.S. 45
Copley, Jim 98
Copley newspapers 101
Cordiner, Ralph 20
Cow Palace 24, 47, 195
Cranston, Alan 235
Creative Society 148–51, 162,
    190
crime 38, 161–2, 212, 215–16,
    224, 232, 251
Cristina, Vernon 41, 45, 53, 56,
    70, 102, 142–4
Cuba 49, 205

Dallek, Matthew 3
Dallek, Robert 15
Dart, Justin 68

Datamatics 95, 261
Davis, Philip 46
*Death Valley Days* 21
defence industry 105
Defenders of the American Constitution 153
Democrats 17–18, 21, 24–5, 29, 31, 33, 36, 40, 52–3, 63–4, 75, 86, 92–3, 134, 140, 141, 156, 160–2, 172, 174, 177, 194, 197, 210, 212–16, 218, 227, 236, 244, 246–7, 250–4, 259, 267–8
Denver 254
*Denver Post* 255
Detroit Economic Club 190
Disney, Walt 58
Dixiecrats 31
Dixon, Illinois 9
drugs 188, 190, 197, 202, 251, 256
Dunckel, Earl 7, 9, 18–20
Dunne, Irene 226
Dutton, Fred 97, 189–90, 195–6, 203–4, 206, 221–2, 224, 237, 243–4, 250
Dylan, Bob 3

education 32, 72
Eisenhower, Dwight 25, 33, 60, 153, 209
*El Grito* 93
Eldridge, Dirk 86
'Eleventh Commandment' 139–42, 167
Enlightenment 187
Erie, Pennsylvania 7, 8
*Esquire* 108
ethnicity 96
Eureka College 158, 204–5
Evans, Rowland 236

Fair Employment Practices Commission 26

Fair Housing Act 34–7, 94, 155–8, 160, 162, 210, 216, 223, 258
Faubus, Orval 29
FBI 153
Federated Republican Women 89–90
Felsenstein, Lee 184
Field, Mervin 174, 210, 219
Field Organization 78, 176
Filthy Speech Movement 180, 184–5, 188, 192, 194
Finch, Robert 251
*Firing Line* 240
Flynn, Errol 8
free enterprise 79
free market 14
free speech 184–6, 188
Free Speech Movement 179, 181–6, 188, 206, 223
freedom 14–15, 29, 45, 49, 203
Freedom Summer 156, 181
Fresno 39
Friends of Ronald Reagan 58–9, 65, 83, 259
Frizzelle, Nolan 39
Fuchs, Douglas 97, 230
Fuck Defense Fund 180
Fuck Rally 180
Fuentes, Thomas 90

Galbraith, John 206
Gallup poll 248
Gardner, Al 62
Gavaghan, Paul 19
General Electric 7–10, 15, 19–23, 32, 59, 125, 126, 132
*General Electric Theater* 8, 20, 21
Gibson, Jim 110
*Girls' Night Out* 172
Goldwater, Barry 2, 24, 37–53, 55–7, 60, 65, 69, 72–3, 75, 80, 86, 90–1, 101, 104, 117,

119, 123, 125, 137–8, 142, 150, 155, 162, 226, 233–4, 238, 241, 245, 253, 257, 259, 267
grassroots campaigning 41, 43, 73, 81, 87, 91, 97, 178, 240, 250, 256
Great Britain 50
Great Society 49, 52, 148, 212
Greenberg, Carl 131, 152
Gross National Product (GNP) 48, 261
Guggenheim, Charles 242–5, 251

Haas, Lucien 37
Hafner, Fred 87, 210
Hall, James 137
Hamill, Pete 161, 248
Hamilton, Alexander 13
Hardin, David 261
Hargis, Billy James 149
Harmer, John 76
Hayworth, Rita 7–8
Hearst, William Randolph 58
Hendrick, Kimmis 217
Heyns, Roger 192, 197
Hispanics 34, 92–4, 236
Hoffa, Jimmy 218
Hofstadter, Richard 13
Holden, Kenneth 98–9, 107–36, 149, 168–9, 198–201, 233
Holden, William 1, 58
Hollywood 1–3, 8, 17–18, 21–2, 68–9, 72, 78, 83, 97, 103, 108, 126, 145, 161, 166, 172, 208, 242, 244, 254, 258, 262, 266
Hoppe, Arthur 108
House Committee on Un-American Activities (HUAC) 17
housing 96, 160
Hughes, Emmet John 2, 248

Hume, Jack 68
Humphrey, Hubert 211
Hunters Point riot 246

individualism 14–16, 31, 149
Inglewood 120, 125
*Issues and Answers* 178, 190, 239
*It's a Wonderful Life* 17

Jackson, Andrew 50
Jefferson, Thomas 13, 49, 187, 242, 260
John Birch Society 25–6, 27–9, 33, 35, 37, 39, 40, 55, 66, 90, 101, 150–6, 162, 210, 226, 234, 236–7, 242, 253
Johnson, Lyndon 2, 38, 40, 48–9, 51–3, 69, 73, 148, 187, 253, 267
Jones, Hardin 199–200
journalists 76, 100–2, 104–5, 114, 122, 125–6, 129, 131–2, 140–1, 163, 166, 168, 170, 208, 214, 227–9, 248, 252, 264
Justice Department 21

Kahn, Roger 46, 55
Kennedy, John 27, 29, 263
Kennedy, Robert 21, 62, 241
Kerr, Clark 185–7, 192, 195, 199, 204
Keynesianism 17
Khrushchev, Nikita 29
King, Martin Luther 161
*King's Row* 8
Kitchel, Denison 47
Kline, Richard 34, 147, 173, 200
Knight, Goodwin 25, 71, 78, 169, 175
Knott, Walter 33
Knowland, William 25
KNX Radio 240

Kossen, Sydney 103, 170, 228
Krassner, Paul 202
Krueger, Robert 116
KTTV 72
Kuchel, Thomas 56, 78–9, 166, 210

labour unions 64, 72, 96, 160, 215–17, 219, 242, 256, 267
*Lady Chatterley's Lover* 180
Las Vegas 8
Lassie 108
law and order 32
Lawrence, David 263
Lee, Eugene 226
Lenin, Vladimir 50
'Letter from a Birmingham Jail' 161
Lewis, Joseph 2, 34, 63–4, 257, 262, 266
Liberace 108
liberals and liberalism 3, 15, 21, 30–1, 37, 45, 50, 53, 64, 79, 105, 121, 212, 225, 247, 250, 252–7, 267
libertarianism 44, 157, 159
liberty 18, 157
*Life* 145
Lincoln, Abraham 243, 260
Littlewood, Tom 260–1
Locke, John 187
Los Angeles 53, 81, 94, 116, 161, 208, 211, 213–14, 218, 236, 246
Los Angeles County 43, 79, 87, 103, 165
*Los Angeles Herald-Examiner* 238
*Los Angeles Times* 66, 88, 101, 131, 152, 171, 176, 219, 228
loyalty oath controversy 199

McBirnie, W. S. 71, 149–51

McCann-Erickson Advertising Agency 67, 102
McCarthy, Joseph 26, 34, 235
McClatchy, C. K. 163
McCone, John 198
McDowell, Jack 70, 128–9, 131, 266
Malibu 109, 116, 124, 127, 129, 132–4, 232
March on Washington 156
Marin County 175
Marx, Karl 27, 50
Massachusetts 162
MCA 21
Means, Marianne 154, 160, 252, 254
media 15, 101–2, 258
Medicare 22, 38, 55, 242
Meese, Edwin 182
*Meet the Press* 115, 188, 239
Melinkoff, Abe 114
*Mexican American* 92
Mexican-American Democrats for Reagan Committee 93
Mexico 220
Meyerson, Martin 185–7
Milias, George 174
milk scandal 173–7
Mills, James 172, 223
Mississippi 181
Monagan, Robert 145
Monterey 151–52
morality 38, 42–3, 183–4, 186, 189, 195, 202, 215, 228, 232, 252
Mosk, Stanley 26
*Mr Smith Goes to Washington*, 17
Murphy, George 78, 90, 108, 210, 226

NAACP 153
National Christian Crusade 235
*National Observer* 143

*National Review* 52, 67
NBC 239
negative campaigning 135, 171–8, 211, 214, 234–43
Nelligan, William 39
New Deal 16–18, 25, 33, 49, 92, 148, 254, 256
New Left 194
*New Republic* 229
New Right 41, 44
New York 162, 179
*New York Post* 161, 248
*New York Times* 103, 248
newspapers and the press 44, 62, 98–101, 105–6, 115–16, 131, 147, 169, 172, 239
*Newsweek* 2, 131
Nixon, Richard 27–30, 39, 52, 67, 77, 137, 153, 162, 211, 231, 245, 253
Nofziger, Lyn 31, 57–8, 69–70, 80, 82, 85–6, 97–102, 105, 121, 125–6, 133, 140, 142–3, 146, 168–9, 171, 174–5, 209, 231, 248, 257–8, 262, 266
Norwalk 218
Novak, Robert 236

Oakland 188, 215
*Oakland Tribune* 171, 197
Obama, Barack 250, 263, 267
Oklahoma 57
Orange County 30–1, 33, 43, 165
Oroville Reservoir 227
Orozco, William 93

Pacific Palisades, California 9, 107, 120, 123
Paine, Thomas 187
Palance, Jack 227
Parker, William 161

Parkinson, Gaylord 29, 35, 52, 59–60, 78, 116, 139–41, 143–5, 163, 208
Patrick, William Penn 167–8, 209
Pattee, Alan 174
Pearson, Drew 103, 175, 218
Peck, Gregory 1
Pennsylvania 162
pensions 92
Perlstein, Rick 16
Perry, James 143
Phoenix 40
Pike, Thomas 86
Plog, Stanley 98–9, 102, 107–36, 149, 169, 174, 199–201, 233, 266
polls 92, 110, 145, 160, 169, 173–6, 187, 210, 212, 214–15, 219, 226, 237, 240, 246, 248, 261
populism 2, 12–13, 23, 30, 225, 255, 265
Posner, Paul 103
Post, Manning 172
poverty 212, 257
Precinct Index Priority System (PIPS) 94–7, 118, 135, 240, 260
press conferences 101, 107, 117
Project Prayer 28
Proposition 14: 35–7, 156, 159
Putnam, George 72

race and racism 34–5, 38, 55, 115, 155–62, 167–70, 212, 215
race riots 38, 161
*Ramparts* 183, 210, 255, 264
Rarick, Ethan 211
*Reader's Digest* 11, 196
Reagan, Nancy Davis 8, 18, 21, 40, 59, 68, 82–3, 90–1, 122, 147

Reagan, Neil 17, 67–8, 133–4, 266
Reagan, Patti 8
Reagan, Ronald
  actor issue 8, 10, 72, 100, 107–8, 112, 115, 121, 130, 137, 166, 170, 172–3, 225–6, 230, 234, 237, 242–5, 260–1, 266
  aloofness 101, 121–2
  celebrity 75, 145, 208, 262
  character 7–8, 66, 102, 144, 162, 209, 217, 262–4, 268
  charisma 53, 75, 83, 94, 121, 123, 127, 133, 142–4, 166, 238, 262, 267
  'citizen-politician' 87, 110, 121, 146–8, 162, 171, 183, 222, 227, 232, 260, 262–3, 266
  compassion 7–8, 263
  conservatism 69, 73, 89, 124–5, 128, 163, 206, 210, 253, 257, 267
  decision to run 56–7, 59, 65–6, 83–4, 137
  distrust of government 12, 48–9, 57, 74, 115, 132, 148–50, 157–9, 232, 245, 254, 256
  dumbing down 123, 164–5, 196, 224, 228–30, 256, 263, 265
  early politics 16, 124
  extremism issue 21, 28, 89, 114, 137, 141, 144, 151–5, 214, 233–9, 253, 257, 264
  freedom 14, 49, 148, 157–8, 190
  fundraising 4, 58, 68, 77, 79, 80–1, 87, 124, 249–50, 259
  gaffes 104, 151
  General Electric spokesman 7–23, 32
  'Great Communicator' 4, 10–11, 19, 33, 48–50, 68, 74, 76–7, 82, 85, 100, 108–10, 124, 130, 133, 136, 155, 165, 230, 238, 257, 263–4, 266
  honesty 75, 100, 143, 154, 237
  humour 77, 105, 151–2, 162
  image and presentation 103, 117, 120, 131, 133, 137–63, 171, 262–7
  inexperience 113–14, 121, 146–8, 165, 171, 217, 227, 263
  integrity 123, 143–4
  intelligence 130–1, 234, 263
  knowledge of issues 12, 68, 72, 76–7, 103, 108, 111–16, 120–4, 129–32, 134, 196, 227–9
  memory 12, 66, 102–3, 124–6, 264
  organization 83
  poise 102, 178, 263
  political philosophy 69, 76, 108, 113, 122–4, 142–3, 155, 158, 267
  populism 4, 23, 48, 87, 121, 132, 147, 183, 186, 189, 205–6, 218, 224, 255, 258, 263, 265
  pragmatism 123, 210
  presidential ambitions 111, 132, 228, 248–9
  Q&A 89, 101, 129–31, 171, 188, 228, 231
  racism issue 155–61, 167–70
  shyness 10, 76, 82, 101
  soundbites 126, 196, 228–30, 254, 256
  'The Speech' 11, 18–19, 20–1, 25, 29, 41, 48, 59, 76, 114, 120

speeches 107, 130, 133, 145, 223
vagueness 126, 150
Reagan Girls 91–2, 208
Reagan Team Barbecue 232
Reaganistas 93
*Realist, The* 202
Reed, Tom 86
Regents, Board of 185, 198, 206
Republican Congressional Campaign Committee 260
Republican National Convention (1964) 24, 45
Republicans 24–7, 30–1, 33, 35–6, 38–40, 45–6, 51, 63–4, 101, 108, 145, 149–50, 163, 208–9, 230–1, 248, 250, 259–60, 266–8
  California 55–6, 59–60, 62, 71, 73, 75, 87–9, 95, 137–8, 174, 210–11, 213, 215–16
  extremists 39, 41, 45–6, 52–3, 55, 79, 119, 127, 136, 145, 153, 162, 194, 209, 233
  moderates 56, 78–9, 138, 162, 165, 174, 214
Ripon Society 260
Riverside County 43
*Riverside Press* 102
Roberts, William 41, 43, 60–2, 64–6, 70–4, 76, 78–9, 81, 83, 85–6, 94, 98, 103, 110–20, 123–30, 134–5, 139–40, 143–4, 168–9, 187–8, 199, 201, 231–3, 239, 241, 258–9, 262
Robinson, Jackie 24
Rockefeller, Happy 42–3
Rockefeller, Nelson 24, 37, 39–43, 65, 69–70, 73, 77, 127–8, 137, 162
Roosevelt, Franklin 16, 133, 148, 254

Roosevelt, Jimmy 212
Rose, Ernest 97, 230
Ross, William 109, 114, 258–60
Rousselot, John 28, 66, 128, 151–2
Rubel, Cy 57–8
Rubin, Jerry 187
Rumford Act, *see* Fair Housing Act
Rumford, William 34–7
Rusher, William 67
Russia 159
Ryskind, Morrie 88

Sacramento 26, 120, 147, 185, 193, 217, 228, 236
*Sacramento Bee* 101, 103, 114–15, 134, 163, 170, 197, 228–9
Saenz, Phil 92
Salvatori, Henry 47, 57–8, 68, 79–80, 85, 98, 116, 119–20, 169, 233
San Bernardino County 87
San Diego 1, 101, 138, 139
San Diego County 30, 43, 165
*San Diego Union* 98, 197, 251, 253
San Francisco 24, 33, 69, 160, 166–7, 176, 222, 246
*San Francisco Chronicle* 103, 116, 154, 170, 172, 177, 202
*San Francisco Examiner* 152, 160, 195, 197, 206, 228
San Joaquin Valley 225
San Jose 192
Santa Ana 208
Santa Barbara 221
*Santa Barbara News Press* 66
Santa Monica 157, 167, 170, 1278
*Saturday Evening Post* 46, 55, 134

Savio, Mario 181, 185–7
Schlafly, Phyllis 25
Screen Actors Guild (SAG) 1, 17, 21, 154, 216–17
Selassie, Haile 48
senior citizens 92
sex 188, 198, 202
Shell, Joe 27, 28, 52, 56, 67, 78, 137
Sinatra, Frank 244–5
Sixties 64
Smith, Al 49
Smith, Gerald 235
Smith, H. Allen 27
Smith, William French 58, 75, 80, 82, 145, 148, 238, 244
Social Area Analysis 95
social welfare 14, 15, 45
social security 47, 235, 242, 253, 256
socialism 22, 27, 32, 50, 254
Sorenson, John 90
South, the 31–2, 38
Southern California Reagan for Governor Committee 117
Southern strategy 253
Soviet Union 22, 25, 32–3
Speakers Bureau 88
Spencer, Stuart 31, 39–42, 44, 51, 57–8, 60–2, 65–6, 69–73, 76–8, 82–3, 85–6, 88–9, 94–6, 98, 101, 103, 110–13, 115, 117–30, 132, 134–6, 143, 146, 150–3, 157, 167–8, 171, 186, 188, 199–201, 206, 209, 217, 231–4, 239, 241, 244, 258–9, 262, 264–5
Spencer-Roberts 3, 41, 43, 60–1, 65, 67–70, 93, 102, 111, 113, 133, 135–6, 143, 154, 155, 198–9, 220, 240, 253, 258–9

Sproul Hall 185, 206
Sputnik 30
*Star News* 239
states' rights 38
Steinbeck, John 256
Stevenson, Adlai 260
Stevenson, Cyril 71
Stewart, James 1, 17, 226
Student Non-Violent Coordinating Committee (SNCC) 201–2
student unrest 105, 121, 179–206, 216, 224, 232, 252, 258
Sturgeon, Vernon 75
suburbia 30
Sullivan, Ed 202
*Sun Times* 260
Sutton, Robert 235

Taylor, Robert 58
taxation 22, 33, 48, 72, 114, 150, 223–4, 232, 252
Tea Party 32
Teamsters Union 217–18
television 44, 64, 97, 133, 147, 178, 190, 215, 228, 230, 232, 235, 238, 242, 254, 260, 262
Temple, Shirley 173
Tennessee Valley Authority (TVA) 20, 47, 253
Thelin, Howard 249
Thompson, John 179–80, 184–6
*Time* 52
Todt, George 238
*Tonight Show* 178
totalitarianism 17, 29
Town Meeting for Freedom 28
Truman, Harry 13
Tuttle, Holmes 57–8, 60, 68, 79, 83, 85, 98, 116, 119–20, 200

# INDEX ★ 311

UCLA 95
unemployment 103, 216
Union Oil 57
United Nations 35, 226
United Republicans of California 71
United States Congress 115
United States Information Service (USIS) 9
United States Senate 79, 108
University Committee for Brown 198
University Consultants Inc. 116
University of California (UC) 120–21, 185–6, 197, 199–206
University of Santa Clara 180
University of Southern California 147
urban unrest 52, 213, 246, 258

Viet Cong 188
Vietnam Day Committee 187–8, 190, 197, 201
Vietnam War 30, 39, 52, 104–5, 181, 184, 187, 206, 211–12, 223
violence 38
Visalia 72
volunteers 3, 40, 43, 46, 71, 88–9, 93–4, 128, 178, 208, 220, 232, 240, 258–60
voter behaviour 63, 80, 94–5, 114, 144, 165, 177, 218, 238–9, 245–7, 261–3

Walker, Robert 46, 74, 139
Warner, Jack 1, 58, 68
Warren, Earl 25, 28, 39, 61, 218
Washington, DC 48, 111, 120, 217, 222, 249, 255
*Washington Post* 32, 38, 230
*Washington Post Intelligencer* 115
water 72
Watts Riots 37, 161, 198, 206, 210, 212–13, 215, 223
Wayne, John 1, 58, 226–7
Weinberg, Jack 181, 185
Weinberger, Caspar 10, 26, 33, 40, 46, 60, 75, 85, 89, 102, 122, 124–5, 130, 147, 217, 219, 225, 238–9, 267
Welch, Robert 25, 149, 151, 153
welfare 17, 22, 32, 45, 55, 72, 74, 92, 103–4, 115, 162, 195, 217–18, 224–5, 232, 256–7
West Covina 82
Western Geophysical 57
Whedon, Peggy 178
White Citizens Council 156
White, William 230
whites 37, 94, 160–1, 211, 213, 216, 246–7, 251–4
Whitaker, Clem 61
Whitaker-Baxter 62
Will, George 15
Wills, Garry 3, 109, 111, 118
Wilson, Richard 228
Wolper, David 242
women 89, 146, 219
working class 194, 216–17, 246–7, 252–4
World War II 30, 226
Wyman, Eugene 134
Wyman, Jane 17

'Ya Basta' campaign 93
Yorty, Sam 211–14, 219–20, 222, 236, 249
Young Republicans 60, 71, 79, 89–90, 123
Youth for Reagan 90

Zebold, Tammy 92